USER INTERFACE DESIGN
FOR COMPUTER SYSTEMS

ELLIS HORWOOD BOOKS IN COMPUTING SCIENCE

General Editors: Professor JOHN CAMPBELL, University College London, and BRIAN L. MEEK, Director of Information Technology, Goldsmiths' College, London, and King's College London (KQC), University of London

Series in Computers and Their Applications

Series Editor: BRIAN L. MEEK, Computer Centre, King's College London (KQC), University of London

Series continued at end of book

USER INTERFACE DESIGN FOR COMPUTER SYSTEMS

TONY RUBIN, M.Sc.
Head of Central Services Group
Communications Facilities Management Division
British Telecom, Ipswich

ELLIS HORWOOD LIMITED
Publishers · Chichester

Halsted Press: a division of
JOHN WILEY & SONS
New York · Chichester · Brisbane · Toronto

First published in 1988 by
ELLIS HORWOOD LIMITED
Market Cross House, Cooper Street,
Chichester, West Sussex, PO19 1EB, England
The publisher's colophon is reproduced from James Gillison's drawing of the ancient Market Cross, Chichester.

Distributors:

Australia and New Zealand:
JACARANDA WILEY LIMITED
GPO Box 859, Brisbane, Queensland 4001, Australia

Canada:
JOHN WILEY & SONS CANADA LIMITED
22 Worcester Road, Rexdale, Ontario, Canada

Europe and Africa:
JOHN WILEY & SONS LIMITED
Baffins Lane, Chichester, West Sussex, England

North and South America and the rest of the world:
Halsted Press: a division of
JOHN WILEY & SONS
605 Third Avenue, New York, NY 10158, USA

South-East Asia
JOHN WILEY & SONS (SEA) PTE LIMITED
37 Jalan Pemimpin # 05–04
Block B, Union Industrial Building, Singapore 2057

Indian Subcontinent
WILEY EASTERN LIMITED
4835/24 Ansari Road
Daryaganj, New Delhi 110002, India

© **1988 T. Rubin/Ellis Horwood Limited**

British Library Cataloguing in Publication Data
Rubin, Tony, *1955–*
User interface for systems. —
(Ellis Horwood series in computers and their applications.)
1. Man. Interactions with computer systems
I. Title
004'.01'9

Library of Congress CIP data available

ISBN 0–7458–0299–0 (Ellis Horwood Limited)
ISBN 0–470–21172–5 (Halsted Press)

Printed in Great Britain by Hartnolls, Bodmin

To Sue and Joshua

Education is what survives when what has been learnt has been forgotten.

B. F. Skinner

Contents

Preface

I have finally decided to write this book after several years of good intentions. It is born out of a desire to provide a simple, easy to read, easy to understand book about issues surrounding the design of user interfaces to computer systems. My aim throughout has been to produce a book that:

a)   I wished I could have bought when I was a student,

b)   I hope I can give to computer scientists and computer system designers – and that they will be able to understand easily.

There are many courses nowadays in Ergonomics, Information Technology, Computer Science, Design and Engineering that have optional course units or a series of lectures on all or part of the subject matter contained in this book. It is hoped that this book will prove to be a useful complement to the material covered on such courses.

This does not mean to say that students are the only audience that might benefit from reading this book. As I have already mentioned, computer scientists, software designers, office automation specialists and any other people involved in the specification, design, production, manufacture, marketing, purchasing or installation of computer-based technology should also learn something to their advantage.

There is little information in this book that is brand new, the material has been gathered from many sources, not least the author's personal experiences of working in human factors research for over seven years. What makes this book different, however, is the variety of information presented in one volume at a comprehensible level. I have tried to steer a course between being too superficial and merely providing a set of guidelines, and the other extreme of being over complex and delving too deeply into the theoretical and psychological precepts of the design ideas presented. Wherever possible I have referred to personal experience or real-life situations to provide the reader with examples or evidence, even if anecdotal, of the point or idea I am trying to put across.

It should be remembered that design is a creative process and hence there are few absolutes that *must* be adhered to. As in all classes of design there are good designs and bad designs (and many in between), there are efficient and inefficient ways of doing things, and there are aesthetically pleasing and purely functional ways of designing aspects of a user interface *and these need not be mutually exclusive sets.*

The design of a user interface is undoubtedly a specialist task; the uninitiated computer programmer or software designer is no more likely to get a user interface right than a person who has never seen a computer terminal before, and *why should they?* We have long recognised the need for people with particular skills to write technical documentation; we do not (or should not) expect the designers and builders of hardware and software to be naturally well versed in written communication skills. *Is user interface design any different?* Indeed, computer specialists have an uncanny knack of making poor assumptions about users, and these assumptions stem from their own experiences and beliefs derived from being too long immersed in the culture of computing. This is not intended to be derogatory, merely a statement of how it often *is*, and to some extent how it is difficult to avoid – we all become immersed in the cultures of our jobs and the particular set of skills required to perform them.

Most users of computer systems have not been subject to the same culture as the computer scientist and are therefore less likely to make the choices, press the keys or provide the input that a software designer expects or designs for. Users have an uncanny knack of their own, which is of finding the one and only sequence of key presses that causes the system to crash! Systems designers have been known to refer to some of their designs as 'idiot-proof' a term I would very much like to see fall into disuse. The phrase itself is often uttered harmlessly, but it does betray a philosophy towards users of computing systems that is completely alien to any 'human factors person'.

This book attempts to make all of us 'human factors people'. Such a statement is not intended to imply that after reading this book the reader will give up whatever profitable employment he/she is currently engaged upon and take up the cudgels on behalf of human factors. We can all be human factors people by merely bearing in mind that *computer systems are built to interact with people.*

If we can remember that simple statement, whatever point of the design process we are involved in, then we are already one step nearer an improved and well thought out design.

Acknowledgements

First and foremost I should like to thank the authors of Chapter 6, Anna Doney and John Seton and the author of Chapter 7, Martin Lea. Their contributions in specialist areas have not only lightened the burden of producing a complete book, they have also enriched the contents with their own insights into areas that are essential to a book with a title such as this one. Also grateful thanks to my co-author of Chapter 5, Dr. Nick Milner, who required some gentle persuasion to be credited for his efforts, his modesty does not become him!

I should also take this opportunity to thank Melanie Leggett of the publishers, Ellis Horwood, who suggested that I write this book and who has since been a valuable source of information and encouragement. I should also say that without the help of the Series Editor, Brian Meek, this book would be far less readable, his critical comments have led to a much improved text.

My colleagues in the Human Factors Division at British Telecom Research Laboratories (especially Richard Taylor) and all the members of the Cosmos project team also deserve a mention for their comments, advice and ideas, many of which I have unscrupulously moulded and then inserted into the text. It would also be impossible not to express grateful thanks to Rachel Birnbaum who runs the Ergonomics MSc course at the Ergonomics Unit, University College London. Her unquestionable authority based on dealing with almost a decade's worth of Ergonomics students (there must be a good collective noun for such a group) has provided valued comments on the level and approach of this book. Since it was that MSc course that designated my career path for at least the past eight years, Rachel and Professor John Long, Head of the Ergonomics Unit, must both bear some collective responsibility for this book too – I hope they are not too ashamed or shy of having such an association made public!

Tony Rubin
Ipswich, Suffolk
April, 1988.

1

Introduction

This is a book that concerns itself with the human-computer interface. If we define an interface as a common boundary or an area of contact, between objects, systems or subjects, then this book is about the area of contact between people and computers.

This area of contact is not confined to a merely physical interaction – the means by which a user interacts with the computer – but as Lee & Lochovsky (1985) remind us, must be extended to include conceptual and perceptual issues. This book deals with various (but not all – an impossibly large task) aspects of each of these manifestations of the user interface.

There are many types of machine and therefore many types of user interface. This book concentrates on computers alone. I would have preferred not to attempt to define the word 'computer' here because of the danger of including, albeit unwittingly, specialized machines or interfaces not directly covered by this book. Are the latest photo-copiers really computers? The laser printer, used to produce the manuscript for this book, can be programmed using a special language[†] is that sufficient to qualify it as a computer? I don't know, but whether the reader chooses to define machines that utilise some aspects of computing technology as computers or not is immaterial – this book still has something to say to people interested in machines that some people would not regard as computers. This book is *not* concerned with photo-copiers or laser printers *per se*, but where such items can be manipulated or addressed from something we would normally recognise as a computer terminal, using a command language, or a menu or some input device, then it does fall into the

---

[†] Postscript is a language used to program the Apple® LaserWriter™

remit of the topics discussed in this book. So, specialised interfaces to particular classes of computer-like machines are not considered here. However, insights obtained from reading the text could prove influential in the design or evaluation of such specialised machines. Moreover, it is useful consider a particular piece of software as the object to which the user has an interface. It is true that the computer hardware in such cases provides the physical interface, but it is the software that will determine the conceptual and perceptual interactions that the user will perform.

There are many occasions in this book where the words 'computer' and, 'software' are interchangeable. In the pages that follow I often refer to the 'computer system' or the 'system'. It is my intention that these terms should be taken to include both the 'computer' and the 'software' together.

Software itself is very interesting 'material' to consider. On the one hand it may be seen as a long list of undecipherable combinations of characters that are somehow input into a computer. On the other hand, the evocation of that list by the computer results in new worlds opening before the user. Alien creatures creeping down the screen, spreadsheet packages calculating interest rates in less time than it takes to type in the data, rocket ships with dazzling armouries, databases holding thousands of records. All these things are so vastly different from each other, yet all are created by software, and can appear on the display of the same micro-computer within seconds of each other as various programs and applications are selected and run.

If software is so all-embracing, so powerful, why is the human factors specialist necessary? What is wrong with putting our complete trust in the mystical and ritual rites used by the high priests of software - the computer scientists and programmers? Well nothing, if computers dealt only with other computers. Of course some computers do just that, and I have absolutely nothing to say about how the computer-computer interface is specified, designed, built or evaluated. However, it is much more common for computers to interact with people, and it is this extra ingredient, the human being, in all its complexity and beauty that makes the case for specialist involvement in the specification, design *etc.* of human-computer interfaces.

The precision and order that are an integral part of most computer scientist's background and everyday experiences suddenly evaporate when the human being is put into the equation. One major reason for so much appalling software is that when that floor is whisked away, when the user *has* to be considered in more detail than merely as an appendage or an intelligent input device, the computer scientist, not unnaturally, grabs at the first thing that comes to hand - his or her own experiences, desires, abilities and expectations. In all our other experiences such a 'personalised data set' tends to be a pretty useless design criterion. Do designers plan door clearances based upon their own stature, do they design bridges that carry stresses based on the weight of the vehicle that they drive, do they design telephone exchanges able to handle a number of telephone calls based on the amount of calls that they tend to make? No, no, and no again.

Why should software and computer interfaces be any different?

In the design examples above, the data required as input to the design process comes in neat, easy to handle, quantifiable packages. It might be anthropometric tables concerning the stature of the population, it might be calculations about the weight of transported loads based upon projections concerning future traffic densities, or it might be data about the telephone traffic in current telephone exchanges.

Data about human cognition, the human sensory system, about attitudes and motivation, about memory is available. However, it is rarely in a form that can be easily handled by designers. This book attempts to present some of that data both for designers to utilise and for students in directly related fields to build upon.

This book, being an introduction, considers only some of the issues concerning human-computer interaction. The issues covered in the remaining chapters were selected for at least one of three possible reasons:

1.) because they were considered so important that to omit them would have been unthinkable,
2.) because they were good exemples of the breadth of approach necessary to make useful judgements and recommendations in user-interface issues,
3.) because they were considered to be of especial use to students soon to become employed in a capacity that will involve them in some aspect of user interface design.

Some of the issues covered in this volume certainly fall into more than one of the categories.

There are four issues that are given separate chapters: task analysis and user modelling (you may argue that these are two issues), menu design, the use of colour, and the evaluation of user interfaces. Two of these chapters (colour and evaluations) are written by guest authors who have specialist knowledge of these specific areas.

There is one chapter (Chapter 3) that deals with four other user interface design criteria in a less detailed fashion. This is not to underrate the importance of each issue, but a consequence of the need to choose only a selective cross-section of the possible issues when writing a book of only 200 pages.

There is a chapter (Chapter 5) that deals with input devices and common methods by which users interact with computers. Chapter 5 also considers WIMP (Windows, Icons, Menus, Pointers or Windows, Icons, Mice, Pop-up menus) user interfaces in general and refers to the Apple Macintosh™ in particular. Such interfaces are still, at the time of writing (1988), relatively new, and there has been a tendency for the Human Computer Interaction (HCI) community to embrace such interfaces with such fervour that shortcomings have been ignored or glossed over. This chapter attempts a more balanced view.

The last chapter is addressed to students and contains anecdotal evidence that there is life after university. It attempts to provide advice about how to adapt to becoming employed in industry as a human factors specialist. Some of the author's own experiences are presented as examples of what not to do!

Chapters 2-7, which contain the meat of the book, treat their subjects in similar ways. There is usually an introduction, followed by a detailed discussion of the topic, divided usually into a series of ('bite-sized'!) issues or sub-topics.

The implications of the topic for user interface design are pointed out as clearly as possible with reference both to the literature and to examples from actual design wherever possible. The end of each chapter contains some guidelines derived from the previous discussions. In almost every case the guidelines are not intended to stand alone, but should be seen as complementary to the preceding discussion of the subject. I make this point at least twice more in this book, but it is worthy of repetition – there are some seriously flawed designs that can be attributed to following guidelines blindly.

Even the in-depth chapters may not be sufficiently detailed for some students or designers wishing to become completely familiar with a subject. All chapters quote many references, and pointers are provided in the text to the most insightful or clearly expressed papers. All the literature referred to in the book is collected together in one large bibliography at the end of the book. I considered having chapter specific references, but ultimately decided that the method chosen is neater, completely self-contained, and can be easily browsed by potential readers (and purchasers?) to get an overview of the topics discussed and the level of discussion.

2

Users and Tasks

One motto much beloved by human factors people, and consequently much quoted is; "Know the user, know the task." Encapsulated in this phrase is a great deal of the philosophy of the user-centred approach to design. It is not just computer systems design that does well to heed such sound advice; *any* design for use by people should be based upon some knowledge of the users and the task(s) they will perform with the designed object.

Design *per se* is not the only activity that benefits from knowledge of both users and their goals or objectives. Many aspects of the service industries require just such knowledge *in a useful and usable form*.

That last phrase is rather important. Merely to state that we need to know about users and tasks is one thing, obtaining that knowledge and presenting it in such a way that designers can make design decisions based upon that knowledge is quite another.

This chapter attempts to make the reader aware of the concepts and models employed in HCI research (for it is mostly studied there rather than in industry) to describe users and tasks. The practical application of such models is often difficult and generally simplified. Wherever possible the applicability of the issues covered to real-world design problems is discussed.

2.1 AN ANALOGY

Instead of thinking about the design of computer systems, let us for a few minutes think about restaurants (this is not the only time that restaurants come to my rescue in this book, see Chapter 4!). In order to run a successful restaurant we would need to know something about people (users); their eating habits, their objectives when eating and what procedures (tasks) they indulge in, in order to meet those objectives, when eating in a restaurant.

Now, depending upon what type of restaurant we wish to run, we would design the restaurant's interior and our *style of working* according some preconceived model of our potential customers. Suppose we wish to run a hamburger/fast food restaurant. We ought to think of the type of people we will be catering for and their objectives once they have entered the restaurant (*ie.* made a decision to obtain food from our premises). In other words, we need to construct a *model* of our potential users. These might be typical of the items that would makeup our model of frequenters of fast-food restaurants:

1.) they want service quickly;
2.) they will queue but only if the queue is fast moving;
3.) they want their food to be cheap;
4.) they want their food to be easy to handle (literally), no cutlery desired;
5.) they often wish to eat on the move;
6.) they like a bright and busy atmosphere;
7.) a great majority are under 30 years old;
8.) 50% are under 20 years old.

The above list is not necessarily accurate, based as it is on personal observation, but it is the *sort* of data we might acquire from a market research company. You might well recognise the type of establishment we are attempting to imitate. Based on this data we might come up with quite a few design decisions:

1.) have several tills (check-outs);
2.) have food already prepared and wrapped and kept warm (not hot – it has to be eaten quickly and without cutlery);
3.) play loud music, use bright colours for walls and floors (cheap and cheerful decor);
4.) minimal emphasis on seating and privacy (fast turnover);
5.) package a limited variety of foods in bright easily recognisable wrappers (image, build-up brand identification);
6.) open early (say 10.00 am) close late (say 11.00 pm).

You can see how building up a model of a user or a user population helped in making design decisions. Try the same exercise, except that instead of a hamburger restaurant, imagine you want to open an 'exclusive' *cordon bleu* restaurant; what might your user model consist of, and how would it help you to make design decisions?

2.2 USER MODELS IN USER INTERFACE DESIGN

If the above analogy is of any use at all, it is in identifying a single, but important, type of user model that is used in user interface design. It is a representation of the user; that is used by the designer to make inferences and decisions about the design. A simple, but very limited, model often employed by systems designers is of a naive, novice or inexperienced (the terms are interchangeable) user. That is, the designer assumes minimal or no knowledge on behalf of the user and that assumption provides some criteria for the design.

If this were the only type of user model employed in this field of work, then life would be all the sweeter, unfortunately it is not. Consider for a moment the following types of user model, all of which appear in the literature from time to time.

1.)   User model   – the designer's model of the user (see above)
2.)   User's model   – the model (in the user's head) that the user has of the system, usually obtained through interacting with the system and the associated training manuals and user guides.
3.)   User model   – the system's model of the user, perhaps built up (by the computer) during an interactive session with a user.

Clearly we cannot continue with such terminology and expect anybody (including the author) to obtain anything other than a headache. However, before I try to make things clearer, perhaps I should throw in a few more terms that you are bound to encounter in the natural course of things; mental model, user's conceptual model, cognitive model. If I can make some definitions clear enough here, you will be able to fit in these other terms as and when they come across them.

As Johnson & Johnson (1987) point out, the term 'user model' has been misunderstood and abused more than any other in the whole area of user interface design and human computer interaction. They refer to Young (1981) who attempted to clear up the morass surrounding the term "user conceptual model" (UCM). However eloquent, Young's attempted elucidation seems to have been ignored as often as it is heeded, and people still make mistakes and get confused. In order to bring about some form of unity I shall use the same terms as Norman (1986), keep my head down and my fingers crossed.

Norman (*op cit*) distinguishes between three models: the Design Model (DM), the User's Model (UM) and the System Image (SI). Let us consider each in turn.

2.2.1   The Design Model
This is the model the designer has of the design as a whole; it is the conceptual model of the system to be built. As Norman (*op cit*) says,

> "Ideally, this conceptualisation is based upon the user's task, requirements and capabilities. The conceptualisation must also consider the user's background, experience, and the powers and limitations of the user's information processing mechanisms, most especially processing resources and short-term memory limits"

Now, don't get confused, but the model of the 'typical' user of the system, such as discussed in the restaurant analogy earlier in this chapter, is something that is incorporated into the DM.

2.2.2   The User's Model
This is the mental model a user holds of the system. If I asked somebody familiar with the London Underground system how to get from Fulham Broadway
to Euston, he or she might conjure up their model (their UM) of the underground system in their head and try to provide an answer. The accuracy of the
answer they give will depend upon their familiarity with the system. What is
certain, is that their UM draws upon the System Image. The UM is each individual's interpretation of the system, no matter how personalised, or in
Norman's terms idiosyncratic, that model is.

2.2.3   The System Image
This is what everybody who interacts with the system sees, hears and feels. The
SI consists not only of the physical entity that is the system but also the
accompanying literature and training material. Everybody gets to see the same
map of the London Underground system, everybody who rides on it experiences
the same trains and lines going to the same destinations (on a good day!) – yet
we each internalise the SI in a personal way – hence the personal nature of the
UM.

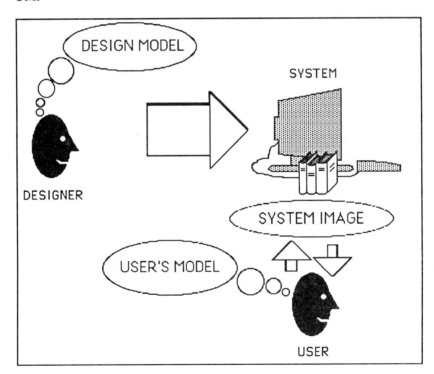

Fig. 2.1 –   The relationship between the concepts of Design Model, System
               Image and User's Model.

(based on a diagram by Norman 1986)

2.2.4   Relating the models

Clearly the three concepts are closely interrelated. Fig. 2.1 above, attempts to illustrate the relationship between the three definitions. The designer's aim is to produce a system and hence a System Image that accurately reflects the nature, potential and the working of the system. The better the SI reflects the designer's intentions – the DM – the closer the model formed by the user – the UM – will be to the DM. If the the UM is close to the DM then the user will be able to exploit the design to its full potential. If the UM is inaccurate because the SI conveyed is poor, then the system will be misused, under-used or just abused.

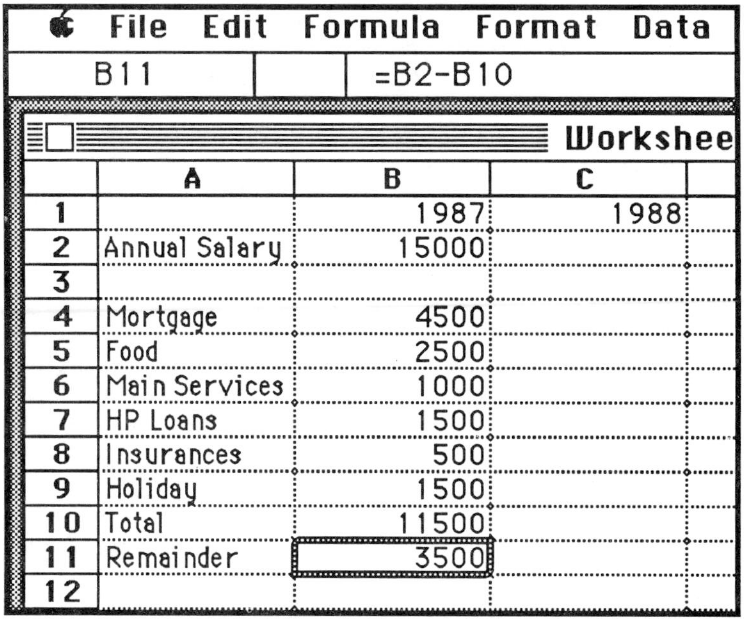

🍎 File Edit Formula Format Data			
B11	=B2−B10		

	A	B	C
1		1987	1988
2	Annual Salary	15000	
3			
4	Mortgage	4500	
5	Food	2500	
6	Main Services	1000	
7	HP Loans	1500	
8	Insurances	500	
9	Holiday	1500	
10	Total	11500	
11	Remainder	3500	
12			

Fig. 2.2 –   Part of a spreadsheet screen. In the figure, it can be seen that a formula for calculating 'cell' B11 is derived from subtracting one cell value (B10) from another (B2).

2.2.5   A good Design Model

One example of a DM that presents the user with a System Image such that the user forms a 'good' (*ie.* close to the designer's) model is the 'spreadsheet' package – there are many such packages around. Spreadsheet applications are aimed at a particular type of user who wishes to perform a particular type of task. The user is often familiar with budgets and/or accounting methods, and uses balance sheets. The task would be accounting, or budget planning. The spreadsheet (see Fig. 2.2 above) presents the user with a series of columns and rows, the user can enter figures into the columns and apply formulae to the columns such that the application can make calculations based on the figures entered. A simple task would be to enter an amount of money you expect to earn in the first column, and then in subsequent rows enter estimated expenses for the coming year. Totalling the expenses and then subtracting them from your salary results in the amount you plan to have left to spend on other things. The effect of say, expecting a 10% pay rise and only a 5% increase in costs in the next year can be easily calculated. The commercial success of spreadsheets is testimony to the closeness of the DM to the UM for many people.

It seems to me that there are very many more design models that present a poor system image to the user than there are good ones. The above example is good perhaps because the intended user population is better known to the designer than in many other cases when a piece of software is made generally available. For example, one might guess that most users of spreadsheets will be numerate and will wish to perform a fairly small set of tasks. If however the software application is a word processing package, is it more easy or less easy to define the user population? My view is that it is less easy. People can use word processing for a wider range of uses and therefore the user population is likely to be larger. What assumptions should be made about such users? Can they spell? Do they know what a 'tab' is? A margin? A forced paragraph ? If the designer knew that the only users of the designed word-processor would be experienced typists who are changing *machines* (*ie.* technology is substituted but their *tasks* are the same or similar – see the Tasks Section below) then the questions about tabs and paragraphs would be answered, and a design model that utilises or *recruits* knowledge the user has already gained in a different machine (but similar task) environment is likely to be very useful.

2.3 FINDING OUT ABOUT USERS

So, knowledge about users is extremely important in design. The next issue that deserves attention is; how do we find out about users or potential users of the design?

There are several approaches that can be taken to find out more about users in order to form a clear picture of the population that is being designed for.

1.) We can observe users of a system or design similar to the new design. The users can be of various population profiles (for example experienced and inexperienced). This approach is useful when there is likely to be a large population of users (and therefore a large variation in user's abilities). It is also useful when building a commercially competitive rival to an existing system. In such a situation the ability to study a set of users of the rival system would indeed be a bonus.

2.) We can perform a full systems analysis to define the tasks (see below) that will be performed, the required abilities of the users of the design and the interface requirements. This approach is useful in some circumstances, when a system to do something quite specific (say, network management) needs to be designed and built. In such cases there is already something known about the users – they will be network managers, thus we can look at what network managers do, and what skills they require to do such a job.

3.)   We can simulate the design and see how representatives of the target pop-
      ulation of users[†] 'get on' with the system. (Chapter 7 – Evaluations
      covers this topic in depth.)

4.)   We can draw up a set of criteria which anticipates or predicts the likely
      range of abilities users of the new system will require. This appears at
      first to be getting the people to fit the task rather than the other way
      around. However there are systems designed that will undoubtedly require
      particular abilities from the users but for which there can be no systems
      analysis because of the uniqueness of the design. For example, the first
      Computer Aided Design (CAD) packages must have looked at what
      designers did, and how they did it, in order to come up with a useful set of
      drawing tools. Thus designers might be expected to know about blueprint
      design, perspective, plan views *etc.* Such a system could incorporate such
      attributes safe in the knowledge that the intended user population would
      not find the concepts difficult to cope with.

   The actual mechanisms by which information about users may be obtained
are many and varied. Chapter 7 on evaluations covers the formal techniques
employed in deriving information from users about systems. The context here,
though slightly different (we are discussing information gathering *before* design
whereas Chapter 7 mainly discusses information gathering *after* design), is still
subject to the same or similar techniques.

   In general such information can be gathered by direct observation, indirect
observation, or by employing some form of survey. This simplified breakdown
does not begin to cover the techniques within each category which can be used,
and the reader is once again directed to Chapter 7. The choice of method will
depend upon the two classic variables; time and money. In industrial projects
the former is normally very tightly constrained whilst the latter is considerably
less limited. In academia it is often the case that the availability of the variables
is reversed – many PhD theses using simple (but often elegant) experiments are
testimony to such a situation. The industrial human factors people (the Ergonomics Society refers to such as *Practitioners*) therefore often use 'quick and
dirty' methods which, though not always academically thorough, provide results
in the time required. The answers obtained will normally have some validity and
are better than not making any attempt at all.

[†] 'Target population' – the intended set of users, the people for whom the system is
primarily designed.

2.4 AN EXAMPLE OF 'QUICK AND DIRTY' INFORMATION GATHERING

Imagine that a design team decide to enhance an accounting software package they are designing, by including with the package a series of 'features'. Each feature is a small bit of software in its own right and will be sold with the main application. The features are:

1.)   A calendar/diary which can be accessed by the user at any time – the user can write brief notes into the diary and can access any day of the year simply by 'clicking' (see WIMP interfaces in Chapter 5) on the date presented in the form of a paper-style calendar (see Fig. 2.3 below).

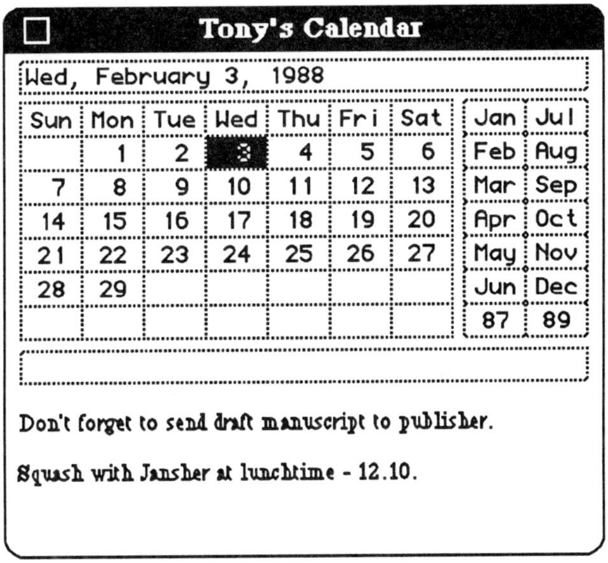

Fig. 2.3 –   A graphical representation of a calendar/diary which might be provided on screen.

2.)   An address book, which can be accessed also at any time, and contains an alphabetical index and a means of searching by name.

3.)   A personal telephone directory. Users can keep telephone numbers of their 'nearest and dearest' or their business contacts in another simple file system which has a graphical/pictorial interface which builds on the most likely model people have of paper-based personal telephone directories (see Fig. 2.4).

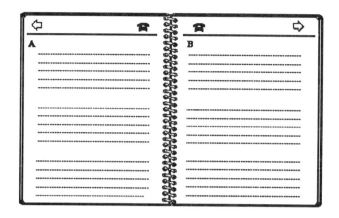

Fig. 2.4 –   A telephone book image which could be displayed to users on
                the screen. Pages can be turned by 'clicking' on the arrows.

Although these features are going to be provided free, there will clearly be a limited amount amount of space in the computer's memory for the storage of addresses and telephone numbers. If the amount of space given to users for storage is insufficient for their purposes this will reflect badly upon the product as a whole. However, if they allocate too much space, they are wasting a valuable resource that could be utilised elsewhere in the package. Also, they need to know how much space to devote to each letter of the alphabet; they can deduce that no-one knows many people with a surname beginning with a 'Z', but what about 'T' or 'N' – are they as common as each other? Does it matter?

In order to solve the dilemma the human factors person is called in. The ideal solution, he thinks, might be to study how well utilised such facilities are on other, similar packages. That is, do users actually use such facilities to store all, some or none of their telephone numbers? Why? What improvements are necessary to ensure users can and will use such facilities? Of course such studies are feasible – given sufficient time – but the designers need some 'ballpark' ideas quickly. What would *you* do?

Of course there is no correct answer to this question, but readers, especially students, might find it a useful exercise to consider what they might be able to do given: two weeks exactly, no other people to help but oneself, a small personal computer, printer, and some statistics, graphics and word-processing packages.

If confronted with a similar problem (and I was a few years ago) I might well take the following course of action. Firstly, I'd consider that whatever the number of telephone numbers people kept in their personal, paper, telephone directories (you know the spare pages at the back of a diary or the purpose-built indexes one can buy) that number would not be exceeded easily or quickly by users of an electronic equivalent. This is not necessarily true, but I would not consider it likely that users would transfer all their existing numbers from paper to machine because the paper version is handy for carrying around, and is always going to be quickly accessible. The system version would only be available more easily if the system was running at the time the user needed to look up a number.

Based on this assumption, I'd design a small questionnaire and administer it to a random selection of 20-30 people who were representative of the lower management levels at whom the package would be aimed. The questionnaire would ask them to go through their paper-based directories, and for each name and number estimate the last time the number was looked up (within the last day, week, month, year), and how frequently it was looked up (daily, weekly *etc.*). Finally I'd ask them to say how many entries they had for each letter of the alphabet.

I might hope to receive about 50% of the entries back with four working days left until my report had to be handed in. All I would have time to do would be to perform some elementary statistics on the data. I'd present the results mostly in pie chart form as in Fig. 2.6 below. I would not produce any significance estimate for the figures (no time) and I'd write a report incorporating the pie charts and tables and including one or two suggestions for the design.

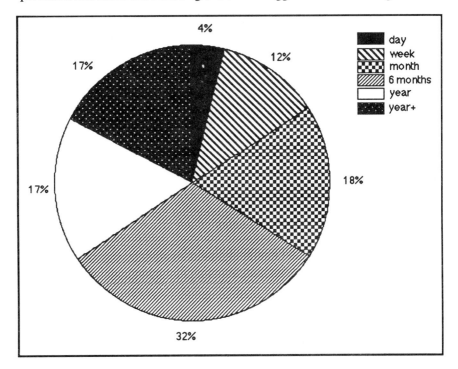

Fig. 2.6 –   Pie chart that might be produced to illustrate the breakdown of frequency of use of numbers stored in personal telephone directories (the values shown here are not based on any survey, they are merely illustrative).

The suggestions might include a facility to allow users to enter a name which would be searched for in order to save users time flicking through lots of electronic 'pages'. Another suggestion might be; the ability to add a new page anywhere in the 'book' should the space under any particular letter become full and provided the allocated memory space was not needed. Finally, I'd provide an initial suggestion for the attribution of pages to letters.

Well, the purists amongst you will probably have a field day pulling such an outrageous example to pieces. Maybe you could do better given the constraints; if you can, well done! The point to be made is that you must do something, it might offend your previously high ideals regarding research, but it will be of more benefit to the designers than if you'd refused on the basis of 'lack of time' or 'scant resources'. As I try to show in Chapter 8, human factors people need to create a niche for themselves. Once the niche is created *then* we can start to demand more time for proper surveys and proper analysis.

Notice how in the example above the designers are choosing to implement a design that relies very heavily on their existing knowledge of the users. The assumption is made that most people understand how to add names to and search through a paper telephone directory – the design reflects that model very strongly.

It may be noticed that, in this example, it is not easy to decide whether the human factors work was performed in order to find out more about users or the tasks they will be expected to perform. This is not entirely accidental – if we attempt to define a user population we do so by reference to some external measure or characteristic. A 'naive' user is naive with respect to something – using a computer is usually implied but it might be a washing machine or a bicycle. The point is, it is important to *define users with respect to tasks*, especially in HCI, where other user parameters (anthropometrics, biomechanics and so on) are usually less relevant to the design process of user interfaces. The rest of this chapter considers the task domain in more detail.

2.5 TASKS

We have seen how knowledge about the user can be useful to the designer in constructing a system. In order to produce a System Image that can be easily assimilated by a user, and that also provides the user with a model of the system that bears more than a passing resemblance to the Designer's Model, the designer needs to know as much as possible about what the system will be used for. That is, the tasks that user needs to perform, and how the system will aid the user in performing those tasks and thereby achieving his/her objectives.

How does the designer obtain information about the tasks that the user is likely to perform? The information is derived from some sort of description of the tasks. The means by which a task is described is thus all important. The technique used is sometimes called 'Requirements Analysis' but more often human factors studies refer to it as 'Task Analysis'.

The reader should understand that it is unusual for a computer system to be devised in order to allow users to do something completely new. In nearly all cases the computer is used as a substitute technology for performing tasks that have already been established. Most new, substitute technologies are more powerful than their predecessors – *ie.* they do all that the old technology could do, but better, or more accurately, or faster, or more efficiently, or cheaper, or some combination of these attributes. Also, it is quite often the case that the new technology is utilised to do other things that the designer had not intended or predicted.

If we consider the case of writing – *ie.* placing information onto some (semi) permanent material. We have progressed from stone engravings, through ink onto parchment and paper, to biros, felt-tipped pens, typewriters and eventually to word-processors. The advent of laser technology has meant that a combination of technologies – word-processing and laser printing – results in a very powerful new technique called 'desktop publishing' (*cf.* Lucas 1987). This combination of technologies allows high quality document production for a fraction of the cost of normal printing. Besides the cost savings there are other benefits; speed, ability to make changes easily, control over the whole production process, *etc.*

So, designers need to know about tasks that users currently perform using some existing technology, in order to exploit those aspects of the new system design or technology in an effective manner. There are several techniques that can be employed to analyse tasks and this section will identify some of the most common ones.

Before considering the essential elements of Task Analysis (TA) the reader should be aware of the two most frequently used forms of TA employed in HCI research.

The two typical forms of TA are:

1.) TA where some design and specification has already taken place. Here TA is used as an early means of evaluation. By making behavioural predictions based upon the system specification, the technique attempts to highlight the consequences of design decisions (Buckley & Johnson 1987). The most commonly quoted example of this type of TA is the Keystroke Level Model (Card, Moran & Newell, 1983) which analyses tasks by examining the actual sequence of key-presses required in order to achieve some objective. Chapter 7 considers Moran's model in more detail.

The aim of this form of TA is to look at aspects of task performance such as 'time taken' or 'errors made' and to predict how these will vary between two or more alternative designs. Of course, in order for such a technique to be valuable the design must be specified in a very detailed form – including the command names, the method of issuing commands to the system, and the effects of issuing such commands.

2.) The other common approach to TA in HCI is to concentrate on the existing task *before* the provision of alternative technology. This maps closely onto the explanation of TA given at the start of this section, and fits in with the description and use of user models provided in the first part of this chapter. Such TA techniques consider in detail, and attempt to describe, how an existing task is performed *in such a way that it is useful for the design of a substitute technology* (Buckley & Johnson, 1987).

2.5.1   Elements of Task Analysis methods
There are some elements of TA that are relevant regardless of the type of TA employed. In order for any specific technique to be useful it must be applicable to a large number of tasks. The ability to apply a technique across a wide var-

iety of task domains is certainly attractive. Such techniques will become adopted because the time and effort spent learning how to use them will be amply rewarded by the large number of times the same technique can be used. Thus a designer will obtain experience in using a method and eventually refine it to suit his/her needs.

The first requirement of any task analysis technique is to provide the designer (let us assume the designer is the person who performs the task analysis, it may in fact be somebody else 'employed by' or 'representing' the designer who actually performs the analysis) with a means of defining and then classifying tasks.

2.5.2   Defining and classifying tasks

Before we can analyse anything, we must have a means of defining that which we are about to analyse. This is true in all spheres of research. Suppose we wished to analyse the 'frequency of smiling' in people being greeted at a railway station. We might gather data by direct observation (*eg.* stand at a platform and count) or we might use indirect observation (*eg.* use a video-camera). Whatever means we use, we shall, sooner or later, need to define what constitutes (and what does not constitute) a 'smile' – probably no easy matter!

In order to make progress in the task arena, we therefore need to define a task. There seems to be no absolute consensus on this matter. Often it is merely a question of level or *grain of analysis*. Consider the following series of events:

1.   A man walks into a railway station.
2.   He enters the ticket office.
3.   He purchases a ticket.
4.   He goes to Platform 8
5.   He boards a train that is headed for Nottingham.

A high level or large grain analysis might say that the task was 'to get to Nottingham' (*ie.* getting a train was only one option).

A slightly narrower grain of analysis might see the task as being 'to get the train to Nottingham' and the *objective* as; 'to get to Nottingham.'

A still narrower grain might consider the above scenario as a *series of tasks* performed in order to achieve an objective. Thus 'enter station', 'locate ticket office', 'purchase ticket' might each be considered as a task in its own right.

We could go further, consider the task 'purchase ticket' that really consists of sub-tasks such as 'state destination', 'find wallet', 'withdraw money', 'place money on counter' *etc.* There are yet deeper analyses that we could perform, right down to biomechanical limb movements and beyond. The value of an analysis that is too broad grained or too fine grained is limited, in the former we encapsulate too much within the task itself, while in the latter we are drawn to consider minutiae of detail which make us lose sight of the whole event.

Many HCI researchers thus try to work somewhere in the middle of this spectrum of task definition. As pointed out before, some models get down to individual keystrokes, but this is too fine for many practical purposes because it is time consuming – the data analysis especially.

A reasonable approach has been adopted by (amongst others) Peter Johnson of Queen Mary College, University of London. He considers tasks to consist of an *action* performed upon an *object*. A series of tasks make up a goal or an objective. The beauty of this approach is that for most user interfaces this allows us to consider a *generic* set of actions and objects.

In a word-processing package a typical generic action would be 'delete'. We could apply that to a number of objects such as: 'word', 'paragraph' or 'document'. Thus, by combining the action with the object we have defined the task – 'delete word' for example.

This method of analysing and describing tasks is referred to in the literature as TAKD – Task Analysis for Knowledge Descriptions – (Johnson, Diaper & Long, 1984, Johnson, 1985) and has been applied to user interface design (although that was not its original purpose). As well as providing the description as explained above, TAKD also provides a formal notation for describing tasks, but that will not be dealt with in this book. Interested readers should follow up the Johnson references.

2.5.3   Source tasks

So far, I have discussed how the tasks might be defined and represented on the computer. Analysis of such tasks is important, especially in evaluation (Chapter 7). However, can we map the 'action/object' model of tasks onto 'real-world' activities that might be required to be replicated or substituted for in the computerised version?

Essentially, we wish to identify the tasks performed currently using 'old' technology which are to be substituted (and hopefully enhanced) in the computerised 'new' technology. By considering tasks as consisting of actions and objects, we can look at what people *do and know* in their current domain in order to identify core or source tasks.

Buckley & Johnson (1987) describe in some detail how communication tasks were analysed in order to provide input to the design of an electronic message system. They divided the domain of structured communication into five categories:

1.)   Communication Channel (the means by which information is encoded).
2.)   Interface (the means of controlling the sending and receipt of messages).
3.)   Activity (the goal of the group involved in communicating).
4.)   Dialogue Support (protocols that help maintain social relations between the communicants).
5.)   Organisation (the institution within which the group exists and its rules).

Buckley & Johnson (*op cit.*) go on to describe how, from this categorisation, they can associate knowledge with such features and thereby derive clues for the design of a user interface that allows users to utilise their existing task knowledge in the new domain. A trivial and untested example follows which it is hcped will suffice.

In order to send a document, we often place it in an envelope and then place the envelope in a receptacle such as a post-box or an 'out-tray'. The question is, can we utilise this existing knowledge of how to perform a task ('send' = action / 'document' = object) in the design of an electronic message system? One way might be to have an small screen image (an icon) of a post-box into which an icon representing the document is placed. The use of such interface 'metaphors' is one partial solution to the interface design problem. It is incomplete because metaphors always break down at some point, often leaving the user unsure as to the result of the action performed. Referring to the above example, we also know that out-trays and post-boxes are emptied, and if they are not, the message remains unsent. So, do we extend the analogy by showing a little postman coming along to empty the post-box icon on the screen in order to reassure the sender? The matter of screen representations will be discussed further in Chapter 5.

2.5.4   Norman's task model
It is worth mentioning here Donald Norman's model of a task, not only as a contrast, but for the sake of completeness. His influential writings are well worth seeking out in their own right.

Norman points out that even simple tasks have a large number of aspects,.as can be seen from the list below. All these need to be taken into account when designing a system, since each task performed by a user on the system will have associated with it the aspects below.

Aspect 1   *Goals and intentions*
                 What the user wishes to get the system to do is the *goal*. The *intention* is formed when a decision to achieve the goal is made, that is when a user decides to *act*.

Aspect 2   *Mapping from goals and intentions to action sequence*
                 In order to specify the sequence of actions the user must translate the psychological goals and intentions into the desired system state, and then determine a course of physical control actions that will bring such a system state into being.

Aspect 3   *Specification of the action sequence*
                 A psychological process whereby the user mentally represents and rehearses the control actions that need to be executed.

Aspect 4   *The state of the system*
                 The physical state of the system, *ie.* what all the variables are at a given time.

Aspect 5   *Control mechanisms*
                 The devices (see Chapter 5) and controls available to the user to alter the system variables.

Aspect 6   *Mapping between the mechanisms and the system state*
                 How varying a control varies the system state.

Aspect 7   *Interpretation of the system state*
                 How the user perceives the system and then interprets that perception in terms of the psychological variables of interest.

Aspect 8   *Evaluating the outcome*
A comparison is made between the perceived system state and the desired system state (the goals). When these are mismatched, a new set of goals and intentions are formulated and the process starts again.

Norman (1986) then uses these aspects to form a seven stage analysis of tasks:

1.)   Establishing the goal.
2.)   Forming the intention.
3.)   Specifying the action sequence.
4.)   Executing the action.
5.)   Perceiving the system state.
6.)   Interpreting the system state.
7.)   Evaluating the system state with respect to the goals and intentions.

Let us consider these in relation to a simple text editing task (human factors literature is replete with text editing tasks!).

1.)   The *goal* is a grammatically correct sentence.
2.)   The *intention* is to edit the existing sentence.
3.)   The *action sequence* is: highlight word, then delete word, then stop.
4.)   The *action* is: move cursor to beginning of word, press control key and the 'w' key (the word is now highlighted), press backspace key.
5.)   The *system state* is perceived by looking at the sentence on the screen.
6.)   The sentence is *interpreted* by reading the sentence.
7.)   The current sentence is then *compared* with the desired goal (a grammatically correct sentence). If the sentence is grammatically correct then the task has been successfully accomplished.

Of course some of these activities run into each other or occur so quickly that it is hard for us to notice the separate stages. That is not the point. By making explicit that there are several (I believe Norman considers this analysis to be still evolving, so there may yet be stages to add) stages to the accomplishment of any task, it should be possible for the designer to consider whether the system is designed to provide optimally for the user to move through the stages easily and gracefully.

2.6 SUMMARY AND DISCUSSION

This chapter has tried to deal with two closely interrelated areas, users and tasks. Both are complex, users especially so. Three models, designer's, user's and system image, have been defined and discussed. Some ideas about how to find out about users have also been presented.

A simplistic but practical approach may be to consider just three classes of user as James (1981) does in a short but interesting chapter. His classes are: the systems programmer (an expert), the engineer / scientist / technologist (regular user), and the general 'member of the public' (inexperienced or infrequent user).

This last class is the largest and for James the class that is likely to be dominant. Of course, (and James makes this point too) in reality these are not
discrete classes but merely identifiable points on a continuum. People will
migrate from one group to another. Indeed, it is my view that we are all mi-
grating towards the expert end of the scale. As computers infiltrate more and
more jobs and more people's lives they will acquire computing skills. As they
do so, their expectations of computers will change, and their expectations of the
user interface will change too. One does not have to be shown a better or improved interface for long before the question, "why don't more systems work
this way?" pops into one's head.

Tasks and Task Analysis have also been considered and although the objectives of users often vary, depending upon where on the continuum of experience
or skill the user resides, the tasks users need to perform in order to achieve their
objectives are often very similar. One method of describing tasks has been
identified in this chapter though interested readers should look at other methods
such as Steve Payne's Task Action Grammar (TAG) (Payne, 1984). Performing
the tasks (for example, deleting the word or sending the electronic mail
message) may be achieved in a vast variety of ways. Assessing the relative
merits of the different means of interacting with a system to perform tasks (and
thereby achieve objectives) is not easy, but has been the subject of much study.
The next three chapters cover many points of interest in this very area.

Finally, Eason & Damordaran (1981) considered four attributes of the human-computer amalgam that are important when considering the naive user,
though it is certainly reasonable to extend these four attributes to other users
too.

1.)   The Task - Tool Relationship
      How well does the system fit the objectives the user needs to reach? A
      system considered good by 99 other users will still be dubbed poor by a
      user who cannot get it to do what he/she wants.

2.)   Expertise in Computer Technology
      What skills are necessary to perform the tasks to achieve the objective?
      Can an experienced user be confronted with an interface which will allow
      him/her to 'cash in' on the expertise acquired or will all users have to deal
      with the same interface? Adaptive interfaces that respond in some way to
      the user either by recognising a user profile (ie. the user logs on and
      associated with the log-on is some information that governs how the sys-
      tem looks / responds to that user) or by some other 'intelligent' means
      have been cited as a solution to this design dilemma. However, work on
      adaptive interfaces has not proceeded as far as it once promised, mainly
      because it is very difficult to do well – at the moment.

3.)   Ease of Use
      This recognises the fact that the user ultimately regards the system as a
      means to an end. The user will often wish to keep the interaction with the
      computer to a minimum. Whilst ease of use will always be an important
      factor to consider in any assessment of a system, it is not necessarily true
      that users will continue to seek to minimise their interaction with the

system. Eminent HCI researchers are suggesting that user interfaces need to be 'more fun'. They cite the example of the computer games industry and how many hours people are prepared to spend interacting with a computer if they find that interaction stimulating, amusing, exciting and just plain *fun*. This author is certainly attracted by this view. Perhaps one day when we are considering the ease of use of a system we shall also consider a complementary function; whether it is also 'fun-to-use'.

4.)   User Support and Training
This book unfortunately will not deal at all with issues such as user documentation and training. It is nonetheless an extremely important area in which human factors people can and should make greater contributions. Pat Wright of the Applied Psychology Unit at Cambridge has been one of the few who have made their voice heard in this domain. Her plenary address at CHI '83 (Wright, 1983) is well worth a read. All users need training, support and documentation. More and more systems are building in help or explanation facilities, but not always particularly well. Chapter 3 deals with the provision of help in more detail.

Although the notions of 'user' and 'task' appear at first sight to be simple and easy to comprehend, it is quickly apparent that these innocent terms contain an unsuspected depth. Knowing the user and knowing the task, which is where we came in, is an ideal which is in fact very hard to meet. Complex models of users, designers and systems, and definition and classification of tasks are prerequisites to such knowledge. Anybody who has worked in the human, biological or social sciences for any short time soon realises how difficult it is to find out real truths or constants about biologically complex systems. We must make that effort, but we should not underestimate the difficulty of our task.

3

Four Common Design Issues

3.1 INTRODUCTION

This chapter considers four interesting issues in the design of user interfaces. They are: system response times (Section 3.1), providing help for the user (3.2), error messages (3.3) and command names (3.4). The critical reader will, with some justification, ask, "why *these* four particular issues, and not four others?". Of course there are many design issues that could be treated in a fashion similar to those selected here. The design issues presented in this chapter are worthy of attention for many reasons, but the reason they have been specifically selected is the frequency with which human factors people have to provide advice to designers on these very issues.

There is a good reason why we are often asked for advice on these specific issues. All four are areas of system design that can often be altered at comparatively late stages in the design process. This is especially true of the last three, but system response time too can often be improved late on in the development cycle by using better hardware *eg.* faster processors or better software *eg.* good compilers.

Now, although human factors people are ever willing to recite a long series of arguments for the importance of taking the user's view into account at the earliest possible stage of the design process, the unalterable fact of life for professional human factors specialists is that such occasions are comparatively rare. It is much more likely that even as late as the first prototype, (or exceptionally, the alpha trial stages of design) problems related to presenting help information, error messages, and command names will appear. A few 'users', or at least people not directly related to the design team, 'have a go' at the system (it is often as vague as that!) and find some user interface issues not to their liking. Panic sets in, what to do? Then comes the rallying cry, "Call for human factors!" And so, like some high tech fire-fighters, we are called in to fight the flames of bad design. The fires we fight are often, but not exclusively, in the areas covered by this chapter.

All the issues here have a considerable research literature, and are still undergoing investigation in human factors laboratories, academic and industrial, in many places throughout the world. The four topics in this chapter; System Response Times, Help Messages, Error Messages and Command Names, are covered in sufficient detail to give all readers a flavour of the nature of the issue, from a human factors perspective. The topics have also been selected to reflect the breadth of topics that come under the scrutiny of the human factors person, and for the uninitiated how any aspect of user interface design has human factors implications. References are made to the literature, and those wishing for more information than is conveyed here should follow these up. Each topic in this chapter also has either some associated guidelines or some issues that designers ought to consider. These are intended to be complementary to the discussion in the text, rather than to be blindly copied – or worse, implemented – without some understanding of the applicability and limitations of such general guidelines. If Chapter 2 made any point at all, it was that users and tasks vary in every situation, and knowledge of both those aspects will help you apply guidelines where appropriate and *ignore them where inappropriate.*

3.2 SYSTEM RESPONSE TIME

3.2.1 The concept
When a user interacts with a computer system, the interaction can be considered in separate phases, which form a cycle. Fig. 3.1 illustrates one way of considering the phases involved in a single cycle of user-computer dialogue.

The user decides to enter something into the computer, either from a self-initiated decision or in response to a prompt of some kind from the computer system. The user then manipulates some kind of input device, typically a key-board, and the information the user wishes to enter into the computer appears on the screen. Very often after one further manipulative action, usually pressing a RETURN or ENTER key, the information entered is processed by the computer. Eventually the computer will respond by providing the user with some kind of feedback. This might be a system message appearing on the screen, or a flashing line or box (the cursor) which often indicates the system is awaiting further input from the user.

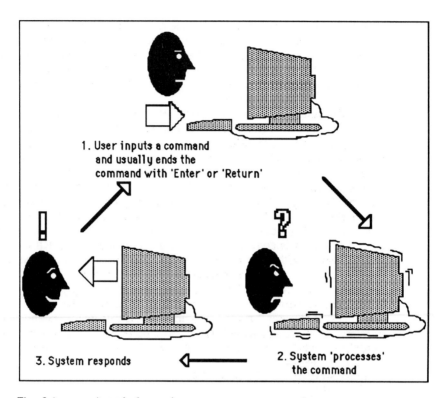

Fig. 3.1 –   A typical user input-system response cycle

This is such a generalized cycle of events that it is almost too vague to be of value. The point is, that there are finite periods of time associated with each event. The system may process the information before displaying it on the screen or it may simply display (echo) a user's input until told (by the ENTER or RETURN key) actually to process that input in some way.

Here are two examples of the cycle for two rather different tasks.

Example 1: Database Request.

1.)   The user decides to request a page of information from a videotex database.
2.)   The user types in the page number required.
3.)   The system displays the number entered by the user.
4.)   The user presses the ENTER key.
5.)   The system 'processes' the page number required by searching through the database and when the associated information is located the system displays it on the screen.

Example 2: Logging Onto a Computer.

1.)   The user responds to a request for a password.

2.)   The user types in the password.
3.)   The system does not display the password (for security reasons).
4.)   The user presses the ENTER key.
5.)   The system 'processes' the password and if it is valid, the system's 'welcome' message appears on the screen.

Each of the stages in these examples takes a finite amount of time, either for the user to process the information presented on the screen, make a decision, and carry out the consequences of that decision, or for the computer to process the data input by the user and to respond accordingly. Note that at this time we are not making any judgement regarding the quality of the information entered by the user or provided by the system. The user might type in a meaningless string of characters or a complicated mathematical equation; the system might respond with an error message, or a series of numbers that is 1000 lines long.

System Response Time (SRT) can be defined as:

"The interval between a user-initiated event and the system's response to that event. That is, it is the time from the last input action until the system responds to the user with some type of output signal."

3.2.2   The issues
There are two main issues that are of concern to ergonomists. The first is the length of the SRT. If it is too short, the user might be rushed to work at an uncomfortably fast pace If the SRT is too long, the user might become frustrated, bored or angry. Thus the *length of the SRT*, can affect how the user responds and therefore it can have a detrimental effect on task performance.

The second issue is that the *variability of the SRT* can affect users too. If users start to expect the system to respond in a given time, whatever its length, and the system varies the response time significantly, users will become uncertain about the system ("has it crashed (*ie.* broken down) or is it still thinking?") which again can result in a degradation in user performance.

Both these issues can affect not only the users' performance but also their attitude to the system. Once a system is regarded as 'untrustworthy' in some way by the user population, because of SRT variability, or they regard it as 'too slow' because of the length of time it is perceived to take to process their inputs, then we are on the very slippery slope of a positive feedback loop. Users may return to the old 'pre-computerization' method if possible, or they might start checking computer outputs, or they might start to make more errors themselves. All these will further lower their regard for the computer system.

3.2.3   Research
A study by Martin & Corl (1986) looked at how user productivity was affected when SRT was reduced. Their intention was to see whether claims made by other researchers, such as Lambert (1984), that large gains in user productivity result from decreasing system response time could be replicated. More radical claims have also been made by some workers, namely that sub-second systems responses produce *dramatic* improvements (*eg.* Smith, 1983) in user productivity.

Of course such extremely fast response times are appropriate only to some tasks, mostly where rapid responses with little processing by the users is possible. That is, in one narrow set, out of a very wide spectrum of user activities, extremely fast SRTs might be valuable. Martin & Corl (*op. cit.*) provide a fuller critique of some of these studies.

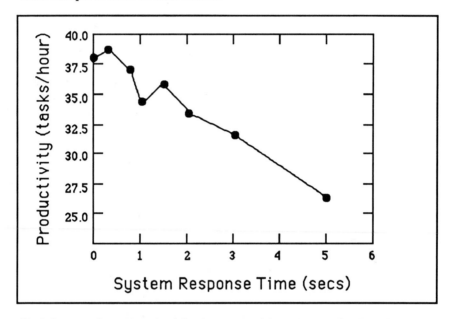

Fig 3.2 –   Overall productivity (as measured by tasks completed per hour) as a function of system response time.

After Martin & Corl (1986)

Martin & Corl (*op. cit.*) varied SRT between 0.1 and 5.0 seconds for 24 subjects. The tasks required of subjects were either a routine data-entry task or a problem solving set of tasks of varying complexity. Figure 3.2 above shows their results for tasks per hour against system response time. Tasks per hour can be taken here to be a good measure of productivity since any loss of accuracy with increasing speed was found to be negligible.

This graph included both types of task. The authors found that user productivity was in fact greater in the simple data-entry tasks when SRT was reduced, *and non-existent in problem-solving tasks*. Martin & Corl (*op. cit.*), made the following important conclusions, from their studies:

1.)   Decreasing system response time does result in an increase in user productivity *in some situations;*
2.)   These situations are limited to simple, habitual tasks;
3.)   Problem-solving tasks showed no improvement, in terms of productivity, with decreased SRTs;
4.)   Many users were unhappy working with the slowest response times and persevered only because they were participating in an experiment, normally they would have logged off and used the system when it was likely

to provide a faster SRT (when there were less users competing for the computer's resources). *Thus long SRTs are not acceptable* even if they do not necessarily affect productivity.

3.2.4   Guidelines

There are several sets of guidelines available, some very vague and generalized (*eg*. Galitz, 1980). When formulating a contribution for the CCITT[†], Human Factors Working Party, I referred to Gallaway (1981) as the main and best offering in this area. Below are the extracts of his recommendations I offered to the CCITT at a meeting of the Human Factors Working Party in Stockholm, 1987.

ACTIVITY	RECOMMENDED RESPONSE TIME (in seconds)
System Activation	3.0
Tracking the movement of an input device such as a mouse or track-ball	0.1
Request for a 'simple' service (*eg*. selecting a menu item)	2.0
Request for a 'complex' service (*eg*. multiple step selection task)	5.0
Response to a 'simple' inquiry (query from a database)	2.0
Response to a 'complex' inquiry (*eg*. search using boolean operators)	2.0 - 4.0
Error Feedback	0.5 - 2.0

Table 3.1 –   Some recommended system response times

(After Gallaway)

Because response time variability is also important, the following acceptable variations in the above SRTs are recommended:
1.)   For system response times of 0 – 2 seconds +/– 5%
2.)   For system response times of 2 – 4 seconds +/– 10%
3.)   For system response times of 4 – 30 seconds +/– 15%.

[†] The initials CCITT stand for the French equivalent of :
' The International Telegraph and Telephone Consultative Committee'

3.3 PROVIDING HELP FOR THE USER

3.3.1   The concept

No matter how well a computer system and the user interfaces are designed, there will be occasions when users 'get stuck' during a task. That is, users will sometimes not know what the correct input to the computer should be. In poorly designed systems, which have been designed without much thought to the user's model of the system, this will happen more frequently than in well designed systems.

One very useful method of dealing with such contingencies is to build into the computer system a 'help package'. In essence these are a series of notes, prompts or hints which the user in some circumstances can call upon to be displayed on the screen. There are a wide variety of help systems, ranging from an 'online' user manual (such as is provided in the UNIX[†] operating system) through context sensitive help systems to elegant knowledge-based help systems. In a large number of applications packages sold today for the major personal microcomputers, and for the larger computing systems, a help package is often provided as an integral part of the overall package.

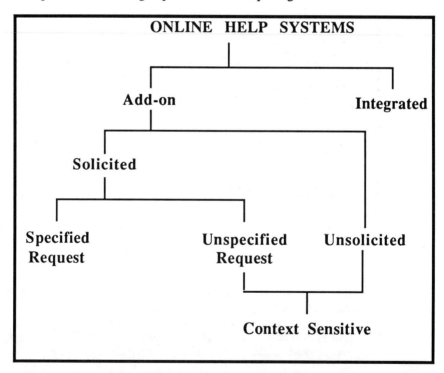

Fig. 3.3 –   Proposed definition of types of Online Help systems.

[†] UNIX is a registered trademark of the Bell Telephone Laboratories

Fig. 3.3 above shows a set of definitions of different types of help systems that the author proposed to CCITT in 1986. This set of definitions was based on those of Hans Bergman (1985).

This definition (which was not completely taken up) clearly separates help that has been integrated into the system from the start of the design and help systems which have come to be added on later. Note that context sensitive help (*ie*. help information that is related to the particular point in the dialogue or place in the system that the user has reached) can be obtained either by solicitation by the user (in which case it needn't be specified because the system 'knows' where the user is or what the user is trying to do), or it can be provided by the system as an unsolicited piece of information (*ie*. the system detects that the user is having difficulties and offers advice or help without being requested by the user). This section will not deal with intelligent help systems, which are usually extensions of the unsolicited type of help, but a paper that does consider this area in some detail was written by Erlandsen & Holm (1987).

3.3.2   The issues
There are two levels of issues to be considered. At the top level, the issue is that some form of computer-based help may be the human factors consultant's only chance to influence a computer system design. Such situations are, of course, regrettable, but it is a fact of life that often our specialist advice is called for when the system design is either 'frozen' (a jargon word for completed or fixed) or too far 'down the road' to incorporate major changes. When placed in such an invidious position, the best the user interface designer can offer may be to design the help system, so that despite the failings of the system design, the poor user has at least recourse to some well-designed help information.

The second level issues are concerned with the design of such help systems, when should help be provided, how should it be requested, how should it be presented. This section concentrates on these issues, which have generated a considerable amount of research.

3.3.3   Research
Magers (1983) reported on an experimental evaluation of online help for non-experts. She found that modifying the help and error messages originally intended for programmers resulted in the system in question being easier to learn. The modifications included the provision of a specially labelled HELP key. Measures included time to complete a task, accuracy and attitudes of users all of which were improved with the modified system.

A good starting point for any reader interested in this particular area is a paper presented at Interact '84 (Williges, Elkerton, Pittman & Cohill, 1984) which reviews several research studies (by subsets of the same authors) on human factors design considerations for online help for novice computer users. I shall precis only one of these studies here.

Cohill & Williges (1982) evaluated nine procedures for initiating, presenting and selecting a help system on an interactive computer system. The main aim of the study was to determine how to apportion responsibilities between a user and the system in retrieving help information. The table below summarises their different experimental conditions.

Condition	Initiation of Help	Selection of Help	Presentation Mode
1	User	User	Hardcopy
2	User	User	Online
3	User	Computer	Hardcopy
4	User	Computer	Online
5	Computer	User	Hardcopy
6	Computer	User	Online
7	Computer	Computer	Hardcopy
8	Computer	Computer	Online
9	Control Condition	-	No Help Available

Table 3.2 –   The nine experimental conditions used by Cohill & Williges (1982).

Their results are summarised in Table 3.3 below.

Conditions Compared	Average Time/Task (secs)	Average Errors/Task
Help Available (Conditions1-8)	376.6	1.4
No Help Available (Condition 9)	679.1	5.0
User Initiated, User Selected (Conditions 1 and 2)	332.0	0.8
Other Help Configurations (Conditions 3-8)	394.8	1.7
User Selected, Hardcopy (Conditions 1 and 5)	330.5	0.9
Other Help Configurations (Conditions 2-4 and 6-8)	392.0	1.6

Table 3.3 –   Comparison of various experimental conditions measured against average time per task and average error per task.

(after Williges et al 1984)

The first finding that can be derived from the data presented in Table 3.3 is that providing *any* type of help brought about a dramatic improvement in operator performance. Look at the first block of data in Table 3.3, which compares all the conditions in which some form of help was provided with the control condition – the average task times without any help were roughly 80% longer and errors were more than three times as frequent. The second important finding can be obtained by examining the second and third blocks of data in Table 3.3. Here it can be seen that allowing users control of when to initiate a help request and when to select help is better in terms of speed of task and frequency of errors. The third interesting finding is that users – novice users at least - seem to prefer hard-copy (*ie.* printed) help rather than screen presentations of help.

3.3.4   Acting on results – a word of caution

This last finding is interesting not least because it demonstrates how laboratory experiments can lead to implementations of ideas or methods into the workplace which are impractical or less successful than the experimental work leads us to believe.

Based on the above study we might well march into an office which is about to implement a new computerised system to be used mostly by inexperienced computer users, and pronounce that we need not bother with online help because the users will prefer hard-copy manuals. Although a straight examination of the evidence might suggest this course of action, a little experience of working in an office would temper this view with a dose of reality.

The reality is that offices are full of books, documents, files, shelves and cupboards, desks, drawers and filing cabinets. Manuals get lost, misplaced, used as plates, made into props for wobbly desks, have coffee spilt on them and so on. Manuals are never (or rarely) where you want them, when you want them (which is next to you and open at the right page). The clean experiment where the subject has one manual placed at his or her side means little in the littered desk environment in which most of us work.

A cynical view? Yes, but it is worth bearing in mind that all findings from laboratory simulations need to be taken with a pinch of salt and a healthy dose of cynicism before practical implementations based on such studies are decided upon.

3.3.5   Some guidelines and some considerations

It is difficult to provide guidelines that cover the variety of eventualities likely to be encountered across the spectrum of computers and their applications. Here are a few generalities that are worthwhile following.

1.)   Make any help information consistent with other instructional material provided (*eg.* manuals). Use terms that the system uses in the same way and with the same meaning.
2.)   Avoid jargon and acronyms; rather use simple, familiar words.
3.)   Use affirmative wording that tells the user what to do, rather than what to avoid. Use the active voice rather than the passive in messages, *eg.* "Scroll the screen by pressing the key marked with a downward arrow" rather than "The screen can be scrolled by depressing the down arrow key".
4.)   Finally, ensure that help information is up-to-date.

Here are some factors that should be considered when designing or advising on the design of an online help system:

1.)   How will users request help?
      Options include: a labelled key, a function key (*eg.* F2), a command entered by the user.

2.)   How will help be presented?

Options include: in a separate window, by over-writing the whole screen, by writing into a fixed and consistent space (*eg.* the bottom four lines on the screen).

3)   How will help be disabled?
That is, how will users get back to the original task?

4)   Should the help provided be hierarchical?
One way of providing levels of help for a variety of users is to provide users who request help with just rudimentary help in the first instance, like some hints. Users who find this insufficient might request help again from this level and be provided with a deeper or more lengthy explanation – a two- tier help system.

5)   Should help be available at all points in the system?
The author has certainly experienced systems which sometimes respond to a help request with "Sorry no help available for this task/command/part of the system".

3.4 ERROR MESSAGES

3.4.1   The concept
If you've worked with computers before, then you'll almost certainly be familiar with the concept of error messages. They are sometimes provided by the system to warn users of an error (rather a harsh term – often it is a mere oversight) they have just made and which may be corrected *eg*:

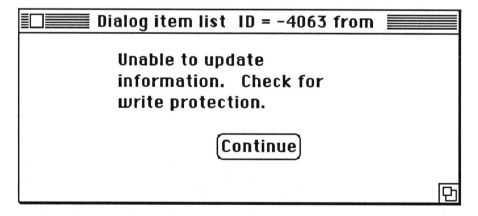

Dialog item list ID = –4063 from

Unable to update information. Check for write protection.

Continue

Fig. 3.4 –   Example of a system warning.

Here the user can 'click' (see Chapter 5, WIMP interfaces) on the Continue button (in fact he has no choice!) and check the file or disk to see if it is 'write protected' (*ie.* unable to be overwritten by new data). Often the message comes too late, for example after the system has crashed. In such cases the message rarely does anything to help the user easily identify the source of the error. Error messages are often badly worded, full of programmer's jargon and indecipherable codes.

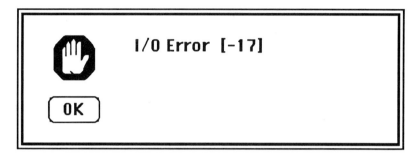

Fig. 3.5 –   Example of an uninterpretable error message.

It is frustrating to be forced (as one is in this example) to say "OK" to an error message that is meaningless, it makes me feel stupid and unquestioning to respond in such a way. (This reminds me of how, as far as I understand, one was to behave at an English public school in the old days At such places you were beaten for doing something wrong, and after the beating you were expected to shake hands with and thank the person who had just administered the thrashing!) In this case, not only am I made all too aware of a mistake, I am made to regret it by being scolded for doing something (an I/O Error?) I don't even understand! Furthermore such a message provides no clue as to the source of the mistake or how it can be corrected and therefore avoided in the future.

Lewis & Norman (1986) question, quite rightly, why such situations are even referred to as 'errors'. They see the use of the term error as an arrogant point of view coming from a system (and hence from some human system designers) designed to be of service to its users. They suggest an apology for getting confused and misinterpreting the information input would be more appropriate – but I think a fawning, apologetic system would be just as awful.

One of the main aims of this book is to help people design computer systems that minimize user errors. It is also useful to accept that people will always make mistakes and we should aim to design systems that allow users to discover easily and quickly that they have made a mistake and to help them recover from the error. The recovery from an error can be made easier by the provision of such things as an 'Undo' command – which is particularly useful in graphical drawing and painting applications, when lines can easily be mispositioned.

3.4.2 The issues
There is insufficient space here to detail the types of studies that have been performed in the domain of error messages and system messages. The Lewis & Norman chapter (*op. cit*) is full of good sense and worth reading. Here I shall just mention some issues that need to be borne in mind when commenting on system messages.

1.)   As with Help messages in the previous section, Error messages should be concise and yet clearly stated.

2.)   They should be polite (apologetic?) and never imply blame on the part of the user (all human-computer interaction is a two-party affair and each must assume some responsibility).

3)   Error messages without constructive advice are of little value. Informing the user of where the error has occurred, what sort of error (if appropriate) and how to recover from the error are all essential parts of a proper error message system.

4)   Provide an 'Undo' facility or a 'Revert' facility if possible.

5)   Warn users. If a user is about to save a document with the same name as an existing document he should be warned before the action is completed. Systems that automatically overwrite files should be a thing of the past.

6)   Consider carefully where to display error messages. Often the bottom two or three lines of the screen (the status area) are used but sometimes fail to attract the user's attention. If they have to be placed in a remote corner of the screen you should consider some way in which the user's attention may be attracted to message – beeps and/or flashing the message are two well known methods. Other systems use a window that overwrites the screen.

3.5 COMMAND NAMES

3.5.1   The concept

The naming of commands that a user has access to has been the subject of study for many years. There are several areas that ought be of interest to students and designers of computer systems. The basic concept of this area is that computer systems are operated by people via some sort of command language. It may be a sparse language of very few words, it may have no words at all but require users to manipulate screen objects or to perform actions upon screen objects in order to perform a certain function (*eg*. 'double-click' a mouse button (*cf*. Chapter 5) to open a file), or it may be a very deep and detailed language. Whatever form it takes, users must communicate with the system via some sort of command language. And once there is a means of issuing commands to a computer then the naming of the commands – usually what the user has to type in to get the computer to do something – becomes of interest to the human factors expert. As Thomas and Schneider (1982) state:

"Discovering how to name these things well can contribute to systems that lead to greater productivity and less frustration."

3.5.2   Issues and a little anecdote[†]

Although some philosophers have, as Carroll (1982) points out, regarded names as meaningless or arbitrary placeholders, there is more than just the philosophical perspective to consider. Carroll (*op. cit*) goes on to say that there is a sense in which names do have some meaning, in that although any *one* name of a file or a command might appear arbitrary when decontextualised, a command *set* or a group of files or system directories do usually have a structure when examined *in toto*. Understanding the structure will often lead to an ability to predict the contents of the file or the result of entering a command.

Furthermore, people derive inferences about commands and file-names which, when incorrect, lead to confusion and frustration. In this context, the consistency of command names is very important. An example that I have retained for moments such as this refers to a line-based text editor. In such text editors, users do not have the benefit of being able to see and edit a whole block of text (as in a screen based editor); rather they have to issue commands to move between each line. In the editor in question the command to move up a line (to edit the line above the one you just edited or displayed on screen) was simply 'U' – which was an abbreviated command for 'Up'. Armed with such knowledge it would be reasonable, would it not, to infer that the command to move down a line would be 'D'? Unfortunately entering the command 'D' would Delete the line you had just edited! In order to move down a line, the command was 'N' – for 'Next line' of course! You can imagine the consternation such a naming convention caused amongst users.

Issues that have been studied in this domain include the following:

1.)   The suggestiveness of command names (*eg.* Rosenberg, 1982).
This issue concerns how well the name of a command maps onto its action. For example the word 'file' is often used as a verb in command sets when it means the same as 'save' or 'put away'. The problem with 'file' is that it is also used as a noun in many systems. The more a command name suggests its function, the more guessable become forgotten or unknown commands.

2.)   How to abbreviate commands (*eg.* Hirsh-Pasek, Nudelman & Schneider (1982).
This issue concerns both when and how to abbreviate commands. It soon becomes tedious for experienced users to type in lengthy commands, so many commands get abbreviated by systems designers. The schemes for abbreviation of command names come in a variety of types. *Truncation* is one method whereby 'one or more contiguous terminal letters of a word are omitted' (Hodge & Pennington 1973) – *eg.* January becomes Jan. *Contraction* is another method, when interior letters are removed and the remaining letters 'coalesce' to form the abbreviated word. Often the letters removed are vowels, repeated letters and one or two consonants –*eg.* Message becomes Msg. Studies have shown that whatever scheme is

---

[†] Carroll (1982) coincidentally, uses a very similar example to help explain his use of the term *congruent* as applied to command languages

used, a rule-based scheme is better than no scheme at all or a confusion of schemes. These commands from a well-known operating system are examples of a confused scheme. Try covering up the right-hand column and guessing what the command stands for – try inferring the next meaning from the last 'rule' you encountered, or thought you encountered!

passwd	means	change **PASSWorD**
pwd	means	**Print Working Directory**
ls	means	**LiSt** all files in current directory
cd	means	**Change Directory**
wall	means	**Write** to **ALL** users
write	means	**WRITE** a message to another user

Table 3.4 – Abbreviated commands and their meanings in a single command set.

3.)   User designated versus system imposed commands (*eg.* Scapin 1982)
There have been attempts not only to suggest a set of command names or file names, but also to allow users to designate their own names. This has been studied, and appears to be less successful than one might guess, since people tend not to use a clear rule-based naming convention. In addition to this issue there are the issues of preference and also how well users perform with what they claim to be a preferred command set. Perry & Lindgaard (1985) investigated this particular aspect of naming.

4.)   Learning and remembering commands (*eg.* Black & Moran 1982, Carroll, 1982)
This topic is almost the essence of this section. How easy are commands to learn and remember? What experiments might be devised to test the memorability of commands?

Most of the above papers appear in a special issue of *Behaviour and Information Technology* : Vol 1 No. 4, which gives a far deeper treatment of the subject than is possible here.

3.5.3   Guidelines
At least some of the excellent work quoted in this section should be read before embarking on the design of command set. However, some of the research studies do allow some guidelines to be tentatively promoted. Other guidelines here are based on that rather overused attribute (in the absence of proper empirical evidence, that is) that 'we' always have more of than 'they' – common-sense.

1.) Use terms and phrases that will be familiar to the user. Task analysis (*cf.* Chapter 2) will often reveal terminology that the user will be familiar with – use this when possible rather than jargon terms.

2.) Be consistent (a familiar cry). Use pairs of opposites whenever appropriate (see 3.4.2). Also make the command structure or syntax consistent. It is better always to have the verb followed by the noun (actually "the operator followed by the operand" is the technically correct terminology here) – *eg.* 'open file' – as that is more like written English, but if the terms *are* to be reversed ('file open') make sure they are *always* reversed.

3.) Make commands guessable. If a consistent approach to naming is applied, users who have not used the system for a while might be able to guess at least some of the commands.

4.) Use short words. In systems where abbreviations are not possible, long commands must increase the possibility of mis-spelling or mis-typing.

5.) Allow users a variety of ways of entering a command. This matter is also discussed in Chapter 4 when menus and 'accelerators' are introduced. If 'control O' and 'Open' and a 'pull-down' menu (see Chapter 4) with 'Open' as a choice can all be offered to the user as alternative ways of achieving the same objective, so much the better. Use the flexibility that computers allow.

6.) Allow users to view self-named objects or files in a variety of ways. If users do name their own files in an incoherent manner, and evidence suggests they do, then we should be designing systems that do not exploit such a 'weakness'. If a user cannot remember the whole name of a file, she might remember part of the name, or the date it was created (approximately). Systems that help users easily search for files in this way are still few and far between.

3.6 SUMMARY

This chapter has presented four typical design issues which frequently confront human factors consultants. This is no advocacy of the piecemeal approach to system design. It is a recognition of how things are to be found in many industries today. The picture is changing, slowly. As design teams realise the effective contributions that can be made from specialist human factors people, they will tend to call them in for advice earlier and earlier in the design. All that we specialists can do is perform the work required of us, whilst making the message of early involvement be heard loud and clear. The other requirement is for us to do good work in order to gain recognition for ourselves, our colleagues and our specialism.

4

Menus

4.1 INTRODUCTION

Most people with little or no experience of computers will probably associate the word *menu* with restaurants and the selection of food. Some short time after being seated at a table in a restaurant we are invariably presented with *the* menu (there is rarely more than one – though it is interesting to note that when choosing wine from a further and separately presented set of choices, the choices are contained in a wine *list*). The menu is usually presented in a textual format (though the author has certainly experienced spoken menus) and it is often structured in some logical order, *eg.* hors d'oeuvres, main course, dessert, coffee.

This chapter will consider the most important human factors issues relating to the design and use of menus in computer systems. In such systems the term 'menu' usually refers to some list of choices available to the user at that point in the dialogue. Whenever relevant, our most common experience with menus, the restaurant scenario, will be used to draw attention to interesting or insightful parallels.

There are a great many issues concerning the design and use of menus in computer systems. The optimal number of choices that should be displayed on a screen (menu size or breadth) balanced against the number of levels of menus (menu depth) is covered in Section 4.3. The alternative selection techniques have also been subject to considerable investigation and some of the latest research findings are presented in Section 4.4. The order in which items are presented to users, and their position on the screen, has also been studied, some of the most recent work is considered in Section 4.5. Section 4.6 looks at the latest trends in menu design, especially the WIMP interface of the Apple Macintosh. The penultimate Section, 4.7, considers other aspects of menu design, in less detail, but points to useful references. Finally, Section 4.8, attempts to synthesize the findings and ideas reported in the previous sections into guidelines which will be of use in the design and construction of a menu system.

4.2 WHAT IS A MENU?

Chambers 20th Century Dictionary (1983) furnishes us with yet one more reason to continue the comparison between menus in computer systems and restaurants, for under a single entry it provides the following definition:

> '... a bill of fare: a list of subjects, options, etc. (*fig.* or *comput.*).'

A computer menu is essentially the presentation of a list of 'things' to the user which can be selected at that point in the user-computer dialogue. The reason the word 'things' is used here is because, as MacGregor & Lee (1987) and Giroux & Belleau (1986) both point out, there are two major applications of menus in computer systems: i) menus for information retrieval and ii) menus for command selection, and therefore the 'things' which the user can select at any given point in the user-computer dialogue can be of widely different types depending upon the application. Section 4.5.2 deals with the implications of these differences in greater detail. In the case of information retrieval menus, the list will contain items which may be as diverse as 'TV programmes' and 'currency exchange rates' but all such items can be classed together as 'information items'. (Note that in this example both items are information items which, if selected, would lead to at least one further menu.) In the second type of menu the list is more likely to consist of a list of commands or actions which will be referred to as 'command items' which the user can request the computer to perform. Typical command items would be: 'File', 'Save', 'Delete', 'Print', *et cetera*.

ORACLE		Microsoft Word	
4-TEL............410	Kids...............550	New	⌘N
Racing............470	Your Money...560	Open...	⌘O
Home File........480	Advertising...570	Close	⌘W
Classified Ads..490	Holidays........580	Save	⌘S
City................500	Buzz..............610	Save As....	
Time Off..........530	What's New...598	Delete...	
Rock & Film....540	A-Z Index......599		

Fig. 4.1 –   An 'information item' menu taken from the ORACLE database and a 'command item' menu taken from Microsoft Word for the Apple Macintosh.

4.3 MENU BREADTH VERSUS MENU DEPTH

4.3.1 What's the issue?

One way of looking at menus is as a means of limiting the options available to the user at any given stage of their interaction with the computer. This might be desirable for a number of reasons:

1.) there might be a very large number of things users could do at any stage, but for reasons of security they are allowed to see or utilise only a subset of the total number of commands;

2.) the user may be attempting to access a very large database which is arranged in a certain way, and hence it may be both technically desirable and, from the user's point of view, cognitively helpful, if access to the information items held on the database is subdivided into sectors that reflect the way the items are stored;

3.) the people that access a database might be infrequent and relatively unskilled users, and therefore presenting a limited menu of options, in which all the things a user can do or access are presented, is a means of limiting the dialogue, which helps to limit the possibilities for error;

4.) by presenting information in a regimented way, the user can devote most of his/her cognitive effort to making the correct selection rather than being burdened with remembering commands and command syntax.

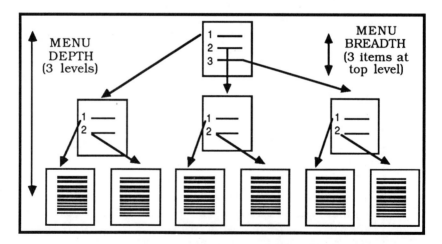

Fig. 4.2 – A simple menu structure, 3 levels deep and with 3 choices at the top level menu and 2 at each of the second level menus

If we accept that menus, under certain circumstances, are *a good thing*, then concerns about both the size of any single menu (its breadth) and how many menus should a user go through in order to obtain the information or issue the command that is desired (menu depth) become apparent. Imagine if we went to a restaurant and the waiter gave us a menu which consisted of five items:

1.	Hors d'Oeuvres
2.	Main Course
3.	Vegetables
4.	Desserts
5.	Coffee and Liqueurs

and we were asked select any single item. Selecting, say, '1.' would result in the waiter providing a second menu upon which all the hors d'oeuvres were listed. After making a selection from this menu we would be given back the first menu and asked again to select an item. This time we select number '2.' and we get a third menu which contains all the available main courses, and so on.

A situation such as described above would be both ridiculous and unacceptable. We would consider it so because the size of the first menu (*ie.* the number of items), is so small that we could have coped with a single menu (rather than the six that would be required in the above scenario) which was divided into separate sections but was presented as a whole. The depth (the number of levels of menus) in the example was only two but the tradeoff between menu size and menu depth *for the task in question* was unacceptable.

One more amusing anecdote will suffice to illustrate the issue. It is based on a TV sketch from some years ago, and takes the form of a dialogue between a customer (CUSTOMER) and the proprietor (PROPRIETOR) of a mobile canteen.

CUSTOMER:	One tea please.
PROPRIETOR:	Cup or Mug?
CUSTOMER:	Mug please.
PROPRIETOR:	Indian or China?
CUSTOMER:	Pardon?
PROPRIETOR:	Would you prefer Indian tea or China tea?
CUSTOMER:	Oh. Indian please.
PROPRIETOR:	Darjeeling or Assam?
CUSTOMER:	Assam please.
PROPRIETOR:	Black or White?
CUSTOMER:	(irritated) White.
PROPRIETOR:	Cow's milk or goat's milk?
CUSTOMER:	Cow's.
PROPRIETOR:	Friesian or Guernsey?
CUSTOMER:	(losing his temper) What?
PROPRIETOR:	Which dairy herd would you like your milk from?
CUSTOMER:	Guernsey.
PROPRIETOR:	Sterilized or pasteurized milk?
CUSTOMER:	Pasteurized.
PROPRIETOR:	With or without sugar.
CUSTOMER:	With.
PROPRIETOR:	One lump or two?
CUSTOMER:	Aaargh!

The agony and frustration of a menu system that has two choices at each level (menu breadth = 2) and nine levels (menu depth = 9) is rather neatly exemplified. As an exercise, perhaps you should attempt to design a menu system that would adequately cope with the choices shown above. Incidentally, you should note that a single menu listing all possible combinations would contain $2^9 = 512$ items!

The issue is how do we compromise between having a menu system that:

1.) at each level contains a number of items that is large enough for the user to scan and select from easily, but not so large that the screen is cluttered or confusing thus increasing the time the user has to take search the list by an unacceptable amount

2.) has sufficient levels to split the task up into manageable sub-tasks, but is not so deep that the user has to go through a long and boring series of screens/menus to get to the target item or command?

4.3.2   Research

Research into this question has resulted in at least two schools of thought who have produced experimental evidence to support their respective claims. One school has produced empirical evidence that the prescription proposed by Shneiderman (1980), that menus should contain no more than seven items, is soundly based. Shneiderman's proposed limit has been presumed, by the authors of a more recent paper (Sisson *et al.*, 1986), to be based on Miller's classic paper (1956) which suggests that the capacity of human short-term memory is limited to approximately seven items or 'chunks' of information. One experiment that supports this school is briefly described here.

Perlman (1984) presented subjects with menus of four different lengths: 5 items, 10 items, 15 items and 20 items. He investigated menus which consisted of numbers ordered sequentially and randomly, and menus of words ordered alphabetically and randomly. The target item appeared at a consistent position on the right of the screen. Subjects were required to locate the target word in the menu, and to indicate when it was found by pressing a key. The results showed that for all conditions the search time increased with list length. Finding words took longer than finding numbers, and randomly ordered lists took longer to search than their sorted counterparts.

A simple experiment, you'll agree, and one that raises as many questions as it answers (read it yourself with a critical eye), but it is evidence of this nature that has supported the claim that lengthy menus *per se* are less than optimal. Lee & MacGregor (1985) produced theoretical evidence, for videotex (PRESTEL is a videotex system) retrieval, that there was an optimal number of items per menu, and that number was about eight items for fast readers and about five items for slow readers. The same authors (MacGregor & Lee, 1987) in a review of the issues surrounding videotex menu retrieval (*ie.* information items and not command items), conclude that there is some consensus amongst experimenters for the optimal number of items being between four and eight. One paper (Kiger, 1984) also found that users preferred the eight item menus.

The other school of thought, which has grown up more recently, conclude that very broad and shallow menus (*ie.* few menus each containing lots of items) are much better than had hitherto been suggested, and produce shorter search times than those normally recommended. Landauer & Nachbar (1985) performed a series of experiments (using only eight subjects – which makes one wonder about the statistical reliability of data based on such a small sample size) which confirmed earlier work by Snowberry *et al.* (1983) that the more items per menu (up to 64) and therefore the fewer menus, the faster the mean search time. This school raises concerns about blindly making recommendations based upon Miller's (1956) paper. In what way is using a menu, where the items can be displayed for as long as required, likely to depend upon short-term memory? Testing for short-term memory usually requires users to remember something like a list and then recall the list (in the correct order) some short time later. Menus make no such demands upon users, the task is primarily a *recognition task* rather than a *memory task*. However, lest the reader gets the wrong idea, the latter school of thought has methodological problems too, some of which are covered in the section below.

4.3.3   Comments

We have seen that research into this area has yet to come to a firm conclusion. Whilst the latest research points towards larger size menus, current computer technology for small systems has difficulty displaying large menus at an acceptable speed. Thus technology currently contrives to help keep the number of menu items recommended per menu nearer that recommended by the earlier work. We should also remember that the context within which most experiments are conducted is somewhat abstracted from the real-life situation.

The optimal tradeoff is usually considered to be the combination of menu breadth and menu depth that allows users to find their target item.most quickly Nearly all of the research described above assumes that the faster the user can locate the target item, the better the menu system (though accuracy is also considered in some of the work). This would be more likely to be true if all users searched all menus for a well defined target item and were accessing the menu with a clear purpose in mind. The practical reality is that users sometimes browse through a database to see what information items are available, they sometimes scan a command menu to see exactly what they can do with say, the document they have just created. That is, users often have no pre-defined target, and their task is also much more fuzzy than in most experimental set-ups. If users indulge in such hard-to-define tasks, then assessing the acceptability of a menu system purely on the criteria of search and retrieval time might be considered somewhat dubious. One can certainly imagine menu systems where a much higher priority is placed on accuracy than speed, or a menu system where splitting the task into logical sub-tasks requires each set of sub-tasks to be displayed separately.

Furthermore, in many of the experiments there is an exact correspondence between the target item and the list(s) which must be searched. That is, the subject is requested to find a target word which is *guaranteed* to appear somewhere in the menu(s) presented. In real tasks there is no such guarantee. A user might wish to find out a particular currency exchange rate. That user has to search the menu tree for a whole list of semantically similar descriptors which might appear: for example: Currencies, Exchange Rates, Money Guide, Rates of Exchange, Banking, all might lead to the information desired. The user has no way of knowing which of a whole range of semantically similar descriptors to use. The cognitive demands of such a task are quite different from the experimental set-ups commonly used.

Apperley & Field (1984) attempted to address some of these concerns by using a complex problem solving task, in which users had to retrieve a number of related items from a database. The results of their work will be discussed later.

The reader is asked to bear these matters in mind when reading the papers quoted. In addition the reader should be aware of the great number of relatively simple experiments yet to be performed that will advance our knowledge in this area. A simple plea: Be critical, but be empirical too!

4.4 MENU SELECTION TECHNIQUES

4.4.1   What's the issue?
In the previous section we looked at how the presentation of a menu or a series of menus, in terms of size and depth, can affect how well they can be used. This section considers the very precise phase in the overall task of menu selection – the act of menu item selection. That is, the way the user indicates to the system exactly which item he/she wishes to select.

In our restaurant scenario we select items usually by one of two methods: we verbally indicate to the waiter the dish or item of our choice, ('I'll have the prawn cocktail') or we point to the dish we require on the menu so that the waiter can see what we would like. Chinese restaurants commonly have numbers next to each dish to ease the pronunciation problems especially when making take-away orders by telephone.

With computer systems we are not quite at the point where spoken choices are a cheap or readily available selection technique. The speech recognition industry will presumably make such systems widespread soon after the publication of this book thus outdating it immediately!

At the time of writing the most common selection methods are as follows:

1.)	keyboard–	the user types in the selection or its indicator
2.)	mouse–	the user moves the cursor over the screen using a mouse (see Chapter 5), and 'clicks' on the menu of his choice
3.)	touch-screen/– touch panel	the user points to item on the screen with his/her finger
4.)	arrow-keys	the user depresses an 'arrow' key which moves a cursor successively over the items available for selection.

The issue is whether any particular technique can be advocated above any other technique for the task of selecting menu items. In attempting to address such an issue, it is impossible not to impinge on the more general area of input devices in human computer interaction. Therefore this section should be read in conjunction with Chapter 5 where some of the more generalizable aspects of input devices are considered.

4.4.2   Research
The reader will, by now, not be surprised to learn that research into this issue has so far proven to be inconclusive. There is less of a clear split in this case between any particular schools of thought. Rather, there has not been enough

work done that attempts to replicate (and thereby validate or dispute) any previous research and the associated claims. Such is the nature of human factors research that altering one variable, however slightly, results in a slightly different experiment often leading to dramatically different results and consequent conclusions. This is not intended to be any more than a mild criticism of the domain, and can certainly be applied to other disciplines too. One can see it as a weakness, in that the research community is trying to answer dozens of slightly different questions using very similar (but not identical) techniques. This results in dozens of partial answers awaiting (often, alas, in vain) verification or enhancement. The alternative view is to see it as a strength, and that the opportunity for new research, using ingenious techniques and methods, is attractive to new researchers. Eventually these separate but related research findings must be drawn together in some grand unifying theory, we await such a day with awe and trepidation (but don't hold your breath!).

Karat, McDonald & Anderson, referred to as KMA from now on, (1986), in a very interesting paper, compared three different menu selection techniques: the touch panel, the mouse and the keyboard. This work was reported earlier (KMA, 1984), but in less detail. KMA were particularly keen to examine the 'naturalness' of the three techniques. Direct pointing using a touch panel might intuitively be considered as the most natural of selection techniques, but it is not quite as simple as that. For experienced users of computers and/or keyboards, using selection techniques other than direct pointing might be no disadvantage. Indeed, for such users, it might be just as 'natural' (*ie.* the behaviour may be just as well-learned) to select items from a screen using a keyboard. KMA in fact found that performance of their 24 subjects (all classified as skilled typists) in selecting menu items using each of the three techniques (after practice) was similar for the pointing and keyboard techniques but significantly worse for the mouse. They also found that subjects liked to use the mouse least for the task required.

Such findings went against the grain of other reports in the literature and worried the authors. KMA thus repeated the experiment and this time took into account other factors namely; sex, typing skill and practice. Their results in the second experiment did nothing to allay their doubts about the findings reported elsewhere. Performance using the mouse improved with the extra practice sessions but was still significantly worse than the subject's performance with the touch panel.

KMA went on to criticise a model or framework suggested by Card, Moran & Newell (1983) which could not predict such results. I shall not reiterate the argument here, but interested readers, particularly with a mathematical background, should look more closely at the work of Card and Moran. (Chapters 2 and 7 explain their work in a little more detail.)

Ewing *et al.* (1986) compared a mouse with the 'arrow' keys on a keyboard. Although the task here was to select a target from some highlighted text in an interactive encyclopedia, there were some similarities with the KMA experiment. They found the arrow keys to be faster than the mouse over a variety of conditions for a variety of subjects. The general consensus among the subjects in the experiment was in favour of the arrow keys over the mouse, though there were some favourable comments about the mouse.

One would have to question how fair the comparison was in this later experiment because of the way the different selection techniques worked. An arrow key when pressed would 'jump' the cursor to the next highlighted word in the direction of the arrow. Thus the subject needed to locate the target word visually and then depress the appropriate combination of arrow keys to get the cursor to land on the target word; finally to select the word the 'Return' key was pressed. The mouse technique allowed the user to move the cursor over the whole screen. To select a target word the subject had to move the cursor to the target word and then depress the mouse key. There is thus an emphasis on accuracy when using the mouse that is not necessary when using the arrow keys. The arrow keys guarantee accurate identification (though subjects may depress the 'Return' key too early or too late). The mouse relies on subjects making sure that the cursor is positioned over the target word by co-ordinating hand and eye to a degree not required in the arrow key condition. One wonders what would have happened if the mouse could have been made to select the nearest highlighted word whenever the mouse key was depressed. This would mean subjects would only have to get the cursor to approach, or get close to, the target word (which, remember, was one of the highlighted words).

4.4.3   Comments

Research seems to be pointing to selection techniques other than the mouse for menu item selection. Again technology itself may determine or limit our options. If the menu is to appear on a particular type of display that does not support touch panels there is clearly little point in recommending their use.

Is it surprising that the keyboard or arrow keys are just as effective or better than the mouse? Setting aside the methodological issue raised in the last section, in general the mouse is probably better for moving around a complex display or for 'drawing' (as in MacDraw) than for selecting from a menu. Most menus are displayed in some regimented fashion, like a single column. It is easy to have cursor keys jump from selection to selection in such a display, guaranteeing accuracy as well as speed.

As will be clear from the last section in this chapter, these techniques no longer need to be made exclusive alternatives. The most up-to-date personal computers have a keyboard *and* a mouse and users can select items presented on a menu in more than one way. Perhaps further research into *the* optimal selection technique is unnecessary, perhaps future research should look at the best *combination* of alternative selection techniques, highlighting the flexible approach and allowing the user a choice. More of this discussion appears in Section 4.7.

4.5 THE ORDER, CONTENT AND POSITION OF MENU ITEMS

4.5.1   What are the issues?

We have already seen that menus consist of a series of items or options from which the user is normally required make a single selection. We have looked at both the size of menus and the methods that can be employed to select menu items.

Another factor that may influence how effectively menu systems are used is the order in which menu items are presented to the user. The content of the menu; the names of the categories and how they relate to items presented lower down the menu structure, is also considered. The positional consistency of items of information on menu screens is also taken into account.

To make the issue of order clear let us briefly return to the restaurant scenario. The waiter provides you with a menu in which the dishes are randomly presented, and appear in haphazard locations (some on the left hand side, some on the right and some in the middle) on the pages of the menu. Intuitively the process of selection of dishes will take longer because you would need to scan the whole menu to establish exactly what the choices of hors d'oeuvres were. If we were searching for a particular dish, again we would have to search the whole menu, perhaps more than once, to see if that dish were or were not available.

4.5.2   Research

4.5.2.1 Order

Perlman (1984) demonstrated that for any size list the search time for a target word or number was longer if the items appeared at random positions in the list than if the list were sorted into a logical (numeric or alphabetical in this case) order. Perlman does make the valid point that: 'Randomness is in the mind of the person doing the searching'. That is, just because a user cannot perceive the logic behind a particular order of items in a menu, it doesn't mean there isn't one. *However, it is a good design principle for menus, where feasible, to have a menu order whose logic can easily be perceived by most users.* (A restaurant menu that ordered dishes based upon the location of food stored in the kitchen with respect to the position of the cooker, such that items nearest the cooker were at the top of the menu, would be logical, perhaps useful to the chef, but pointless and impossible to perceive for the customer.)

4.5.2.2 Content

Giroux & Belleau (1986) make a strong case for a distinction to be drawn between command item menus and information item menus. They argue that in the latter case the search through a variety of categories requires different cognitive demands and that the selection process should depend upon factors such as semantic distance. They point out that whereas it might be useful to order commands alphabetically as Card (1984) did, information item menus would be better organized semantically. Finally they suggest that users' search strategies will be different for each menu type. Their initial report of the empirical evidence (1986) was a short paper and we await their more considered verdict with interest. However, their paper reported that the closer the semantic distance between the general category at a high level in the menu structure (*eg.* bird) and the target concept residing at a lower level in the menu structure (*eg.* robin) the shorter the decision time.

4.5.2.3 Positional Consistency

Teitelbaum & Granda (1983) varied the position of five pieces of information appearing on menu screens: the menu title, the page number, the topic heading, an instruction line and an entry area. Their work demonstrated:

"... a clear performance advantage in searching for screen-presented information in a multiple screen interface, when that information is present in a positionally consistent manner, as compared with a positionally nonconstant [*sic*] presentation."

The reader should bear in mind that the one thing *not* positionally varied was the menu itself with respect both to the other screen items and to the internal order of items within the menu.

4.5.3   Comments
In information retrieval systems most of the items that appear on the next screen are usually different form those that appear on the current screen. There are some systems in which one or two items appear on each and every menu. Such menu items might be : 'Previous Screen', 'Help' or 'Quit'. *In such menus it is advisable that items such as these appear in the same place in the menu and should be selected by the same means at each menu in which they appear.*

The author has seen more than one menu system where there is no consistent position of a constant menu item. For example, the 'Quit' option is selected by pressing '0' in menu 1, but is selected by pressing '2' in menu 2, and '0' again in menu 3! The inconsistent position of the item in the menu and the variable 'selector digit' places a higher cognitive demand upon users than a menu system where say, 'Quit' is always at the bottom of the menu (*ie.* the last) and always selected by pressing a '0'.

4.6 TRENDS IN MENUS

4.6.1   Multiple selection techniques
Many personal computers offer the mouse as a standard part of the system hardware (for example the Mac) or as an optional extra for use with particular PC and software packages (for example the IBM pc).

The integration of the mouse (sometimes referred to as an 'off screen pointing device') and menu systems has led to a change in how menus are presented to users and how users select menu items. These are probably trends (hence this section's title) rather than final and frozen designs, Apple's latest (1988) update to the 'Finder' has brought about a new trend sure to be followed by other 'Maclike' interfaces. (The whole topic of WIMP design is dealt with in detail in Chapter 5 but where this impinges upon menu design it is dealt with in this section. There is undoubtedly some reiteration of the principles of WIMP design here but both parts of the book are intended to be complementary and both should be read to obtain the most complete understanding of the topic.)

In the Mac interface, the menu headings are permanently displayed in a strip along the top of the screen, called the menu bar. By using the mouse to place the cursor over the menu heading desired and then depressing *and holding down* the mouse button, the menu heading is inversely displayed (white letters on black background) and a window containing a vertical menu of options is displayed. By moving the cursor (via the mouse) down the menu, each menu item is sequentially highlighted by being inversely displayed. When the item to be selected is reached, the user releases the mouse button, and the process or command requested is carried out. Fig. 4.3 illustrates the steps in this process.

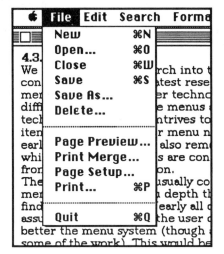

Fig. 4.3 – On the left, the 'File' menu is 'pulled down', and on the right, the 'Open' option is highlighted by moving the cursor down the menu.

As can be seen from the menu illustrated in Fig. 4.3 some of the menu items have a symbol '⌘' followed by a letter. Depressing the command key on the Mac keyboard (which is marked with a '⌘') and simultaneously pressing the appropriate letter has the same result as going through the menu process described above. It is a short-cut or 'accelerated' procedure. The use of such 'accelerators' is entirely optional, but by displaying them alongside their complementary menu option users will, in theory, come to learn them and eventually use them. Thus, experienced Mac users do not have to go through the process of moving the cursor to the menu and selecting 'Save' via the mouse; many will have learnt the accelerator for this command (⌘ S). The point is that the user can choose. This flexible approach to menu selection has many advantages:

1.) No single method is imposed upon the user.
2.) Users can switch between methods at leisure.
3.) Experienced users are provided with a short-cut.
4.) Users always have the accelerator option displayed which will help them to learn the accelerated options.
5.) The common provision of an 'Undo' facility means that normal selection errors are recoverable, which encourages users to experiment since the potential cost of error is low.

Point 5. above is covered in Chapter 5, but briefly, the 'Edit' menu on the Mac usually contains an 'Undo' option which often (though not always!) allows the user to revert to the condition the screen was in before the last command was issued.

Before the reader gets the impression that the solution to all menu problems has just appeared, a word of warning might be appropriate. Because there are usually quite a few accelerators available with most software for the Mac, and because there is little or no standardization for the production of accelerators, the following two problems occur:

1.) the letter used in association with the ' ⌘ ' key rarely bears any close semantic relation (*ie.* is a lousy mnemonic) to the menu item (for example, in the program used to type the manuscript for this book the menu item 'Footnote' has the accelerator ' ⌘ E' and the menu item 'Glossary' has the accelerator ' ⌘ K');

2.) the use of accelerators across different software packages is not standardised, so that in some cases the same menu item will have a different accelerator depending upon the software package used ('Print' is ' ⌘ P' in one word processor and ' ⌘ T' in another), and the same accelerator will certainly evoke different responses in different packages (' ⌘ W' means 'Close' in one WP package and 'Show Space' in another).

4.6.2   Visible sub-menus
A new (in 1988) method of accessing sub-menus is also being made available on some WIMP systems. Some menus will have sub-menus in future, but these will be accessed via the main menus in the same way, except that to access a sub-menu the user moves the cursor to the left or right after having moved the cursor down to the selected item. This will allow the 'collapsing' of some menus, thereby making more room on the menu bar for new menus.

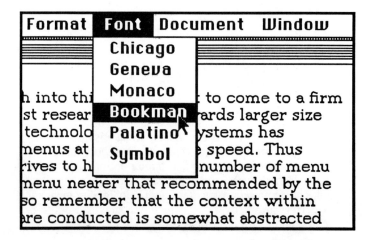

Fig. 4.4a –   Sub-menus on the Mac. The user first pulls down a menu, and selects a font.....

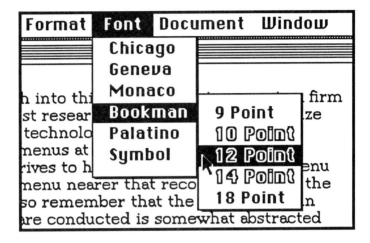

Fig. 4.4b –   ...the user then moves the cursor to the right and a sub-menu
                allowing the specification of font size is displayed.

Time will tell whether or not this trend catches on and is replicated in other
menu systems. The ability to see the main menu whilst accessing a sub-menu
seems to be a useful aid to the user, and earlier work (Apperley & Field, 1984)
on navigation through menu systems certainly recommended some trace or reminder of previous menus be displayed to users.

4.6.3   Unavailable options
Guidelines have, in the past, mentioned that menus should only contain options
which the user is legitimately able to select. The idea behind such a guideline is
to prevent a user going through two levels of menus to reach a third level,
identifying and selecting an item, waiting 10 seconds and then receiving a system message such as: "The information on the item you require is not available".

In our restaurant scenario, we have all experienced the frustration of spend-
ing ten minutes reading a menu, selecting and ordering a particular dish, and
then salivating for a further five minutes in anticipation of the forthcoming de-
light, only for the waiter to return to inform you: "Sorry sir, the dish you ordered is off".

In respect of this ideal, the WIMP interfaces (see Chapter 5) have a problem.
Some of the software (actually nearly all) provides large numbers of options
under a variety of conditions. For example the options 'Cut', 'Copy', and
'Paste' are very often provided under the 'Edit' menu. However, in order to be
able to perform any of these three functions, some screen item; a character, a
drawing, a word etc. has to be selected or highlighted first – otherwise there is
nothing to Cut, Copy or Paste. The problem is that, given the technical limitations of a machine like the Mac, it would take too long to rewrite the menu to
include or exclude these options depending upon whether the conditions for their
inclusion or exclusion had been met.

The Mac gets around this problem by 'greying out' menu options when they are unavailable for selection. Thus the menu need not be rewritten, merely some of the options are displayed in half intensity. This technique has a couple of advantages too:

1.)   menu lengths remain constant, allowing users to learn where to look for an item, thus reducing search time

2.)   users can always see the full list of options that *could* be available under certain conditions – they become aware (and are constantly reminded) of the full potential of the system (if some options are not displayed under condition 'X' how do I know they are available under condition 'Y'?)

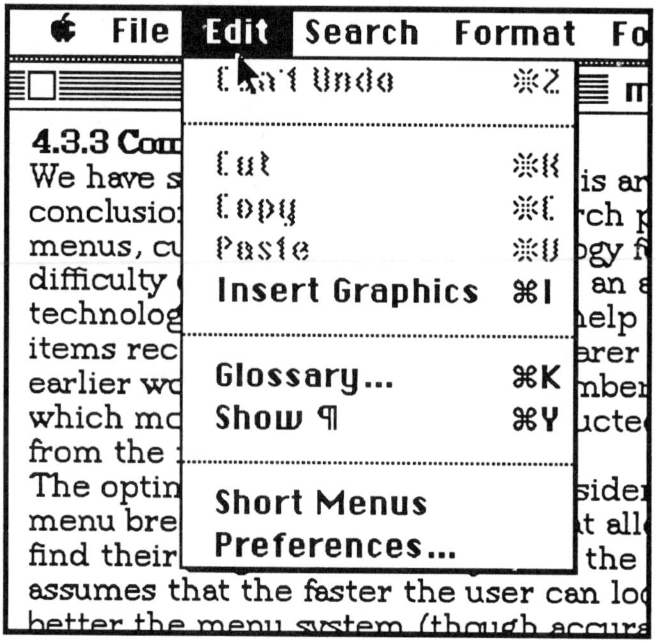

Fig. 4.5 –   The 'Edit' menu showing some 'greyed out' menu options.

4.6.4   Confirmation of selection(s)

Another commonly quoted guideline is that menu selections should be fed back to the user to confirm the item selected. This ideally occurs before the user enters a 'Return' or other key entry that tells the system to find or perform the option selected.

Whilst this guideline is useful in some circumstances it can be extremely tedious for users, whether novice or expert, to have continually to confirm all selections. It is far better to have users confirm only those selections which might have a serious consequence were they selected inadvertently (see Guidelines in Section 4.8).

The most common catastrophe that befalls most computer users is quitting or exiting the current task without having saved, filed or stored the work that has just been done. Most system designers have now built-in 'confirmation routines' that the user must go through in order to bring about the selected option. Fig. 4.6 shows how one word processor does it on the Mac.

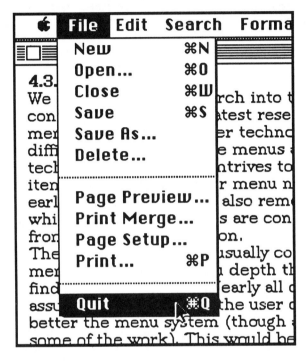

Fig. 4.6a –   The 'Quit' option is selected

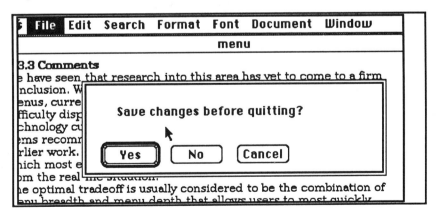

Fig. 4.6b –   The system asks the user to confirm that he/she wishes to quit saving the changes made to the current document. The default choice is to save the changes.

There is another useful function that arises as a consequence of having a menu bar permanently available. The menu items currently in use or selected can be marked so that the menus can be pulled down at any time in order to establish the status of the system or the options currently in use.

In the Mac, a tick ('check' in the USA) is placed alongside those options currently selected, this is a quick and useful means of ensuring the system is in the expected state. For example, most word processor packages on the Mac come with a large variety of fonts and font sizes. A user can quickly make sure that he/she is using the correct font by selecting the 'Font' menu and looking to see which font and font size are ticked (checked).

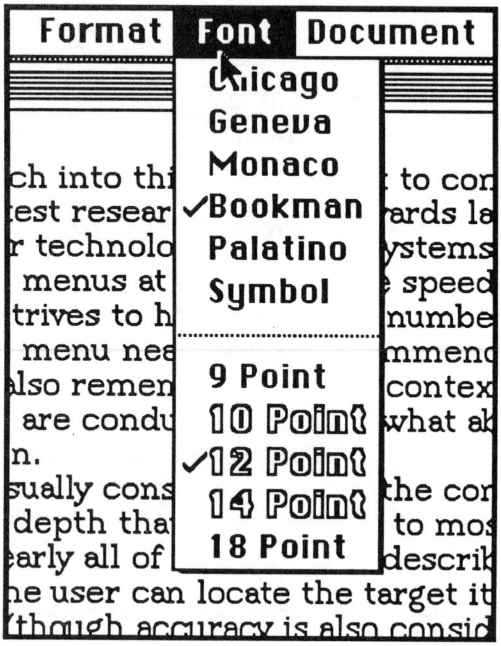

Format	Font	Document
	Chicago	
	Geneva	
ch into thi	Monaco	to cor
est resear	✓Bookman	ards la
r technolo	Palatino	ystems
menus at	Symbol	speed
trives to h		numbe
menu nee	9 Point	mmen
also remen	10 Point	contex
are condu	✓12 Point	what a
n.	14 Point	the cor
ually cons	18 Point	to mos
depth tha		descri
arly all of		
he user can locate the target it		
(though accuracy is also consic		

Fig. 4.7 –   The 'Font' menu with currently selected options ticked

4.7 OTHER CONSIDERATIONS IN MENU DESIGN

The are several other matters related to the design of menu systems that have been studied, and are worthy of consideration here. They are dealt with in less detail than the aspects considered above, either because they have been subjected to less study, or because they have less of a bearing on the current theory of menu design. Reference to more comprehensive literature covering these topics is made throughout this section.

4.7.1   Performance measures
Some mention of performance measures was made in Section 4.3.3. As Mac-Gregor & Lee (1987) point out, there are four main measures of performance that are measured in most menu retrieval experiments:

1.)   errors

2.)   efficiency
3.)   success rate
4.)   search time

4.7.1.1 Errors

These are often measured in terms of the probability of error, which is calculated by dividing the total number of correct menu choices made by the subject by the total number of choices. However some research has merely counted the mistakes made by users that would have led to an error in a 'real' system. Hauptmann & Green (1983) compared commands, menus, and natural language programs as different methods of interacting with software that plotted data entered into different types of graphs. They counted user inputs that were undecipherable by the software as errors. The probability of error at least provides the experimenter with an indication of the degree of difficulty for a particular task (it is usually applied to information retrieval rather than command menus).

Pure totals of errors may be less useful, but in experiments where we were testing whether users could perform a series of sub-tasks (say editing a piece of text via a menu-based command system) the sheer number of mistakes might be a simple, direct measure which might help make your point to the system designers – especially if the experiment is recorded on video (see Chapter 7 on Evaluations for clarification of this point).

4.7.1.2 Efficiency

In information retrieval systems there is often more than one route that will lead the user from the top-most level menu to the target item. There is usually an optimal or ideal route which is the minimum number of menus it is necessary to go through to get to the target item. Efficiency is measured by taking the number of menus required by the optimal route, and dividing it by the actual number of menus accessed by the subject. Such a measure is useful when assessing whether subjects learn to use efficient search strategies over a period of time. Their efficiency before and after training could be measured in this way.

4.7.1.3 Success Rate

This is a relatively simple measure of the number or percentage of target items successfully retrieved during a session. It would provide a good 'feel' for how well users might get on with the system.

4.7.1.4 Search Time

Many research papers measure speed in one form or another. Some merely record the length of time taken to retrieve the target item or to select the correct command on the menu. In retrieval systems it is better to divide the search time by the total number of menus accessed to get a 'search time per page' parameter. It is even better if the system itself can measure the search time for each specific menu (it could be made to run a timer from when the menu was called up to when a new menu was requested). Analysis of such data might indicate particular menus as being more of a problem than others, perhaps prompting the design team to re-evaluate how the descriptors for those menus are phrased.

One should bear in mind that all systems take some finite time to retrieve the information requested. Also users go through at least two phases which might be separately timed: a decision phase, when they are scanning the menu and deciding which option to select, and a selection phase, the time taken to press a key, or point and click on a mouse. Measuring both phases is difficult but might provide useful additional information about the task.

4.7.2 Training

This is an area that has suffered from a surprising lack of research. If you accept the premise that human factors experts (or cognitive psychologists or ergonomists) are still having difficulty influencing the actual design of menu systems, then perhaps we should at least devote some more effort into how to best train users of menu systems.

One of the few papers that directly addressed this issue (Parton *et al.*, 1985), looked at four different training schemes. Subjects were split into four groups. The first group (Trial and Error) allowed the subjects access to the system for 12 minutes and invited them to browse through and explore the system. The second group (Command Sequence) were given a sheet of paper that contained a list of the pathways that led to the target items. The third group (Frame Presentation) were given a sheet of paper that showed all the frames (menus) they might encounter, whilst the fourth group (Global Tree) received a diagram showing the overall structure of the menu system. The results showed that on at least two measures the Global Tree group out-performed all the others on all the measures but was only significantly better than the Command Sequence and Frame Presentation groups in two of the measures. The Trial and Error group performed surprisingly well on all measures too. This study certainly indicates that, where feasible, a structured view of the menu system might pay dividends.

4.7.3 'Navigation' through menu systems

This has been a topic of interest for some time but research into the specific topic of navigation is less easy to find. There is much published in the area of keyword searching through databases (*eg.* Pluke, 1983 and Weerdmeester *et al.* 1985), and even some comparative studies on keyword or command versus menu selection techniques (*eg.* Antin, 1986). The reader interested in the use of keywords *per se* is encouraged to pursue the references above, but there is insufficient space in this book to do the subject justice.

So, users can navigate through databases by use of keywords, which allows experienced users to 'jump ahead' to the desired menu or information page without going through the intermediate menus. The method of navigation is not the only issue here. Despite MacGregor & Lee's (1987) doubts, my experience is that users can manage to 'get lost' in large databases with relative ease. Apperley & Spence (1983) have shown that, by providing the user with a trace of the previous choices made, some traditional navigational problems can be resolved. The use of visible sub-menus as covered in Section 4.4 is also a solution that may find a rapid uptake in digital displays particularly with high resolution graphics.

The guidelines presented in Section 4.8 further show how this potential problem can be minimized.

4.7.4   Category names

4.7.4.1 Textual Descriptors
An important, and yet under-emphasized factor in successful menu design is the categorical descriptors that partition the information available. This matter was touched upon in 4.5.2.2 when semantic distance was briefly mentioned. Rogers & Oborne (1985) reported on a very interesting study of various semantic attributes of a set of verbs with respect to the psychological processes involved in a naming task. In particular they looked at how easy it was to elicit from subjects 'command' verbs when the subjects were given a verbal description of the command verb. The verbs had already been evaluated in terms of imagery and concreteness-abstractness in an earlier experiment – and many verbs used as commands were found to be low in imagery and high in abstractness.

Dumais & Landauer (1983) looked at information retrieval categories rather than commands and command verbs. In a simple, but revealing study they looked at how well people could place items into pre-defined categories when just a category name was given and also when 1, 2, or 3 example items from that category were provided. They found that providing three example items, even in the absence of an overall category name, was at least as good a way of describing a category as providing just a category name. The authors make the point that, in large databases, it is sometimes difficult to categorize items (especially at the topmost levels) with an appropriate descriptor and that often an *ad hoc* name is given to a set of items. In such cases say the authors:

> "We think that the use of examples to describe categories presents a possibility for overcoming some aspects of this problem."

4.7.4.2 Graphical Descriptors
This topic is likely to grow rapidly as the use of icons (small pictures or symbols – see Chapter 5) spreads across applications and technical improvements in display resolution become cheaper and therefore widely available.

Muter & Mayson (1986) have looked at the use of graphics in the selection of items from videotex menus. They found that the inclusion of graphics with textual descriptors had no effect on the search and selection time of subjects but it did improve the accuracy of items selected, halving the mean error rate. They did not use a graphics only condition which would probably have yielded some more interesting data. One of the authors' proposed explanation for their findings was that the graphics provided extra relevant information and helped users avoid making the wrong decision. Often the graphic information was in the form of an exemplar (category: clothing, graphic: a coat) which ties in with the findings of Dumais & Landauer (1983) mentioned above.

4.8 GUIDELINES

It is appropriate to reiterate the point made in the introduction, that this book is not mainly about guidelines. There are other sets of recommendations and guidelines written by experts (*eg*. Smith &Mosier, 1986) which provide a range of advice for a large variety of design issues. Often guidelines are provided without any background information as to what they are based upon. They are often so general, as Smith &Mosier (*op. cit*) point out, to be of little use to anyone. Furthermore, as Tijerina (1986) makes clear, no guidelines currently assess the cost of *not* incorporating an ergonomic design feature, or guidance on *when* to use *what* guidelines.

The guidelines provided below can at least be placed in context by referring firstly to the earlier sections in this chapter, and secondly by following up the references cited. The reader should bear in mind, before blindly applying any guidelines, what Schell (1986) says:

> "...the only method of ensuring good design is a properly conducted usability test."

4.8.1   Menu breadth and depth

It seems unnecessarily restrictive to cite either a single value or an upper limit for the size of a menu. As we have seen in Section 4.3, opinion about menu size is divided. Often the computer system will take so long to show a large number of choices that users will become frustrated. This is one limitation on menu size. Another limitation is the way the database is partitioned: it may be that the most feasible way to divide the information is in menus of less than 20 items.

1.)   Menus should, where possible, be less than 15 items in breadth (*ie.* 15 items long), although it is more important to ensure that a menu contains a set of logically related items. The limit given here should ensure that search times are not excessively long, and that items can be displayed quickly.

2.)   The depth of a menu structure clearly depends upon the size of the database, but for databases that are not complex three levels seems a reasonable maximum. This is not so deep that users might get lost or are forced to go through interminable menus, but deep enough that each menu can be reasonably broad. In very large databases the depth will necessarily be greater, and concomitant improvements in 'where am I?' and 'where have I just come from?' type aids should be seriously considered, as should short-cuts for experienced users.

4.8.2   The menu

1.)   Each and every menu should have a meaningful title that is clearly displayed at some upper central screen location.

2.)   Menu items are best displayed in a vertical, left-justified column, with the short code selector (a number or mnemonic) clearly displayed, usually on the left of the item descriptor, but certainly all selectors should be consistently positioned with respect to the menu item.

3.)   The place where the users' keyed input appears on the screen (the input area) should be clearly marked with some appropriate wording such as: 'Item Number Selected:' or 'Enter selection and press Return:'.

4.)   The input area should appear in the same place for each menu, regardless of any difference in size between menus.

5.)   In information item menus especially, it is a good idea to always provide the user with means of returning both to the last menu, and to the start (topmost) menu. Where such options are provided they should appear in the same place (*eg.* the bottom or top) in each menu, and should be selected by the same means.

6.)   Items are best ordered in a logical way. If some options are likely to be used more frequently then they should be displayed at the top of the menu. Where there is no obvious item order, menu items should be arranged alphabetically. Only one menu item should be displayed per line.

7.)   Menu items and their categories should be named with care, and where feasible, exemplars or text name supported by a graphical or iconic representation of an exemplar might reduce errors.

4.8.3   Selection techniques

1.)   Wherever possible provide users with more than one method of making a selection. Accelerators (see 4.6.1) should be indicated to users on the menu proper and are best used in 'pull-down' or 'pop-up' menu systems.

2.)   Current literature suggests that touch screens (technology permitting) are a good alternative to keyboards. Provide a mouse only if an alternative selection technique is also available. Expect new mouse users to take longer to assimilate manipulation skills. Provision of training and/or practice with direct manipulation devices should result in improved performances.

3.)   Arrow-jump keys to move the cursor between menu items is a useful, and apparently acceptable, selection technique. The speed of cursor movement between each menu item should not be so fast that users have difficulty stopping the cursor on the desired menu item.

4.)   Keywords are a very useful short-cut method for experienced users and should be provided in large information databases in particular. The choice of keywords, the possibility of user defined keywords and number of keywords are all issues that must be considered carefully. Follow-up the literature references cited in Section 4.7.3 if further information on keywords is required.

5

Input devices and WIMP interfaces

Written in collaboration with Dr. Nick Milner, Human Factors Division, BT Research Laboratories.

5.1 INTRODUCTION

This chapter attempts to present the reader with issues relating to the more physical aspects of the human-computer interface. The first part of the chapter considers some common input devices: keyboard, mouse, joystick, trackball, touchscreen and light-pen. The most common devices; the keyboard and the mouse, quite rightly receive the lion's share of attention, for it is these which are most often used in computing. Other devices, in particular the trackball, joystick and touchscreen, are dealt with in enough detail for readers to comprehend the important issues. First of all a simple, four component model of a user interacting with an input device is presented. Then each input device/technique is described with reference to the model. As usual, research findings and interesting studies are identified in the text, and should be followed up where in-depth information is required.

The second part of this chapter concerns WIMP interfaces (WIMP stands for: Windows, Icons, Menus and Pointers *ie.* interfaces that contain these features). Some general observations are discussed and some critique of such interfaces or at least the metaphors that WIMP interfaces employ is brought to the reader's attention.

5.2 INPUT DEVICES

Input devices, as their name suggests, are used to input data (either alpha-numeric or graphical) onto a visual display screen. The word 'data' is used here in the broadest possible context – characters typed onto a screen, pictures drawn using a drawing package or numbers entered into a spreadsheet (see Chapter 2), are all 'data'. Input devices actually do quite a bit more than merely permit the user to input data. They can be used to select and also manipulate data which already appears on the screen. Furthermore, the devices allow the user to input commands to the system in order to get the system to perform some task (*eg.* display a file, calculate a sum, send a message). The commands input may be alphanumeric (*eg.* 'file') or use some other form of dialogue such as menu sel-ection (see Chapter 4). In essence, *an input device is the means by which the user communicates with the computer system.* It is clear then that, if the input device is the communication link between human and machine, its design is crucial for users to be effective in getting systems to meet their requests, however they are made.

5.2.1   A simple model of user interaction with an input device
So, input devices are important. As it is we humans who have to use these de-vices, it is useful to construct a simple model of such use in order to assess the human factors implications of any device. The model presented below has four components:

1.)   the cognitive component
2.)   the perceptual component
3.)   the motor component
4.)   the sensory component

5.2.1.1 The Cognitive Component
This is where the user, in Norman's (1986) terms, 'forms an intention' (see also Chapter 2). The user, having decided upon an objective, needs to get the system to bring about that objective. The cognitive component selects what, where, when, why and how the input is used. The psychological processes that should be considered at this level of the model include: memory, expectancy, learning, information theory and decision making.

For the sake of simplicity let us assume that, for users, all inputs start at the cognitive level. In some cases, there may be reference back to the cognitive component if the user reaches the perceptual stage but has a problem (*eg.* they forget what they were trying to do). In such a case the process starts again.

5.2.1.2 The Perceptual Component
Perception may be defined as:

> "...the way in which we interpret the information gathered (and processed) by the senses. In a word, we sense the presence of a stimulus but we perceive what it is.."
>
> (Levine & Shefner 1981)

The perceptual component in this model locates the object upon which the user wishes to perform an action. For example, if the user is an inexperienced typist then the perceptual component is the visual search performed in order to locate each required key on the keyboard. Alternatively, if the user is a touch typist, then the perceptual component is proprioception, *ie*. they do not have to look for it because they have a spatial awareness of where the keys are in relation to their fingers. (Proprioception is a mental map which allows us to position our fingers and limbs accurately without looking.) The types of perceptual processes that should be considered here are: vision, hearing, kinesthetics, proprioception, tactile.

In order to be comprehensive we should also consider the perceptual senses of smell and taste. However these human senses have, so far, not been made use of in human-computer interaction. Perhaps computers of the future will use all our senses, but for our current purposes only the commonly used senses are considered.

5.2.1.3 The Motor Component
Motor activity is a broad term referring to the physical actions of the body. The motor component described in this model contains all the aspects of physically bringing about an input such as depressing a key on a keyboard, or clicking a button on a mouse. Among the factors considered important at this level are: force, distance, size, speed, repetitiveness, duration and voice. (The last factor applies only to one particular type of input technique which is covered in a note at the end of this chapter.)

The motor component in this model is not 'intelligent'. The cognitive and perceptual components determine the action to be made and the motor component simply ensures that the appropriate action is performed. Before the next motor action is initiated, evidence that the first action has been performed correctly must be provided. This feedback is provided by the sensory component.

5.2.1.4 The Sensory Component
Sensory information is delivered from the sense(s), which have monitored the execution of the motor action, back to the brain. The sensory mechanisms which are most commonly used to provide feedback are: visual, tactile, and aural.

In skilled users, the feedback component very rarely takes place after every motor action. This is an efficient method of performance that generally comes with experience and skill. This phenomenon is by no means exclusive to human computer interaction: it is common in most forms of skilled motor activity. For example, watch a beginner's class at a gymnastics lesson. Walking on the beam is a slow, uncoordinated activity, as the beginner needs to monitor his/her relative limb positions after every step in order to maintain her balance. Contrast this with an experienced gymnast, who rarely needs to look down to see where the beam is in order to take the next step. In a relevant domain we could consider touch typing; here the typist rarely checks that each character typed is correct. Instead he/she checks complete words or even larger chunks of input data.

5.2.2   The keyboard

5.2.2.1 Introduction
Over a century ago, in 1866, an event occurred that was destined to change the nature of work for millions of people; the typewriter became a commercial success (Noyes, 1983). It was developed by two Americans, Sholes and Glidden, who were attempting to design a mechanical device to number rail tickets, bank notes and pages of books consecutively. In 1886, they patented their invention, the Sholes, Glidden and Soule typewriter (Richards, 1964). The layout of keys in the original patent remains the most widely used format today for typewriters and computer keyboards alike. The layout is usually referred to as the QWERTY layout, after the first six keys on the top row of the keyboard.

According to many investigators the QWERTY layout (Fig. 5.1 below), which was designed to reduce the typing speed of skilled users in order to minimise the jamming of the mechanical keys, is neither the easiest layout to learn nor the most efficient to use. Considerable time and resources have been spent developing alternative keyboard layouts but it appears that the QWERTY configuration will continue to be extensively used due to the massive expense and disruption (in hardware exchange, drop in typing efficiency and retraining) that would be entailed by replacing the QWERTY keyboard with a more up-to-date design. Let us consider the keyboard in terms of the model developed in 5.2.1.

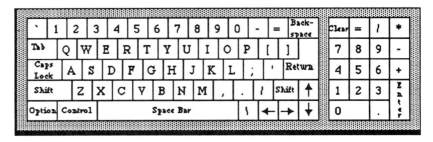

Fig. 5.1 –   A typical QWERTY layout on a computer keyboard.

5.2.2.2 The Cognitive Component
Any layout of keys will impose demands upon the user's memory. There is little doubt that the QWERTY keyboard layout places a notable demand on memory primarily because there is no inherent logic to the layout or position of the keys relative to each other. There is no other existing model that user's knowledge can draw on to help them locate keys on a QWERTY keyboard. An example of such a model would be the alphabet. If keys were placed on the keyboard in alphabetical order one might expect the time taken to learn the position of the keys to be less than on a QWERTY keyboard. An example of this principle was used by Texas Instrument's 'Speak and Spell' game for children, which asks the child to type in a word spoken by the computer. The keyboard is laid out alphabetically.

The argument for using existing stereotypes to minimise learning is also one of the main reasons for retaining the QWERTY keyboard, because of the number of individuals who have had so much experience of it. For those who have not yet used QWERTY there may be a good reason to consider an easier layout to memorise. However, attempts in the past to introduce an alternative to QWERTY have met with extremely limited success – in order to get manufacturers to change we need more than research findings and psychological theories, we need to reach a *critical mass* of users brought up on an alternative keyboard layout – this seems unlikely to occur.

5.2.2.3 The Perceptual Component
Most keyboard users employ a 'hunt and peck' typing style (*ie.* looking at the keyboard for the keys) rather than touch typing where the typist looks at the screen (or piece of paper). Users can become quite proficient at this way of inputting text (the authors count themselves in this category) and typing rates of 20-30 words per minute are quite common. To reach this rate requires a lot of practice, so why do users not learn to touch type (where typical rates would between 40 to 80 words per minute)?

In most cases the reason is that their typing loads have evolved with the increased availability of office automation equipment rather than being planned. The net result is a very large number of users (literally millions in the United Kingdom) who cannot operate a keyboard without looking at the keys. For this reason they must be able to see the characters they want quickly and easily.

In order to maximise the the typing performance of the hunt and peck typist, the following three rules should be observed;

1.)   minimise the search area,
2.)   maximise the target visibility,
3.)   place it where it is expected.

Keyboard design can take account of these rules with minimal cost. Colour coding particular blocks of keys (like the numeric keypad often included in computer keyboards) both reduces search areas and helps target visibility. Labelling keys clearly and using key size and shape as an indicator of function are two further design techniques that can be influential.

5.2.2.4 The Motor Component
The key has to be large enough to allow a big (99th percentile male) finger to hit and depress a key without accidentally activating the key next to it. The limit on maximum key size is the need to keep all the keys within a space small enough for a typist to reach all the keys easily by finger movements (as opposed to wrist movements). For standard QWERTY keyboard layouts the recommended key dimensions are 12mm to 15mm square (Cakir *et al.,* 1980) with a spacing of 19mm +/- 1mm between the centres of adjacent keys (ISO R/1091). Beaumont (1985) reported in an investigation of different input devices that the reaction time was faster on the 'SPACE' bar than any other key on the QWERTY keyboard. The reason for the superior performance was because the key was "large and easy to locate".

Function keys
Many keyboards have an additional set of keys which are called function keys (sometimes referred to a 'F-keys'. These multi-purpose keys are often utilised by

the software as a means of allowing users to access certain computer functions without needing to type in a string of text (a common example is F9 = 'help'). Poor design or inconsistent use of the function keys can cause more problems than it solves.

The location of keys is important. They have to be sufficiently spaced from the alphanumeric keys to make them distinct, whilst still within easy reach of the operator. Shneiderman (1987) reported that "some users would rather type six or eight characters rather than remove their fingers from the home position" which demonstrates the delicacy of the relationship.

Cursor control keys
A particular type of function key are the cursor control keys. There are usually four keys which can move the cursor up, down, left and right. In certain cases there are eight cursor keys to simplify diagonal cursor movement.

There are several different types of cursor control key available. The two most widely used configurations are shown in Fig. 5.2 and are preferred because they are compatible with arrow directions. The layout in Fig. 5.2 (i) is used on the IBM 'PC' superimposed over the numeric keypad. Cursor movement or number generation can be selected by depressing one of two keys, but neither of them have any means of letting the operator know which mode has been selected. Hence the likelihood of character generation instead of cursor movement, and vice versa, is greatly increased. This illustrates that, whereas cursor key layout is important, an initially correct design can be easily undermined by inadequate consideration of usability requirements.

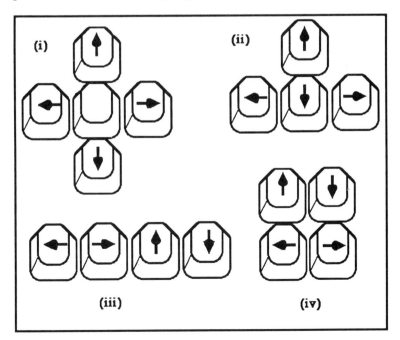

Fig. 5.2 –   Four possible layouts of cursor control keys.

Experiments have been performed to determine the configuration which is fastest and least prone to error. In separate studies (Foley, 1983 and Emmons, 1984) both the configurations 5.2 (i) and 5.2 (ii) were found to be faster for novice users than that laid out in figure 5.2 (iv). However, Emmons (*op. cit.*) noted that frequent users could use configurations 5.2 (iii) and 5.2 (iv) equally quickly.

5.2.2.5 The Sensory Component

There are three main ways that a key can provide feedback to the user without the user having to look at the screen for confirmation that the activation was successful. The three ways are pressure (force), displacement and sound.

In practice there are two basic types of keyboard; one which uses both force and displacement for feedback and a second type which uses pressure (force) only. In both types of keyboard, the option for additional auditory feedback exists in the form of a mechanical click or an electronic sound. The type of pressure feedback can vary according to a pre-defined relationship between the amount of key pressure required for any amount of key displacement.

5.2.2.6 Summary

The keyboard is an essential input device for current computer systems. It may be supplemented by one or more of the input devices described elsewhere in this chapter, but it is difficult to imagine a single device that could replace the variety and flexibility of inputs that a multi-key device can provide. Some systems have keys that represent a complete command (*eg.* a key labelled 'file' or 'delete'), but for this approach to provide a flexible method of communicating with a system *and* maintain a large vocabulary of commands would require an impossibly large set of keys. So, keyboards are here to stay, at least until voice recognisers show a great degree of improvement. As this section has attempted to show, just because we are stuck with keyboards does not mean improvements in their design cannot be made, easily and relatively cheaply.

5.2.3   The mouse

5.2.3.1 Introduction

> *"The mouse is a small device, about the size of a cigarette packet, with [one to] three buttons on top. This is attached to a display terminal by a thin cord"*
>
> (Huckle 1981).

The purpose of the mouse is twofold. Firstly, the mouse can be moved about the surface of the desk or pad to control the movement of the cursor on the screen. Secondly, with the use of the buttons, the mouse can be used to perform some action on objects on the screen. For example, the mouse can be used to move an arrow-shaped cursor to point at an icon (see Section 5.3) on the screen, pressing the mouse button might then be used to indicate to the system that the user wishes to see what is 'inside' the icon (*eg.* the icon might represent a file or list of files).

The most widely used mouse at present contains a small ball which rotates as it is moved over the desk surface. These movements are translated into the movements of the screen arrow.

The forerunner of today's mechanical mouse was invented by Douglas Englebart in 1964. The device had two wheels underneath it set at right angles to each other which were translated, via potentiometers, to X and Y movement on the screen. The commercial optical mouse was invented by Steve Kirsh of Mouse Systems Corporation in 1982 (Comerford, 1984). Fig. 5.3 shows some typical mouse designs.

Fig. 5.3 –   Three types of mouse design in common use.

5.2.3.2 The Cognitive Component

One of the major advantages claimed on behalf of the mouse is that it is easy to learn to use. It was reported by Apple Computer Inc. that computer-naive users could become familiar with the mouse in 15 minutes. In contrast, it required an average of 20 hours to operate similar software using a keyboard. How Apple Computer Inc. relate their findings to contrasting results reported by other researchers (see Chapter 4, Section 4.4.2) is not clear[†].

Generally the mouse is a popular input device. It allows the user to work in a comfortable position with the hand supported. Engelbart (1973) also noted that working with a mouse allowed the user to change posture easily which is important during long periods of interaction with any machine.

In addition to the positive reports of comfort and physical ease of use, the mouse is popular because it appears to make human-computer interaction easier. The perceived improvement cannot really be attributed to the mouse alone, but is more likely to be due to the combination of a pointing device and good software to support its use. It is likely that any interface supporting the same software plus a pointing device (eg. joystick, touch screen etc.) would be preferred to an interface which required typing in keywords and commands for most applications. Some of today's computers use the mouse as an integral part of

---

[†] Apple are clearly convinced about their findings – in March 1988 in the UK they based a large newspaper advertising campaign on this very point, depicting learning curves in the ad.

the system – it is not an add-on device that the user can take or leave as he/she desires – rather, to get even partial functionality from the system a mastery of the mouse is required.

It is surprising how much can be achieved with the mouse alone on some systems. For example, a colleague of ours once used his Macintosh for fully 45 minutes before he realised that he had not plugged his keyboard in! That is, the computer was found to be fully operational for a large number of tasks without the keyboard even being required.

5.2.3.3 The Perceptual Component
The movement relationship between the mouse on the horizontal desk top and the pointer on the screen is important for the efficiency of the device. As one might expect if one moves a mouse to the left at desk top level, the majority of people expect the pointer to move in the same direction. The same relationship exists for movements to the right. But what is the *expected* relationship between the up/down pointer movement and the fore/aft mouse movement? If I pull the mouse towards me will the arrow move up or down on the screen?

Evidence from control-display relationship experimentation has shown no clear 'natural' preference. Spragg *et al.* (1959) measured tracking ability with different relationships between control and display and found performance very similar for both types of control. In office automation, there is an analogy drawn between the screen and the desk top (Smith *et al.* 1982). The screen is a vertical representation of the horizontal desk top. If one imagines placing the screen in a horizontal position, then the relationship between moving the mouse forward and the pointer moving up the screen seems quite natural. In the usual position, with screen upright, a forward movement of the mouse sends the arrow up the screen. It is this relationship which all commercially available mouse input devices use.

5.2.3.4 The Motor Component
There are many different sizes and shapes of mice and so far no standard has emerged. Basically all the commercially available mice require a smooth, flat surface on which the hand can rest and easily operate the mouse button(s). No evidence currently exists that one design is faster, more accurate or more comfortable than any other.

It is interesting to note that the inventor of the mouse intended that it would be held between the thumb and little finger leaving the other three fingers in between free to manipulate the buttons (Comerford, 1984). There were three buttons on the original mouse, one for each finger, but it was felt that control of the device would be lost if it was held with the little finger and thumb. Most mouse users hold the body of the mouse between the thumb and middle finger, leaving the index finger to operate the button. Thus some controversy exists as to the optimum number of buttons.

Button design
Mice have either a single control button (*eg.* the Apple Macintosh), two buttons (*eg.* Microsoft, Sun) and three buttons (*eg.* Mouse Systems). It has been suggested that the performance of a mouse is faster and more accurate using different buttons rather than different numbers of clicks (Price & Cordova, 1983).

Positioning
Card *et al.* (1978) compared the positioning time and the error rate of selecting text using four different pointing devices (step keys, text keys, rate-controlled isometric joystick and a mouse). The mouse used in the experiment was an old design consisting of two wheels at right angles to one another on the underside of the mouse. As the mouse moved over the table one wheel coded the amount of movement in the X-direction, the other the movement in the Y-direction. The results showed that the mouse was quicker to position and resulted in fewer errors than the other devices investigated. In addition, it was reported that as the target distance increased so did the positioning time. However, the effect of the target distance had a much lesser effect on the overall positioning time for the mouse than it did for the other devices.

5.2.3.5 The Sensory Component
When the mouse is moved across the desktop, the pointer moves across the screen. The ratio of the mouse movement across the desk to the pointer movement across the screen is termed the gearing. There are two observations to make about gearing.

Firstly, as a mouse moves across a desktop there is often some slippage. In the case of the mechanical mouse (*ie.* a mouse that uses a rolling ball to interact with mechanical transducers inside the body of the mouse that translate the ball's movement into electrical signals that move the screen cursor appropriately) slippage is due to the ball inside the mouse not turning at an even rate over the desktop. The result of this is that it may require different mouse movements on the desk to achieve the same pointer movement on the screen. Optical mice (*ie.* a mouse that works by pulsing light at a dark and light graded surface and sensing the reflected light to determine its speed and direction) are prone to slippage in a different way. If the optical mouse is moved faster than the pulse sensors can interpret, then accuracy is lost and slippage occurs.

The second observation is that gearing is dependent generally on screen size. The smaller the screen, the lower the gearing. From measurements made of existing terminals, the gearing ratio of mouse movement to arrow movement is in the range of 1:1.3 to 1:2.5 for screens measuring 9-19 inches. The gearings across the sample were considered to be rapid whilst sufficiently sensitive for accurate manipulation. Note that the Mac has 'configurable' gearing – the user can set the gearing himself, within limits.

Feedback
The feedback of successful or unsuccessful mouse manipulation is provided on the screen. The mouse itself provides feedback on the activation of the button(s) only by the snap action or the ramp action of the button. Information about the successful positioning of the arrow comes from the screen, which means that the most important aspect of the feedback is that it must be instant. Any delay in the visual feedback of the arrow moving across the screen, or a menu appearing after the button has been depressed, would cause error of operation and slow down the overall performance of the mouse system.

5.2.3.6 Summary
The mouse is a popular device, that is rapidly becoming commonplace in many computing environments. Because it is designed to be an integral part of some systems, the software written for use with a mouse allows users a very fine grained control, especially with bit-mapped display screens. Provision of software designed to make the most of the mouse means users getting to easily utilise more of the computer's potential, which cannot be a bad thing. Thus users tend to be happy with the mouse because of the ease with which they can perform tasks that were formerly much more difficult.

A simple example will suffice. In early screen drawing tools, drawing on the screen even something as simple as a rectangle was a difficult operation. The coordinates for the top left corner of the rectangle had to be entered (often in number of pixels) in numeric form, and with the correct syntax, then a line was drawn to the top right corner of the rectangle by specifying where the line should end, and so on. Assuming one eventually got a rectangle on the screen, moving it to another part of the screen was another lengthy task since one had to add X number of pixels to all the horizontal co-ordinates to (say) move the rectangle to the right. In WIMP interfaces (see later in this chapter), which normally use a mouse, both drawing and moving a rectangle is much simplified. The task is also changed in nature, from a numeric calculation task to a manipulative task – and generally speaking we are pretty good at co-ordinating our eye and hand movements (it is natural and something we do all day). In this case it is true that it matters little what pointing device is used, although the mouse is certainly the most common. Furthermore, direct manipulation of screen objects using a mouse does not carry with it the same penalties for error that a wrong calculation inflicts on the hapless user of a highly syntax specific command language.

5.2.4   The joystick

5.2.4.1 Introduction
The joystick concept has a long history which begins in car and aircraft control devices (Shneiderman, 1987). The notion of using a joystick to control cursor movements on computer systems has been accepted for a long time too and this is reflected in the variety of devices that are currently available. Although there are three basic types of joystick; the displacement joystick, the isometric (or force-operated) joystick and the switch activated joystick, they all look essentially similar. They consist of a short lever mounted in a base. Movement of the stick results in a movement of the cursor or arrow on the screen. The differences between the three types of joystick become apparent when the user attempts to move the stick.

Displacement Joystick
The displacement joystick allows the user to move the stick in any direction and the cursor moves in direct proportion. The displacement joystick tends to operate in absolute mode rather than in a rate-controlled fashion. The difference between these two modes will be described below.

Isometric Joystick
The isometric (or force-operated) joystick looks the same as the displacement joystick but when the user applies pressure against the stick it does not move. However, strain gauges located in the device sense the pressure and translate this into cursor movement. When the user stops applying pressure to the stick, the cursor stops moving. Pressure can be applied to the stick in any direction and the cursor will move accordingly.

Switch-Activated Joystick
Unlike the other two joysticks, the switch-activated (or digital) joystick detects movement only in eight directions (north, north-east, east, south-east, south, south-west, west, and north-west). This is because the stick is in contact with eight switches at its base and when the user moves the joystick it closes one or more of the switches. The switch status information is simply converted into cursor movement. When the user takes pressure off the stick, the stick usually returns to the centre position but the cursor remains where it is. The cursor usually moves at a fixed velocity in the direction in which the joystick is pointing.

Fixed Velocity vs Rate-Controlled
There are two possible joystick/cursor relationships. Firstly, there is the fixed velocity relationship where, no matter how fast one moves the joystick (or how much pressure one puts on it in the case of the isometric joystick), the cursor will move at a fixed velocity. The second type of relationship is termed rate controlled. In this case the cursor speed can be controlled by moving the joystick at different speeds or applying more or less pressure against the stick.

5.2.4.2 The Cognitive Component
There have been no reports in the literature of users finding it difficult to learn to operate joysticks. The widespread use of joysticks for various home-computer games is testimony to the ease with which people can learn to use the device as well as to its relative cheapness and durability. There is minimal learning required in the use of a joystick, especially if one is familiar with the control display relationships of the mouse or trackball.

5.2.4.3 The Perceptual Component
The considerations of movement stereotypes discussed in relation to the mouse apply equally to the joystick. The common control display configuration assumes that the operator considers the VDT screen as a vertical desktop, with fore and aft movements of the joystick causing upwards and downwards movement of the cursor respectively.

The joystick requires little space and can usually be made small enough to fit into a keyboard, allowing easy location and thus minimal perceptual demand on the user. This allows full visual attention to be paid to the events on the VDT screen.

5.2.4.4 The Motor Component
There is some disagreement about what the physical dimensions of the joystick shaft should be. The length of the shaft has been reported as being between 1-2

inches (Huckle, 1982) and 1-4 inches (Greenstein & Arnault, 1987). In both studies the references were describing the joystick dimensions rather than prescribing the optimum design. No comparative studies have been found to suggest determine the critical dimensions of a joystick.

It has been suggested that the joystick should incorporate a palm or handrest so the device can be used for extended periods without fatigue. Ritchie & Turner (1975) provide an illustration of a joystick which has the shaft mounted in a hemispherical base which they suggest will "reduce fatigue for lengthy interactive routines." It is important to consider supporting the hand during and between joystick use to minimise the build up of fatigue, since this could affect accuracy as well as the time required to complete the task.

It has been noted that the joystick is particularly good if rapid changes in cursor direction are required. In the case of tracking tasks, this may be an important feature, and indicates why it has been so successful as a device for arcade games as well as home computer games.

5.2.4.5 The Sensory Component
As with mice and trackballs (see next section), the gain (ie. the ratio of joystick movement to cursor movement) of the joystick may be changed. Jenkins & Karr (1954) found that the optimal control to display movement ratio was approximately 0.4 (ie. for each 10 units of joystick movement the cursor moves 4 units of the same scale on the display screen). However, the size of the joystick that is required for this level of accuracy would be impracticable for most modern display screen and keyboard sizes.

Accuracy
It is generally reported that the joystick is not a very accurate input device and has low resolution (Rubinstein & Hersch, 1984, Scott, 1982). For computer applications, joysticks are thus most suited to more coarse pointing or tracking tasks which do not require a great deal of precision.

Isometric versus Displacement Joysticks
When the shaft of the displacement joystick is moved, the user is provided with proprioceptive feedback proportional to the pressure applied. The isometric joystick is advantageous in that it removes the travel time inherent in the use of a displacement joystick. However, the lack of proprioceptive feedback means that accuracy is generally poorer in both rate of movement and higher order levels of control. Paradoxically, isometric joysticks are more generally used to encode velocity information and displacement joysticks, absolute distance information. The reason for this mismatch between user and input device is hard to determine but it has been suggested that it may be a consequence of the technology used in displacement joysticks which slows cursor positioning.

5.2.4.6 Summary
The joystick is not commonly provided with mainstream personal computers. It is more likely to be purchased as an add-on device, for special applications. The best example is home-computer games, for which a joystick is very often required. Most home computer joysticks either have a button in the handle as a trigger to be squeezed or a button on top to be pressed with the thumb. The

button often operates a 'gun' in 'shoot 'em up' type games. Industrial joysticks, apparently, have failed to utilise this idea, and there seems to be no reference to such joysticks in the literature. Can it be that in years to come single, or even multi button joysticks will become more common? I doubt it, because the mouse now has a firm position as a popular device, and the accuracy of a joystick still leaves something to be desired when very fine control is needed – but one never knows.

5.2.5   The trackball

5.2.5.1 Introduction
The trackball (or trackerball or roller ball) is a cursor control device in the form of a mechanical rolling ball set into the work surface, the keyboard or a special box near the display terminal. Rotating the ball causes the cursor to move on the screen. The direction and speed of the cursor is determined by the speed and direction of the trackball. For those who have not had experience of a trackball but who have used a mouse, the trackball could be described as a static, upturned mouse.

The trackball only positions the cursor. A further feature (*eg.* a button or a keyboard) is required to perform any action on the object located. Because of the method of operating the trackball, it would be difficult to operate the ball and a button simultaneously.

5.2.5.2 The Cognitive Component
Most authors reporting on the trackball have commented on the ease and speed which most subjects have learnt to manipulate a pointer using a trackball (Huckle, 1981). The movement relationship between the trackball and the cursor is the same as the mouse (*ie.* forward ball movement for upward cursor movement, backwards for down, left for left and right for right).

Another attribute of trackball operation is its 'feel'. Feel refers to the inertia and damping of the ball, which varies between models due to the size and weight of the ball used and the way that it is mounted in its holder. Reporting on the literature, Jackson (1982) concluded that users adapt very quickly to the different feel of different trackballs.

The trackball is often used as input device in potentially stressful environments such as air traffic control (Shneiderman, 1987), radar and other military applications (Greenstein & Arnaut, 1987). However, no research exists to suggest that an user performs quicker or more accurately under stress with a trackball than with any other input device.

5.2.5.3 The Perceptual Component
During normal usage of a trackball the user's eyes are fixed on the screen and the hand operates the ball. Since the ball is fixed in a container or, in some cases, into the working surface, there is no proprioceptive (or sub-cutaneous) perception. Other input devices make use of this perceptual ability to facilitate speed and/or accuracy, *eg.* touch typing on a keyboard and operating a mouse.

The trackball has certain qualities which makes it popular in dark or otherwise demanding environments. Firstly it can be fixed in one place on the work surface which makes it easy to locate. In darkened environments, such as air traffic control rooms, quick and accurate location may be critical. Secondly, the hand may rest on the ball so that in bumpy or similarly difficult conditions the operator may keep contact with device. In addition to this, the fact that the trackball can have a relatively small 'footprint' (a footprint is the amount of desk space a device covers) makes it an attractive pointer control device, particularly in military applications.

5.2.5.4 The Motor Component

The trackball can be manipulated in a number of ways. The fingers can be placed upon its surface and moved, drawing the ball along in continuous contact, or the ball can be flicked into ballistic motion by the fingers, with further flicks for additional motion components. Friction pressure is used to halt the ball abruptly. Similarly the palm of the hand can be used for continuous contact or to impart an impulsive force.

The 'feel' of a ball is determined largely by the inertia and by the extent of damping on its motion. In most current rolling ball mechanisms both friction and inertia increase with ball size.

Trackball Dimensions

There is some confusion about the optimal physical dimensions of the trackerball. Ritchie & Turner (1975) suggested the ball is "up to 75mm in diameter", whereas Shneiderman (1987) gives a much broader range of ball diameters of approximately 25-150mm. Jackson (1982) reported a smaller range of 25mm-115mm. As far as can be determined, no comparative study has been performed to determine the effect of different ball diameters on device performance.

Fatigue

During normal operation the fingers are used to turn the ball. When the cursor does not need to be moved the hand rests on the box containing the ball. Operating the trackball with short rests interspersed as described above is reported to be an acceptable work routine for "an extended period of time" (Greenstein & Arnaut, *op cit.*).

Speed

It is widely accepted that the trackball is one of the quickest target selection devices available (Mehr & Mehr, 1972, Gomez *et al.*, 1982). However, the maximum velocity varies as a function of the direction of the movement. This may be due to the different strategies of using the fingers or the palm for moving the ball in different directions.

5.2.5.5 The Sensory Component

It has been reported that very fine levels of accuracy can be achieved with a trackball. Ball *et al.* (1980) compared the error rates for selecting targets displayed on a CRT screen for three different input devices; an on-screen touch input device, a touchpad and a rolling ball. In general there was little difference in the error rate in positioning where the 'resolution' (*ie.* the radius of the circle surrounding the target which is considered to be a hit) was coarse. However, the trackball out-performed the other two input devices for the task being studied where the resolution required was fine. The crucial comparison (for us) would be with a mouse, which was not made.

The most important limitation of the device itself is its resolution, *ie.* the smallest ball movement which will be registered by the system. Newman & Brown (1958) have shown that operators can track consistently to 0.25mm and the device should not limit this too severely, even if the screen resolution produces different criteria. The resolution of the ball will depend on its internal mechanics and the way in which it communicates with the computational part of the system. Most rolling balls operate on the same principle of transferring motion, by friction, onto two cylindrical shafts set at right angles to one another. The resolution depends on the diameter of the shaft and the number of gradations which can be read from the disc per rotation. Jackson (1982) points out that, since the ball is employed as an infinite surface, the resolution is quite independent of ball size. On a common commercial, optically (as opposed to magnetically) encoded ball with 48 disc slots, the resulting resolution is 0.5mm which compares reasonably with Newman & Brown's (*op. cit.*) value for tracking performance level.

5.2.5.6 Summary
The trackball is well regarded in military and air traffic control environments where is has been around for many years. It provides a high resolution of movement and is therefore quick and accurate in the hands of a skilled operator; which it is not difficult to become. Modern computing systems use input and cursor control devices for far more than just tracking or targetting objects on a screen. In particular, on-screen drawing is widely used nowadays and this device cannot in reality be used for such tasks. To use a trackball with many of today's personal or mini-computers would require the creation of both a special interface and software – an expensive undertaking given its limits and the easily available mouse.

5.2.6   Touch sensitive screens

5.2.6.1 Introduction
This technology has arisen based upon an intuitive notion of 'what we do naturally', and it is not the only technology based upon such half-truths, myths and 'plain common sense'. The assumption is that we all point at objects in the world around us, and, as this chapter testifies, technology has provided several devices which permit us to do the same to screen based objects. If we can actually eliminate the intermediate pointing technology; the mouse, the joystick *etc.* by allowing users to point at objects on the screen directly, surely this would be an advance? This is the intuitive notion whose validity is discussed in the section below.

There are several different types of Touch Sensitive Screen (TSS). Although the enabling technology differs between devices, they all operate in the same way from the user's point of view. With a TSS a series of options is presented on the display screen. The options are often framed in touch sensitive boxes called light buttons. The user indicates his/her choice by touching the appropriate box on the screen with a finger and a new or revised set of choices appears on the screen.

The problems with this method of pointing at objects on a screen are partly to do with the anatomy of the user and partly because of the technology employed. The limitations of a person's anatomy are fixed and cannot be changed. Provided designers appreciate what human attributes limit current TSS's then there is no reason why a new generation of improved TSSs, could not be designed. In order to understand why users experience problems with the current TSSs, the different technologies need to be appreciated. These are very briefly described here:

1.)   Acoustic Touch Sensitive Screens
       use ultrasonic waves which are generated over a sheet of glass which is placed over the CRT screen. When a user touches the screen the waves are interrupted and reflected back towards their source where they are detected.

2.)   Conductive and Capacitive Touch Sensitive Screens
       are sensitive to the touch of the user's finger on the screen. The conductive screen is really just an ordinary VDT screen with two grids of conductive material placed over it in an X and Y direction. When the screen is touched the grid shorts in that location and information about the co-ordinates is sent to the system.

       The capacitive device uses a capacitive film which covers the back of a glass overlay set in front of the CRT screen. When the finger touches the screen, the body's own capacitance causes an electrical signal to be generated which is converted into co-ordinate information

3.)   Infrared Touch Sensitive Screens
       use a series of infrared emitting diodes and detectors which are positioned around the edge of the screen. When a user touches the screen the flow of infrared light is blocked by the finger between certain diodes and detectors.

4.)   Pressure Sensitive Touch Sensitive Screens
       use a glass overlay with strain gauges placed between the CRT screen and overlay. Pressure on the glass is measured in X, Y and Z directions before being converted into X and Y co-ordinates.

5.)   Touch Wire Touch Sensitive Screens
       the oldest TSS, are made up of rows of copper wires mounted above an overlay containing further wires. When a user points to an area on the screen they press the top wire against the lower wire and earth the circuit through his/her own body.

5.2.6.2 The Cognitive Component

An indication of the relatively low load imposed by the act of pointing was described by Martin *et al.* (1984) who reported that pointing took half the time of speaking in a primary tracking task *ie.* that the cognitive *and* motor components of pointing took the same time as the cognitive or articulation element of speaking. This may be interpreted as evidence that pointing is a more compatible low-resolution system input, requiring only limited cognitive processing and imposing a minimal cognitive load. (Children can point before they can speak.)

It has been noted that the learning the principle of operating a TSS is very easy (Usher, 1982). This means that many agree with Greenstein & Arnaut's (1987) sentiments that if one uses a TSS then training is minimised. Although learning may be quicker and easier than for other low-resolution input devices, this does not mean that training is unnecessary.

There is clear evidence that the subjective responses to using a TSS are positive *if it is used for an appropriate task* (Pfauth & Priest, 1981). There appears to be some disagreement why the TSS is popular. Greenstein & Arnault (*op. cit.*) suggest that it is the ease of learning which may be the cause of high user acceptance.

In a comparative study of five different touch screen technologies, Schulze & Snyder (1983) recorded performance and subjective ratings. Of the five different devices (acoustic, capacitive, conductive, cross-wires and infrared), the cross-wire received the highest subjective ranking as well as being first equal in performance tests with the infrared device.

5.2.6.3 The Perceptual Component

One of the main problems associated with the TSS is that of parallax. Parallax is defined as an "apparent displacement of [an] object due to [the] different displacement of [the] observer" (Oxford Pocket Dictionary, 1969). With a TSS the problem occurs when an users locate the area or menu item that they want to select on the screen and touch what they believe to be the corresponding sensitive area. If the distance between the touch sensitive area and the actual object on the screen is great enough, the visual system may be fooled, and user errors occur. Another problem is that, as one reaches to touch the screen, the object that one wants to select becomes obscured by the hand or finger.

With any overlay (which some TSSs use) there will be a reduction in the image quality. The quality may be impaired by making the screen fuzzier (making labels, text and the edge of boxes harder to determine), reducing screen luminance, or affecting the colour on the screen. All these factors will have an effect on the ease of visual perception.

Screen Design

The method of operation and the technology involved do cause some perceptual problems. However, in the desire to maximise the potential power of a TSS system, many currently available commercial applications have introduced further perceptual problems by overloading the screen with information. Some screens are covered by identical touch sensitive boxes with small, short coded labels. To the occasional user, or the expert working quickly, errors can easily be made because of overloaded screens.

5.2.6.4 The Motor Component

One of the major problems with using Touch Sensitive Screens for extended periods of time is the fatigue caused by regularly reaching out and touching the screen. The regular action of pointing causes local fatigue and discomfort not only in the muscles of the active arm but often in the muscles of the shoulder and neck, which are in a state of contraction to support the arm.

There are two considerations in determining the optimum target dimensions of the active touch area from the motor point of view. Firstly, there is the static consideration of the size of a finger. The critical dimension is more than the area of the end of the finger because for some devices (as with infrared devices) the sensitive area lies on a plane several millimeters above the screen surface. The finger is wider at this point, which increases the minimum area for a target. The minimum area is further enlarged because it has been observed that the finger strikes the screen at an angle (especially with vertical mounted screens).

Secondly, pointing is a dynamic activity, and this means that the finger will not hit *exactly* the same place on the screen each time the operator points. The error is not great, but it does exist and must be considered. It has been reported that off-set pointing varies depending on where the object lies on the screen. Beringer & Petersen (1985) have reported that the higher an object is on the screen, the lower in the touch sensitive area the user is likely to point and consequently the greater the error rate.

5.2.6.5 The Sensory Component
As with all input devices, feedback should be provided in the form of an acknowledgement from the system to the user. Unlike the majority of input devices, the touch sensitive screen has no moving parts so no tactile feedback can be provided. In the normal mode of operation touch sensitive screens provide visual feedback by highlighting the light button or menu option selected or by changing the whole screen configuration. Whilst this may be adequate as feedback if it is registered immediately, the heavy use of a system may result in much slower response time, thus leaving the user uncertain whether the system has received the input or not.

5.2.6.6 Summary
The touch sensitive screen does have its advocates, although at least one of the authors is not one of them! Such a technique can be employed only for registering a user's request from pre-specified options. The actual input of data cannot be practically employed using a TSS. So, in any general purpose computer system the TSS would have to be supplemented by at least one other device and possibly two (*eg.* a mouse *and* a keyboard), in order to get the maximum potential from the system. This rather defeats the object of having an extra input device. The likelihood of fatigue, difficulties in target acquisition caused by viewing problems and lack of general applicability combine to limit the use of such a device to specialist tasks and environments.

Finally, a word about the 'naturalness' of such a device. Although we learn to point at objects very early in life (my son, Joshua (Rubin), started pointing at objects from about 9 months) it is rarely with the intention of bringing some action about as a result of the pointing. That is, we usually point in order to direct someone's attention to an object or scene. Thus the question of how natural it is to point to screen areas and bring about some action must remain open. We prefer to make the analogy with button pressing on vending machines, since this seems closer to the mechanical equivalent of TSSs. Of course, today's technology has made remote control devices for TVs, VCRs and stereos commonplace domestic equipment, and these probably ease learning for pointing devices though the fatigue experienced with TSSs is removed by allowing the users to make their choices from a distance.

5.2.7   The light pen

5.2.7.1 Introduction
The light pen is an input device that looks much like an ordinary pen but its tip is used to point to areas of the display screen and thereby cause a signal to be generated for interpretation by the computer. The operation of the light pen is simple; a small photocell in the pen has light emitted from the screen focussed onto it. As that part of the screen is refreshed by the electron beam, the increase in brightness is detected and a signal to the computer is generated. By providing a switch (usually finger operated) the user can decide when to cause activation of the signal. The computer detects exactly where the signal occurred based on the time of the signal since the last refresh and so the display screen co-ordinates can be calculated. Because of their method of operation, light pens can be used only with cathode ray tube (CRT) displays.

5.2.7.2 The Cognitive Component
The light pen is easy to learn. It draws on existing stereotypes in that all users have used pens and pencils, and, as with the touch screen, pointing at a screen area is not difficult to learn to do. It is also reasonable to assume that some 'unlearning' must take place too: we usually use pens on horizontal or near horizontal surfaces, whereas light pens are used in the (near) vertical plane. We have an expectation that we need to press down with a pen in order to bring about its successful operation, and this is not the case with all light pens.

5.2.7.3 The Perceptual Component
The need for the overlays required by TSSs is removed, and therefore so is the problem of fuzzy images. Parallax may still cause problems, especially if the user sits at a less than optimal orientation to the display screen. Indeed, the finer point of the light pen allows both for a greater number of screen areas that can be activated by pointing, and these for areas to be correspondingly reduced in area. These factors combine to increase the possibility of error in target acquisition; as with the TTS, the user's hand and the light pen will at times obscure parts of the display. One perceptual advantage is that the light pen does not require the user to scan the screen in order to locate and then move a cursor (Galitz, 1980). Again, as with TSSs there is a tendency for designers to clutter the screen with too many sensitive 'buttons' or selectable screen areas.

5.2.7.4 The Motor Component
Fatigue is again reported to be a concern when the device is used over long periods. The constant reaching up to point at a display can be reduced by locating the screen horizontally. In addition, Engel & Granda (1975) point out that light pens are cumbersome devices and especially awkward to use for left handed people.

5.2.7.5 The Sensory Component
Engel & Granda *(op. cit.)* also report that the 'feel' of the pen is not as natural as normal pens and pencils, and that there is a lack of precision because of the pen aperture and the distance the pen is from the screen surface. Feedback can be fast with single selection type tasks, but with a user working quickly over a large menu, selecting several items, it is possible for the system's response to slow considerably.

5.2.7.6 Summary
Light pens again have a limited usefulness. The need for CRT's, their use as selection rather than data input devices, and the special hardware and software, all contrive to reduce the number of applications where the light pen has a distinct advantage over other devices. An experiment by Haller, Mutscler & Voss (1984) showed that the light pen was superior to other devices (including a mouse, trackball and cursor keys) when the task was positioning a cursor on the screen, which illustrates that, in specialist, limited tasks, the device has a definite use.

5.2.8   A Note About Speech Input Devices
The use of voice as a means of controlling or directing a computer is a fast growing topic. More than that, it is such a specialist area that it would be inappropriate within the confines and scope of this volume for a non-specialist to comment or summarise work in this area. Instead the reader is referred to another book published by Ellis Horwood: *'Speech and Language-Based Interaction With Machines'* by Waterworth & Talbot (1987).

5.3   WIMP INTERFACES

5.3.1   Introduction
Since about 1983 there has arisen a new breed of user interfaces to some small computing systems – the WIMPs: interfaces that use Windows, Icons, Menus and Pointing Devices. Several years before this, larger more powerful, computers such as the Xerox Star (the original WIMP) and ICL's Perq had their interfaces built around the now common WIMP features. As computing power became cheaper, and chip design allowed a further reduction in the physical size of storage devices, it became possible to provide WIMP interfaces on personal computers as well as specialist and very costly workstations and mini-computers. Apple's Lisa, which was launched in 1983, though not cheap, was an early attempt by Apple Computer, Inc. to educate users as to the potential merits of such interfaces. Of course there are also disadvantages to such systems, and when our office first had a demonstration of a Lisa, the demonstrator left us to 'play with it' for a couple of hours over lunch. When she returned we had managed to throw the 'alarm clock' (a screen object that told the time) into the 'wastebin' (a screen object into which discarded files and documents were put), from which it never returned!

This chapter will cover those aspects of WIMP interfaces that have not been covered so far in this book, and point out issues that are, or should be, the concern of human factors people. Lastly some criticism of some of the philosophy behind such interfaces is put forward, both to stimulate debate and also as an attempt to inject some balance into what has become a rather one-sided argument in human factors circles during the mid–1980's.

5.3.2   The general philosophy of WIMP interfaces

Before WIMP interfaces came along the user of a computer had a only a very restricted way of having a dialogue with a computer. A language often had to be learned, though some databases could be interrogated with a minimum of learning using a database query language. The language might have been very 'low level' where the user had to learn a language that was close to the computer's way of interpreting information. That is, if we consider that ultimately, all information processed by a computer is a series of 1s and 0s (binary), a low level language such as 'machine code' literally means a code (usually hexadecimal or 'Hex') that the machine understands almost without any translation. As we move up and away from the machine there are other languages which need increasing amounts of conversion in order for the machine to carry out the instructions received. Most common computer languages: Pascal, C, Fortran *etc.* are termed 'high level' in that they are quite remote from the instructions directly understood by the machine. However, to mere mortals like ourselves such computer languages are still a considerable stumbling block that has to be overcome in order for us to get a computer to do anything worthwhile.

The computer industry around the mid 1970s seemed suddenly to recognise that the materials for computers were dramatically reducing in price; memory was becoming cheap and single chips and processors were becoming more and more powerful. This led to low cost computers being sold in their hundreds of thousands, and meant that computing was about to be removed from the hands of the specialist and delivered to us ordinary mortals, on our desk, (in shiny little boxes, and with shiny little screens!)

If computers were about to be distributed to the masses, the major stumbling block had to be overcome. It may have been all right for specialists to be forced to learn the required arcane incantations of a highly structured, syntax dominated computer language, but Joe and Josephine Soap were not going to be bothered to go to the trouble. Something had to be done to ensure a wider user population – WIMPs were a heaven sent shot in the arm to the computing industry.

WIMP interfaces utilise what Shneiderman (1983) has termed 'direct manipulation'. He presented an 'integrated portrait' of the features provided by direct manipulation and summarised these four principles:

1.)   Continuous representation of the object of interest.
      ('WIMP-talk' refers to things that appear on the screen as 'objects'.)
2.)   Physical actions (movement and selection using the mouse) instead of complex syntax.
3.)   Rapid, incremental, reversible operations whose impact on the object of interest is immediately visible.
4.)   Layered approach to learning that permits usage with minimal knowledge. Users are encouraged to 'expand their knowledge gracefully'.

We shall return to the advantages bestowed upon users of systems that embody these principles later in this chapter. Suffice it to say here that, users have taken up WIMP interfaces in a big way, Apple Macintoshes are very popular machines and IBM PC's (and their clones) although not 'naturally' WIMP-like have special software available that makes them so; Microsoft Windows and Digital Research GEM are two common proprietary operating environments that support WIMP interfaces.

Although it is the interworking of the WIMP features that bestow the interface with its directly manipulable nature, it is valuable first to consider each WIMP feature separately, or as separately as possible.

5.3.3 Windows

The window, or 'windowing' is one of the fundamental features of WIMP interfaces. In essence it is the facility whereby the display screen can be divided into smaller sub-screens or windows each of which can display different objects. The object might be a spreadsheet, a text file, a drawing or any other of the myriad possibilities available. There are usually limits to how many windows can be displayed, the limits being both technical (has the system enough memory to remember the contents and run the applications in all the windows?) and pragmatic (given a finite screen size, how many windows can feasibly be displayed and still be useful to the user?). Fig. 5.4 illustrates a display screen with several windows open. As can be seen, the windows can represent a folder (*ie.* a screen object containing other folders and documents), or a disk, or even a document (not shown). The items inside a window can be displayed as various lists, or as icons.

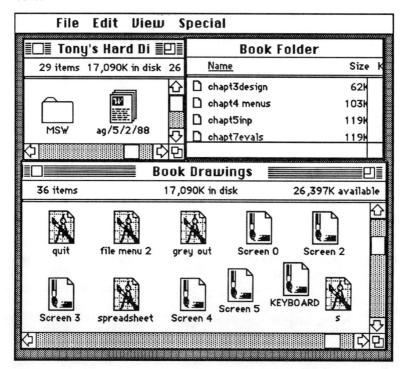

Fig. 5.4 –   Three 'tiled' windows showing various contents.

5.3.3.1 Overlapping and Tiled Windows
In a system capable of displaying windows, the designer may have to choose a method of displaying such windows as they are opened by the users. There are two basic methods employed by most designs: overlapping and tiled. Fig. 5.4 above shows tiled windows.

Tiled
If windows are tiled, two options for the positioning of windows on the screen are available, either the use of fixed columns or the use of an arbitrary rule. The design of any tiling algorithm will present problems in defining what happens to information that was designed for full-screen presentation and needs to be fitted into the smaller tiled windows. If the image (text or graphics) is presented with the same physical scale and layout, then only a portion of the original image can be displayed (it has been 'clipped'), and a mechanism must be provided to scroll the window (see later in this section). If the image is scaled to fit the new size tiled window, then either the text could become too small or distorted, or a graphical image could be severely distorted. In the example above the windows only show a portion of their contents *ie.* they are clipped views.

Fixed columns are more straightforward for the user to understand, but large high-resolution displays are needed to guarantee that the first few windows generated are of usable size.

The more arbitrary rules give more flexibility for the user to arrange the windows manually to maximize the height or width of a specific window to suit their assessment of the task requirements. The disadvantage of arbitrary tiling is that when scaling the displayed image to fit the tiled window, it is totally unpredictable what distortions may occur to that image.

Where it is necessary to display transitory information (*eg.* an error message) then it is impractical to rearrange the tiled windows, and an overlapping temporary window must be provided. Such windows are usually classified as dialogue boxes, message boxes, alert boxes, *etc.* – see Chapter 2 for some examples.

Overlapped

Fig 5.5 below shows the same information as in Fig. 5.4 except some of the windows overlap others. The extent of overlap often depends upon the application software, but it can vary from total (where the user cannot see the windows below the top window at all) to non-existent. Users can usually move and 're-size' overlapping windows.

The use of unlimited numbers of overlapping windows can soon lead to excessive screen clutter. However, the ability to move windows around the screen and resize them as required is valuable.

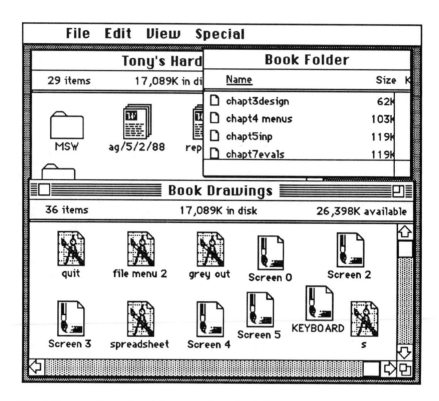

Fig. 5.5 –   Example of three overlapped windows.

It is not possible to make absolute statements about the relative merits of overlapped or tiled windows. The decision on when to use either type of window is controlled by many factors, including the following:

(1)   The overall resolution of the screen is important. Where a large number of pixels are available in both the horizontal and the vertical direction, tiled windows can realistically be created.

(2)   It may be necessary to distinguish between related views of the same information and between different sets of information or a different process. It can be useful to use overlapping windows to distinguish between unrelated sets of information or different processes, and to reserve tiled windows to show related views of the same information.

(3)   Tiled windows ensure that all windows can be seen, but problems can arise in presenting the information in sufficient quantities within a small tiled area. This will lead to a decision being made on reducing the scale of the information presented or on reducing the amount of information being displayed. When displaying graphics, these operations are scaling and clipping respectively.

(4)   Overlapping windows can be easily hidden, and the user can rapidly lose
       track of which window contains which information.

5.3.3.2 Sizing
If windows can be varied in size by the user they must be manipulable by the
user. Thus, some form of size control must be provided. One method often used
is to provide what Apple Computer, Inc. (1986) call a 'size box'. This is the
small box in the bottom right hand corner of a window, see Fig. 5.6 below.

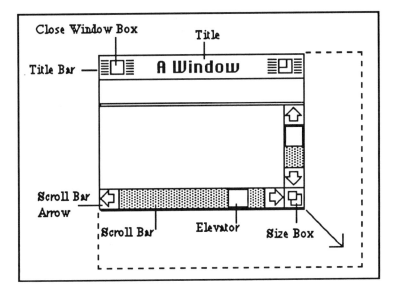

Fig. 5.6 –   A window with a size box. Clicking and dragging the size box
                will alter the size of the window in the direction of the dotted
                perimeter.

   If the user positions the cursor on the size box (usually using a mouse) and
then depresses ('clicks') the mouse button *and holds the button down*, then
moving the mouse ('dragging') will change the size of the window. It will still
remain rectangular but its dimensions will be altered.
   Another method is to provide 'handles' around the window. These are four or
six tiny black squares that appear on the perimeter of the box. Selecting (by
clicking on) and dragging any of the handles will change the shape of the window appropriately.

5.3.3.3 Scrolling
There is little point in providing a window system if the windows which display a reduced portion of their total amount of information cannot be made to
reveal all the information within them. This is made possible by allowing users
to 'scroll' the windows.
   Imagine a small picture frame, say 10 cms square. Place the frame in the top
left corner of a spread out newspaper. Read the contents within the frame only.
Clearly, you can only read a bit of the newspaper. To read the rest of the page

through the frame, one of two things must happen: either you must move the frame over the newspaper, or you must move the newspaper below the frame to reveal a new, and as yet unread part of the page. Of course, logically both these methods are the same – *ie*. whatever method is used, the result is the same: new parts of the paper appear in the frame.

Consider the information 'in' or 'behind' or 'belonging to' a window as the newspaper, that is, it is more than can be displayed in the 'frame 'of the window. Scrolling is the mechanism by which the user moves the information around *relative to the frame* so as to bring it into view through the window. Scrolling is often achieved by providing 'scroll bars' – the two shaded bars running across the bottom and down the right-hand side of the windows (see Figs. 5.4, 5.5 and 5.6). Clicking on the arrow at either end of either scroll bar will scroll the contents of the window in the direction opposite to that in which the arrow is pointing. Quick scrolling, say from the top of a long document to the bottom can be performed by moving the 'elevator' (the white box in the scroll bar) by clicking and dragging it in the desired direction.

5.3.3.4 Title Bar
The title bar is the prime method of indicating to the user details of the contents and the status of a window. The information displayed in the title bar normally contains the name of the screen object the window represents (*eg*. a folder or a document). 'Live' windows (the window in which the cursor is active) need to be clearly depicted.

5.3.3.5 Closing a window
If users can open windows onto the screen then of course they must be provided with a mechanism for closing them. One way is to provide a 'close box' button in the top left-hand corner of the screen: clicking in that box will normally close the window. However, if the content within the window has been altered since the window was opened (especially if the content of the window is a document or a drawing) then the user is usually asked if the changes made to the contents of the window should be saved (*ie*. made permanent).

5.3.3.6 Summary
Windows provide users with multiple views of their working environment. Integrated software applications, (so that drawings (say) can be created using some software, and then 'cut' and 'pasted' into a text document created using some different but compatible software) become much more useful and useable. The ability to see both (or even several) applications at the same time is a great advantage in many circumstances.

The ability to change the size of windows and scroll windows to see what they contain are essential elements of any windowing system. Human factors issues that should be considered when designing windows and a windowing system include the following:

1.) Manipulating – how the window is moved and altered in size
2.) Selecting – how a particular window is selected, opened and closed
3.) Scrolling – how the information is presented and moved relative to the window frame

5.3.4   Icons

The high resolution (the ability to display high quality images) of most WIMP
system displays meant that 'objects' that a user can interact with could be displayed on the screen graphically, often as small pictorial images. Thus, in a
text only system, the user might have a file which he/she names 'Letters'. The
file will be used to store all correspondence created on the computer. To store a
new letter the user might have to enter some text command *eg.*

'SAVE 'New Letter' > FILE'Letters'

Such a command would probably have very strict syntax: a space in the wrong
place or the incorrect inverted commas would mean the command would fail
(see Chapter 3). In a WIMP system, the file called 'Letters' could be represented
by a screen object – an icon, which bears the title 'Letters'. The text file called
'New Letter' created by the user could also be iconically represented. To store
the file 'New Letter' in the filestore 'Letters' needs no syntax or typing at all by
the user. The user merely clicks and drags the icon representing the text file
until it overlaps the icon representing the filestore (a folder in this case) and the
text file is stored. Fig. 5.7 illustrates this series of events.

(a) The filestore is represented by a
'folder' icon on the left. The text–
file is on the right.

(b) Fred selects the textfile 'New Letter'

(c) Fred drags the textfile until it lies
over the folder.

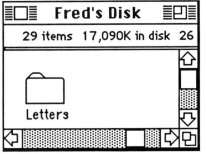

(d) He lets go of the mouse button
the textfile icon disappears from
view – it is 'inside' the folder

Fig. 5.7 –   Text file icon being selected and dragged and placed over a
filestore icon and then stored within the folder.

Icons can be used to represent many objects in a WIMP interface. Applications (specialist software packages), disks, files, clocks, running processes can all be depicted graphically by icons.

5.3.4.1 Icon Size

There seems little reason for allowing wide variations in the size of icons presented in the same window. For this reason, the conventional method of creating icons within a fixed size rectangular pixel map appears a satisfactory model to use. Within this rectangular area, it is possible to produce icons of varying shape, but the size is fairly constant.

The user is normally at liberty to reposition the icons, and the window manager (software that controls what happens on the screen and in the windows) will subsequently replace the icons in their newly defined positions. Icons are usually moved by selecting and dragging the object using the mouse.

5.3.4.2 Pictorial and Textual Icons

Early Xerox systems used textual icons, but pictorial ones were used in later systems. Textual icons have the advantage of being (potentially) unambiguous in their meaning. The considerable disadvantage of a large number of textual icons is that it is very difficult to scan them rapidly in order to locate the desired target icon.

The human ability to recognize pictorial images rapidly facilitates quick scanning of icons to locate one (or more) with a particular picture. The disadvantage of pictorial representation is that it is very difficult to construct more than a few unambiguous pictorial icons. This has not prevented some very creative and imaginative icons being created – as well as many poor and unrepresentative icons too!

The convention, adopted by many systems, of using pictorial icons with a textual title displayed underneath the icon combines the best of both methods. Users are able to use their ability to scan pictorial information to select those icons of the correct type, and then read the labels of that subset to locate the precise target being searched for.

5.3.4.3 Icon Representation and Meaningfulness

The use of icons to represent a document (data entity) is useful in providing the user with a visual method of representing both document types, and the hierarchical representation of filing systems. This is the model used by the Apple Macintosh and Digital Research GEM.

Superficially, this model is different to the most common model employed by computer systems, since in most systems, documents (data entities or files) are represented by a textual label (eg. the Unix filename). It is easier to relate the two models if it is considered that a document has a (default) application associated with it, and that the icon represents not only the document, but also the appropriate application needed to produce the contents of the document on the screen. Opening a document will open a window that will also start up the application required to view the contents of the document.

There is currently little or no standardisation of icons. Thus it is possible that the same object will be represented by different icons on different systems. It equally possible that the same icon will represent different objects on different systems. This means that moving between WIMP interfaces on different systems will not be as easy as it could be, or should be. It seems that the time is ripe to agree a standard set of generic icons for the most commonly represented objects: folders/files, documents, drawings, spreadsheets, disks and so on.

Yvonne Rogers (1986) compared six different sets of icons each of which represented a range of word processing commands. The sets varied on an abstract-concrete scale, and users were asked to predict what object or action each icon was intended to represent. She concluded that a large variety of command operations were able to be successfully comprehended when represented in an iconic form. The most successful icon set was one where the commands were pictorially represented by concrete objects which were directly operated on. Readers are encouraged to seek out this paper which outlines many of the important psychological issues in icon design and the representativeness of icons and symbols)

Whereas many of the symbols that we see and comprehend in our everyday lives have been designed by graphic designers, relatively few screen icons have been through this process. The upshot of this is that a powerful means of representation might be weakened by poor design. There is also a needless tendency to represent everything as icons, which becomes increasingly more difficult to do well, since the number of designs is limited by the size of the icon and the resolution of the display screen.

5.3.4.4 Summary

Icons are pictorial representations of screen objects. These graphical images can be manipulated (moved, opened, labelled) directly by users and some actions that were conventionally performed via a command language, such as filing and copying, can now, in 1988, be performed by manipulation of objects on the screen. As Rogers (*op cit.*) says:

"Underlying this idea is the popular notion that since we live in a strongly visual and spatially organised environment it seems more compatible to learn interfaces which also use visual and spatial information representations."

and,

"...graphic images in general are often regarded as a potentially universal means of communication and are assumed, therefore, to be able to overcome some of the problems associated with verbal language."

Of course, the universality of graphical representations depends upon agreed conventions for symbolic images. CCITT[†] do already provide recommendations for 'symbols and pictograms' that are displayed or used in the telecommunications environment. However, at the time of writing these recommendations refer only to paper-based images, not screen-based ones.

[†] The initials CCITT stand for the French equivalent of :
'The International Telegraph and Telephone Consultative Committee'

5.3.5   Menus

Chapter 4 dealt with Menus exclusively and considered the type of research and the predominant issues surrounding the design of menus. This short section merely considers menus in WIMP interfaces and what they have to offer that is different from traditional menu interfaces. This section should be read in conjunction with Chapter 4 and Section 4.6 in particular.

In WIMP interfaces, the 'windows approach' means that not all available or usable information needs to be displayed to the user all the time. This has meant that menus too need not be made 'public' to the user all the time, only when they are required. There are two methods by which this is normally achieved: 'pop-up' menus and 'pull-down' menus.

5.3.5.1 Pop-up Menus

These are menus that do not appear in a fixed position on the screen. Such menus usually appear at the site of the cursor. They are normally rendered visible (*ie.* made to 'pop-up') by a mouse click. The user clicks the appropriate mouse button (this type of menu often occurs in systems with a multi-button mouse) and holds down the button. This allows the user to select one of the now displayed options. Such a method means the user does not have to move the cursor (and mouse) in order to see what options are available. This is more of an advantage on large display screens than small ones, where the distance the cursor has to move is always small. Users will tend to take longer to learn how to use pop-up menus.

5.3.5.2 Pull-down Menus

These are menus that are made visible by moving the cursor up to a 'menu-bar' which is (nearly always) displayed at the top of the screen. The menu bar contains a set of general headings such as: File, Edit, Search *etc.* The actual headings in any menu bar are dependent upon the software application. In a word processor application, for example, there are often menu bar items such as 'font', and 'document'. Clicking on the menu bar item results in a menu appearing. (see Section 4.6.1 for more detail). Such menus are ideal for novice and infrequent users, and by the use of accelerators (*ie.* short codes that can bring about the same event – see 4.6) more experienced users can be accomodated too. It has been pointed out that the menu bar might be considered as a horizontal menu, which is therefore in contravention of many human factors guidelines! This is not really true since the items displayed on the menu bar are not themselves selectable; they really represent a row of fixed buttons. One advantage of a menu bar is that it is a continual reminder to the user of the main facilities available.

Although the menu bar is limited by the width of the screen, the number of menus available in such systems is still potentially large. The ease with which a user can move from menu to menu, by moving the mouse, makes it easy for users to browse the menus for the item required.

5.3.6   Pointing devices

The major features of most common input devices have already been covered in detail earlier in this chapter. The important companion to a pointing device that has not yet been explicitly mentioned is the 'cursor'. The cursor is the small, often flashing, screen image that moves in response to the movement of the pointing device. In some systems there are a variety of cursors used depending upon the state of the system, or the action the user wishes to perform. Fig. 5.8 illustrates five common Macintosh cursor designs.

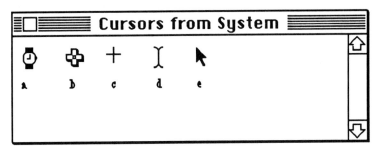

Fig. 5.8 –   5 common cursors used on the Macintosh: a) is displayed when a lengthy wait ensues, b) selects cells in spreadsheets, c) is used to draw graphics, d) is used to select text (the ibeam cursor), e) the arrow cursor or pointer used to select objects and pull-down menus.

The use of a pointing device in WIMP interfaces is clearly fundamental to the whole design of the interface. The emphasis on direct manipulation means that a methods of performing such manipulations must be provided.

5.3.7   Buttons

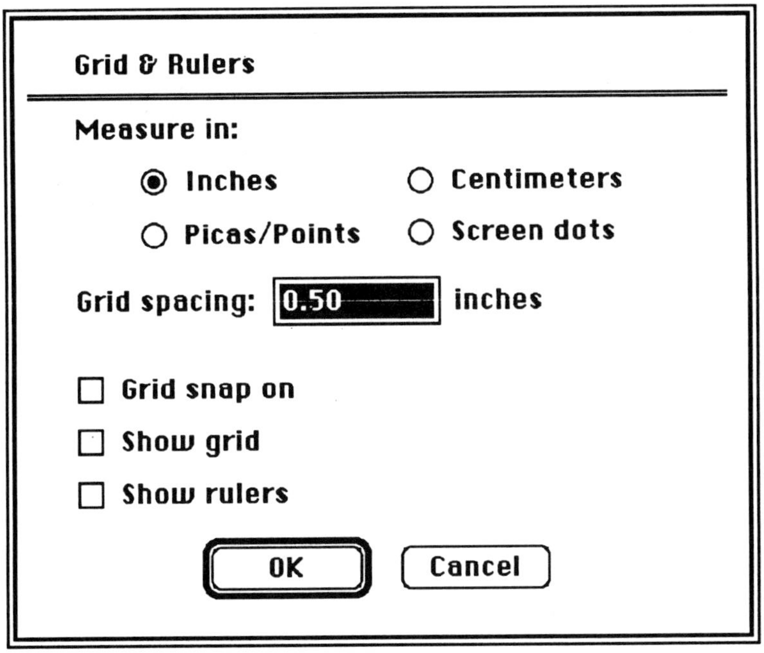

Grid & Rulers

Measure in:

◉ Inches   ○ Centimeters

○ Picas/Points   ○ Screen dots

Grid spacing: `0.50` inches

☐ Grid snap on

☐ Show grid

☐ Show rulers

OK   Cancel

Fig. 5.9 –   A window showing a variety of buttons and 'check boxes'.

Many of the controls available to a user in a WIMP interface are presented as 'buttons'. Buttons come in various shapes and sizes, but have the same fundamental design principle. That principle is essentially a presentation of the complete command vocabulary available to the user. This vocabulary can be limited to a single command (*eg.* 'OK') which appears in a button in a window (see Fig. 3.5 in Chapter 3 for example) or it may be several alternatives any of which can be selected. There are also control buttons and 'check boxes' which can be turned on or off by clicking in them. Control buttons are usually presented when the user can choose a combination of several parameters. Figure 5.9 above shows a window with several types of buttons.

5.4 DISCUSSION

The previous section attempted to elucidate the essential features of a WIMP interface whilst occasionally alluding to some of the human factors issues that surround the design of such interfaces. It is certainly hard to contend the fact that WIMP interfaces are here to stay. In general they have been warmly embraced by both users and human factors specialists. They have certainly made a large variety of facilities available to an audience who previously had extremely limited access to such powerful technology. This book has been prepared and written on a WIMP based machine including all the illustrations except the photographs used in Chapter 6. It would not have been feasible before about 1983 to do this on a system costing less than £10, 000 and occupying less than the space of a desktop (and that includes the laser printer).

It is certainly hard to argue with the general principles of WIMP interfaces and as Shneiderman (1983) points out, the following advantages accrue to users of such systems:

1.) *Documents appear in their final form.* This is also referred to as 'what you see is what you get' or WYSIWYG (pronounced WIZZYWIG). In purely text based systems, documents appeared with a large number of embedded formatting commands for how the text will finally appear. It was impossible to view the document on the screen as it would appear on the paper.

2.) *Cursor action is visible to the user.* The use of cursors allows users to focus their attention on the relevant part of the screen.

3.) *Cursor motion through physically obvious and intuitively natural means.* The use of pointing devices to move the cursor is a natural physical mechanism that relies on users' eye and hand co-ordination rather than their memory for command names – we only have to remember *how* to do it, not *recall* what it is called.

4.) *Labelled buttons for action.* The permanent display of the current command vocabulary in buttons or the optional selection of menus is again *action*, not *memory*, oriented.

5.)   *Immediate display of results of an action.* The clicking on buttons, the movement of screen objects all occur instantly. The result of deleting a word or any other sized piece of text is made immediately apparent.

6.)   *Rapid action and display.* Scrolling windows, moving the cursor, and performing most actions is very quick. The response to a request to open a file is dependent upon the size of the file, but is rarely more than a few seconds.

7.)   *Reversible commands.* Mistakes can be easily reversed, especially in word processing applications: backspacing, deleting and general editing is fast, smooth, and efficient. Major errors like deleting the wrong file can usually be 'undone' if nothing else has been performed since the error occurred. This reduces anxiety about errors and frees users to concentrate on the creative side of the task.

These are some of the main reasons for the all-embracing welcome afforded to WIMP interfaces by most of the human factors community, but is it really so simple?

The general philosophy of WIMPs of course has to appear in commercially available systems, and it is here that perhaps an extra degree of objectivity has been lacking. The Apple Macintosh especially has tended to be seen by many people both inside and outside the computing industry as the ultimate machine. This book has used it for many of the examples of WIMPs presented in this and the previous chapter, but that does not mean that we regard all its features as never-to-be-changed virtues. One of the main dangers to future interface design as it is currently represented by machines like the Mac is this: it tends to blinker creative design, it makes it too easy to follow the current trends and actually stifles radical alternatives. When discussing possible interfaces for new systems with designers, it is sometimes very difficult to conceptualise non-Mac-like ways of doing things, so influential is its design.

It is not hard to see how such a state of affairs has come about. After years of complaints about the difficulty of using software, of the incompatible nature of software, and of the incomprehensibility of user manuals, what happens? A new piece of software arrives for the Macintosh, the disk is unwrapped and inserted in the disk drive, and after one or two mouse clicks, there, on the screen, up and running is the software – it's a miracle! No need to LOAD, no need to RUN, no need to type a single command. The appeal of such a situation is hard to resist.

However, we should remember that all the issues and design principles discussed in this book apply to *all* interfaces, WIMPs and Macs are not excluded. It is possible to produce lousy interfaces on the Mac, although the effort required to get it wrong may be greater than the effort required to get it right! Let us briefly consider two aspects of the Mac that rankle even with enraptured users:

1.)   *Consistency* is a much valued principle in UI design, and a much vaunted attribute of the Macintosh. However there are occasions when the consistency is lacking. To move a document from one file to another file on a disk requires the user to select the icon of the document and move it to the folder icon of the new file. If this process is repeated in order to move a file from one disk to another, the result is not a *move* but a *copy* (*ie*. the creation of a duplicate document now on both disks). To delete a folder or a document the user selects the document icon and moves it over the wastebin icon. To eject a disk the user can move the disk icon over the wastebin icon. To allow the commands *delete* and *eject* to be brought about by same action dependent only upon the object must have caused more than user a worrying moment as a disk is placed over a wastebin icon.

2.)   *Desktop Metaphor*. The common approach of WIMP interfaces has been to use a 'desktop metaphor'. That is, the display screen, at the topmost level, is intended to represent a person's desktop. Documents can lay open on it, as can folders and files. It purports to be a desk turned through 90 degrees. However, as Thimbleby (1984) points out, what office worker keeps the wastebasket on their desk? Given the breadth of applications, one can also question the validity of promoting a system image (see Chapter 2) that will be clearly inappropriate for many of the users.

So, WIMPs are a generally a good thing, but the application of good design principles is just as important in their construction as it is to any other type of interface.

6

Using Colour

ANNA DONEY† and JOHN SETON
Human Factors Division, BT Research Laboratories

The purpose of this chapter is to make the reader aware of the differences between a well designed colour display and a poorly designed one. The chapter is in four main sections. The first section discusses why it is appropriate to consider using colour in computer displays. The second section discusses some of the basic properties of colour, and some of the problems associated with trying to carry out scientific investigations using colour. The third section describes some of the problems which are specific to computer colour display equipment. The fourth section describes some of the properties and limitations of the human visual system, which impact upon how colours should best be used. Finally, some general guidelines are given. It is only in becoming aware of the limitations of guidelines that a true understanding of the subject can be gained. It is hoped that the information in this chapter will enable readers to formulate their own ideas about good display design. There is also a glossary of relevant terms at the end of the chapter.

6.1 INTRODUCTION: COLOUR COMES TO THE MAN-MACHINE INTERFACE

Until the 1980's, colour played little part in the majority of man-machine interfaces, with computer displays being produced on monochrome screens. Since the mid–1980's we have seen a range of rapid advances in the technology which is available to the man-machine interface designer, many of which have already been discussed elsewhere in this book. The former 'glass teletype' *genre* of exclusively alphanumeric computer monitors have evolved into the current

---

† Anna Doney is, at the time of writing, working in Sri Lanka

higher resolution pixel-addressable displays, which can be used to present either text or graphics just as easily as each other.

Developments in display resolution and flexibility have been matched by developments in display colour. More and more computer systems now offer the option of adding colour. On the face of it, this gives the designer of a system much more scope for producing an eye-catching and commercially successful product. As we shall see, however, the addition of colour to computer interfaces raises a whole new set of potential problems for the designer. Whilst appropriate use of colour can make for a more effective man-machine system, it is also possible to abuse colour, and produce systems which are much less well adapted to their users' information processing capabilities than a corresponding system using a monochromatic display.

In this chapter we shall examine how colour can be used to enhance the effectiveness of a man-machine interface, as well as discussing some of the pitfalls which can await those who make indiscriminate use of colour. In order to appreciate why particular types of colour use are either helpful or risky for the designer of a system, it is necessary to have at least a limited appreciation of the specialised vocabulary and concepts of colour science. The few essential, more involved concepts are explained in the chapter itself, but a number of straightforward technical terms are defined in a glossary at the end of this chapter.

Many papers have been written on the use of colour on computer screens, and few deny the benefits that colour can bring. Colour has aesthetic appeal, it is eye catching, and it can be used to clarify relationships between items of information on a screen. With a well designed display, the use of colour can greatly reduce the time taken to spot particular items of information, particularly where the information content of the screen is high. The majority of papers written on the subject of colour in computer displays are important not because they question whether or not to use colour, but because they investigate which colours work well together and which work badly. However, few authors explain why these differences in suitability exist, so this chapter attempts to give the reader a clear understanding of the area by tying together two disparate research areas: human factors and physiology.

6.1.1   Colour in everyday life

Highly developed colour vision systems are to be found in many fish, bird and mammalian species. The human half of the man-machine system is no exception to this general trend. Adult humans with normal vision are able to distinguish colours which are physically very similar to each other: under optimal conditions we can discriminate wavelength differences as small as 0.2 nanometres (Hilz, Huppman & Cavonius, 1974). This difference represents about 1/1500 of the full range of wavelengths to which the visual system is sensitive.

The fact that the human visual system is so exquisitely sensitive to colour difference suggests that colour is an important aspect of visual perception, and one which could be exploited to make displays of information easier to understand.

Colour cues are used in detecting and recognising objects in the visual world, and become all important where other visual cues such as luminance, texture and depth cannot be used. Ripe fruit on a tree may not necessarily be lighter or darker than its leafy background, its shape may be obscured by the surrounding leaves and surface texture cues may not be noticeable from a distance: nevertheless the fruit is immediately obvious because it is a different colour from the background. This is a form of qualitative colour coding; if it's red it's fruit and if it's green it's a leaf. Furthermore, the fruit can also be quantitatively colour coded for degree of ripeness; green may mean unready to eat, and stages of ripeness may be indicated by shades of yellow through to red.

There are many examples of qualitative and quantitative colour coding in the world, and the ability to perceive these codes will have been vital to our evolutionary success. Poisonous snakes are often colour coded; meat with a greenish tinge may contain toxins; a person with a yellowish pallor or red spots may be infectious. Colour coding rules are equally important in our man-made world. Traffic signs signifying danger are often colour coded in red, and cyclists try to make themselves conspicuous by wearing colourful clothing.

Other colour codes exist just to facilitate our day-to-day lives. A black and white London Underground map is much harder for people to decipher than a version in which the different lines are shown in different colours. The advantage of the use of colour for this application is shown in Plates 1 and 2 where a black and white and a colour version of the London Underground map are available for comparison. People might spend twice as long trying to find their favourite brand of breakfast cereal at the supermarket without the use of distinctive brand-specific colours.

6.1.2   Colour - aesthetics and commercial potential
The use of colour can liven up an uninteresting display and, it is sometimes claimed, create particular moods (Bobko, Bobko & Davis, 1984). When colour television sets became available they were much preferred to the black and white sets. Videogames in black and white were soon ousted by their full-colour counterparts in games arcades. Similarly, now that colour screens are available for computers, the advantages compared to monochrome screens are rapidly becoming appreciated.

A number of writers make wide ranging claims made for the benefits of colour in displays, which are not so well supported by rigorous scientific evidence. For example, Shneiderman (1986) mentions that colour displays can "evoke more emotional reactions of joy, excitement, fear or anger". We have not experienced this rich quality of experience with many displays, and this type of thinking is perhaps somewhat reminiscent of that found in the paperback books available at railway stations which predict personality and mood on the basis of colour preferences.

As colour displays become more advanced with higher resolution and better colour rendition, it is becoming possible to create realistic computer-generated images of natural scenes and people. Advertisers are now able to manipulate photographic representations to add in colour washes, take out unwanted detail and so on, and then print the adjusted version of reality.

The use of colour for simple alphanumeric displays is not so necessary as it is for more complex displays. Nevertheless, conservative and considered use of colour may improve the look of any type of display and can generally enhance its functionality. Screens can be made more eye-catching than those of competitors, and company logos and a house style will be more obvious on a coloured display. A software product is often judged to a large extent on the perceived quality of its user interface. A customer is likely to be more impressed by a well designed colour screen than by its equivalent in monochrome.

For general reviews on the use of colour in the design of the computer interface see Robertson 1980, Galitz, 1980, Durrett & Trezona, 1982, Foley & Van Dam, 1982, Kron & Rosenfeld, 1983, Marcus, 1983 and 1984, Weitzman, 1985, Brown, 1986 and Shneiderman, 1987.

6.1.3   The growth of colour coding on computer screens

When colour screens first became affordable, the general feeling was that while the addition of colour made computer games more enjoyable, business users were not gaining much by paying extra for the addition of colour to office automation systems. This may have been the case when business applications were rather more restricted and involved word processing and number crunching. However, in the last few years, the proliferation of business graphics packages has been enormous and colour has added greatly to the intelligibility of information displays such as pie and bar charts.

While computer games and the advent of business graphics saw the first real use for colour on the lower priced, lower resolution personal computer (PC) monitors, high resolution colour monitors were rapidly gaining importance in the high technology and advertising industries. It is these powerful, high resolution computer displays which provide the greatest potential for the use of colour, because it is in these systems that a wide choice of different colours is available. High resolution colour displays have found their way into a wide range of control room settings: for example, in telecommunication network management centres, gas and electricity supply plants and air traffic control rooms.

Colour displays can be very important tools in control or design environments and consequently the need for good display design becomes essential. This need is all the more important because the powerful computers with high resolution displays can produce wider ranges of colours, and therefore carry a higher potential for the misuse of colour. Lower cost PC based colour systems often offer only sixteen fixed colours, in two ranges of eight, one brighter than the other. Only the darker range can be used as a background. This has the effect of limiting the possible combinations of colour, which cuts out a wide range of both suitable and unsuitable combinations which might otherwise be available.

6.1.4   Ways in which colour can help on a screen

A number of researchers have studied the use of colour as a coding mechanism on CRT screens. Colour is very good at improving performance on visual search tasks (Christ, 1975, Carter, 1982). Information can be organized very effectively on displays (Engel, 1980). Colour can have many uses on the screen. Some of these are as follows. It can:

1.)   Emphasise the format and partitioning of information on screens. *Eg.* to make a title stand out as being different from other information or to make scroll bars and icons easier to differentiate from the subject content of a screen.

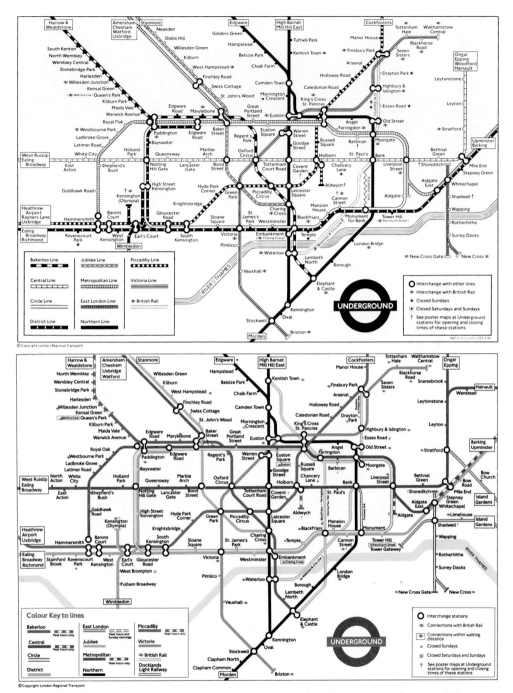

Plates 1 and 2. Colour coding. A black and white and a colour version of a part of the London Underground map. Notice how much easier it is to follow the different routes in the coloured version of the map. This everyday example indicates the benefits which can be obtained by using colour coding.

Plates 3 and 4. Colour assimilation. If you view these plates from a distance of more than about 0.5 metres, the thin coloured bars on the left hand side of each plate become purplish. In each case, the colour of the lines interacts with the colour of the background. The thicker lines on the right hand sides of the plates retain their colour.

red on blue   red on blue   red on blue
red on blue   red on blue   red on blue
red on blue   red on blue   red on blue
red on blue   red on blue   red on blue
red on blue   red on blue   red on blue
red on blue   red on blue   red on blue
red on blue   red on blue   red on blue
red on blue   red on blue   red on blue
red on blue   red on blue   red on blue
red on blue   red on blue   red on blue
red on blue   red on blue   red on blue
red on blue   red on blue   red on blue
red on blue   red on blue   red on blue
red on blue   red on blue   red on blue
red on blue   red on blue   red on blue
red on blue   red on blue   red on blue
red on blue   red on blue   red on blue

Plate 5. Colour combinations and isoluminance. This plate shows some of the problems which occur when colour names are used to describe combinations of colours. All the combinations in the plate can be described as red on blue. Some of the combinations are easy to read, whilst others are difficult. The intensity of the blue background increases from the bottom of the plate to the middle, and the saturation of the blue decreases from the middle to the top. The three columns of text increase in intensity from left to right. The text is hardest to read when the luminance of the text matches that of the background (ie. when the text and background are isoluminant).

2.)   Draw attention to significant information such as a warning message, or a
        single target item which is to be detected.

3.)   Be used to categorise information, *eg.* annual leave and sick leave in a
        colour display for a staff payroll system. By colour coding similar items,
        related information of interest can easily be perceptually grouped by the
        user.

4.)   Be used to locate information at different positions on a quantitative scale.
        For example, a gradation from blue, through yellows and oranges to red
        could be used to indicate temperature.

5.)   Be used to associate headings with information, as on a graph key for ex-
        ample.

The consensus is that while colour can improve performance, in certain
conditions it can impair performance (Christ, 1975, Aretz & Reising, 1983, and
see Reising & Emmerson, 1985). It is, therefore, important to consider the observer's task before making decisions about the application of colour to displays
(Weitzman, 1985) – a point also brought out in Chapter 2.

6.2 BASICS OF COLOUR SCIENCE

This section is intended to introduce some basic concepts of colour science, as
briefly as possible, in order to make the later descriptions clearer.

6.2.1   Sub-components of colour

In everyday life, we tend to talk about colour fairly loosely. It is useful to subdivide the concept of colour in order to describe various colour effects in more
detail. A useful way to subdivide colour is into hue, saturation and lightness.

6.2.1.1 Hue

The hue of a colour is the aspect of colour which is most strongly related to the
wavelength of the light involved. The colours in a rainbow, from red through to
violet, represent a continuous change in hue, as the wavelength of the light
varies from long to short.

6.2.1.2 Saturation

The saturation of a colour is the aspect of a colour which varies as the amount
of white light in it varies. The colours of a rainbow are highly saturated.
Adding increasing amounts of white to a pure colour will cause it to become
progressively desaturated. A fully desaturated colour has no apparent hue: pure
blacks, greys and whites are all fully desaturated.

6.2.1.3 Lightness

The lightness of a colour is related to its perceived brightness. An increase in
the objective intensity of a light source produces an increase in its perceived
brightness. Often, in the real world, a change in lightness will be compounded
with a change in hue and saturation. For example, as more power is applied to a

filament electric light bulb, the brightness of the light given off increases, the hue of the light emitted changes at first from red, to orange to yellow, and the saturation of the light decreases until a bright white light is produced.

6.2.2   The colour solid and CIE space

The values of hue, lightness and saturation of a particular colour can be thought of as defining a unique location in a three dimensional space, or colour solid. A number of models of colour space have been devised, each differing from the others in detail. These models generally have pure black at the bottom, and pure white at the top. A straight vertical line (which could be thought of as a z-axis) between these points represents a family of fully desaturated colours of increasing lightness. At any lightness, a family of colours exists, which can be represented within x- and y- axes.

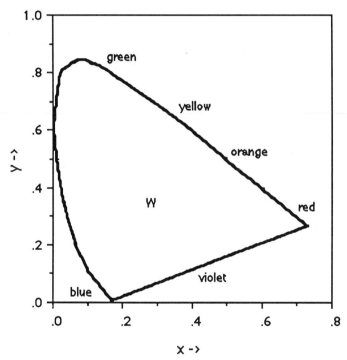

Fig. 6.1 –   A representation of the CIE colour space. Locations within the bold 'horseshoe' represent visible colours. Pure colours are located on the edge of this space, some common pure colours have been shown. Moving towards the middle of the space colours become more washed out or desaturated. 'W' marks the location of a white within the colour space.

Colours can be more precisely defined using the CIE space to make objective measurements, though this is too specialised and involved a process for most software designers to concern themselves with. A basic understanding of CIE space is nevertheless helpful. The CIE colour diagram is shown in Fig. 6.1 above. It takes the form of an area in a two dimensional x-y space bounded by an inverted U shaped curve, with a straight section across the bottom. Points within this area represent colours which can be detected by the normal human colour vision system. Points outside the area represent electromagnetic emissions which the average human observer cannot detect. The pure colours of the visible spectrum (*ie.* the colours of the rainbow) are arranged around the edge of the colour space. The point marked near to the middle of the colour space represents white. A line moving from the edge of the CIE space to the white point represents a continuous range of colours from a pure colour to a progressively more desaturated shade.

An important property of the CIE space is that it makes clear the effects of mixing different colours. If two light sources are mixed, then the possible set of resulting mixes will lie on a more or less straight line between the points representing the two colours. Similarly, if three different colours are mixed, the possible colours which can be produced will lie within the triangle defined by the locations in CIE space of the three colours concerned. Colours outside such a triangle cannot be produced by any combination of the three colours represented by the triangle's vertices.

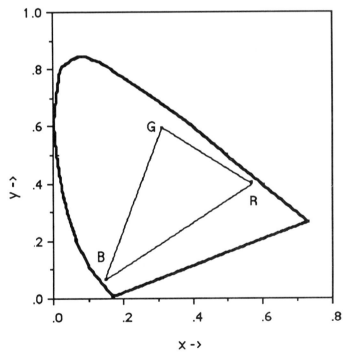

Fig. 6.2 –   A CIE chromaticity diagram showing the locations in colour space of the red, green and blue phosphors of a typical colour monitor. The total range of colours which can be seen is contained within the bold 'horseshoe'. The range of colours which may be made using the phosphors of the colour monitor is contained within the triangle between points R, G and B. Note that many colours which we can see cannot be reproduced on a colour monitor.

6.3 LIMITATIONS OF COLOUR GRAPHICS TECHNOLOGY ON DISPLAY DESIGN

6.3.1   The possible colour gamut of the colour screen

Computer colour displays are produced by light emitted by three coloured phosphors, which are referred to as 'red', 'green' and 'blue'. The locations of these points are shown on the CIE chromaticity chart in Figure 6.2 (above) by the letters R, G and B. These points represent the approximate locations of the P22 family of phosphors, which are commonly used in colour monitors. As can be seen, the possible gamut of colours which can be produced by a colour monitor is considerably smaller than the range of colours which can be detected by the visual system. This is an important property of colour monitors: there are some colours which we can see in the real world which simply cannot be reproduced accurately as a result of the physical properties of the light given off by the phosphors of the cathode ray tube.

6.3.2   Computer screens cannot produce a true black

Another limitation of the cathode ray tube is in the reproduction of the darker shades. If you look at a computer monitor or a colour television set screen when it is switched off, it will appear a mid grey colour under normal office lighting. The grey colour is produced by the reflection of ambient light in front of the CRT rather than by any light produced by the tube itself. This is the darkest shade which can be reproduced on the screen, corresponding to a zero input to the red, green and blue guns. It is therefore not possible to use a true black on a colour monitor screen. The appearance of blacker colours than that of the switched-off screen is produced by contrast and, where appropriate, expectancy effects. These latter effects are more pronounced in viewing real scenes and objects: for example, we know that car tyres, coal, or night should look black, whereas there are no such helpful real world clues to apply when looking at an abstract business graphics display.

6.3.3   Maximum brightness of CRT colours is limited

The dynamic range of cathode ray tubes is also restricted. Even when the maximum possible drive level is applied to a cathode ray tube, the luminance produced is relatively low when compared to that produced by for example, natural daylight. It is not possible using a CRT to reproduce the physical hue and intensity of, for example, a vibrant red flower illuminated by bright natural sunlight.

The range of possible colours which can be reproduced on a computer monitor is therefore significantly restricted compared to the range which occurs in the natural world. For this reason, certain colours and combinations of colours which are easy to view, and which would be effective if used on a colour display, are simply not available to the display designer.

6.3.4   Resolution and image sharpness: Colour v Monochrome

It is often assumed that a colour monitor of a given screen resolution (resolution: the number of separately addressable points across the screen) is in some way automatically better than a monochrome monitor with a similar resolution. As was mentioned above, colour monitor pictures are made up from light given off by physically separate patches of three types of phosphor: usually a regular pattern of dots, but sometimes an array of vertical stripes. When, for example, a white straight edge is to be produced on a colour monitor, it has to be made up from light given off by phosphor patches of three different types, with slightly different relative locations. In order for a sharp edge to be perceived, the relative separation of the different colours making up the white edge should be small enough for the fine structure of the edge not to be noticed.

Because of the discrete nature of the phosphor patches on a colour monitor, it is generally necessary to have a CRT of higher resolution in order to produce an image which will appear as crisp as one on a particular resolution of monochrome tube. The effect described above occurs to the extent of the spacing of the discrete phosphor patches even when the three CRT guns are perfectly aligned: if this is not the case, the red, green and blue components of the image can be still further out of register, so that definite coloured fringes are seen. This effect, called misconvergence, produces disturbing visual effects, and can degrade performance on a range of tasks (Milner *et al.*, 1987).

6.4 PROPERTIES AND LIMITATIONS OF VISUAL PROCESSING

In the previous section, we examined some of the differences which exist between the colours we see in the everyday world, and the colours which can be produced by a computer monitor. In addition to limitations imposed by the available technology, there are a wide range of properties of the human information processing system itself which need to be taken into account by the designer of a system which makes use of colour screens.

One type of factor which needs to be considered in designing visual displays has already been discussed elsewhere in this book: the general cognitive capacity of the user has to be taken into account. It is no use presenting the user with more information than he or she can deal with at the same time. In 1956 Miller wrote a paper called "The magical number seven - plus or minus two" which gave evidence for the fact that, using various sensory modalities, people can recognize approximately seven items or chunks of information simultaneously. This classic finding has been replicated and refined numerous times in the intervening years, and the basic finding seems fairly robust. The effect of this on the display designer is that, for example, menus should not bewilder the user with a long list of unrelated options (see Chapter 4).

Other guidelines are based on the fact that the visual system has certain limitations. Again, some of the effects are discussed elsewhere in this book: screen formats and layouts must take account of the abilities of the user. This section concentrates on effects which are related to the limitations in our ability to process colour, which must be taken into account if we want to make displays which are useful as well as colourful.

6.4.1 An overview of the visual system
Some basic knowledge about the visual system is needed in order to appreciate some of the reasons why problems can arise if colour is used indiscriminately in computer displays.

6.4.1.1 Image formation, and the visual receptors
The image in the eye is formed by a lens. The image is formed on the retina at the back of the eyeball. Images of objects at different depths are brought into sharp focus by muscles which act to change the shape of the lens. The retina contains a large number of receptor cells, which convert light input into changes in activity in nerves which are joined to them. The receptors contain different types of photo-pigments, which are substances which reversibly change state when they absorb light. The different types of pigment are each best at absorbing light of different wavelengths.

Rod receptors
There are two main classes of receptors, which are named in accordance with their physical appearance. Rods are receptors which are used for vision in low light levels. There are relatively few rod receptors, and this explains why our acuity (the ability to see small detail) is lower in low light conditions. The rod receptors all have the same characteristic pattern of sensitivity to light of different wavelengths, so rods cannot be used to detect differences in colour.

Cone receptors
In the sorts of conditions in which computer screens are usually used, there is generally enough light for the other type of receptor, called a cone, to operate. The cones generally belong to one of three sub-classes. The three different types of cone contain different pigments, each of which absorbs different wavelengths of light most strongly. The three main cone types have a peak sensitivity to light of long, medium and short wavelengths respectively. The cones types are generally referred to as red (long) green (medium) and blue (short). These names are slightly misleading, since there is a large overlap between the areas of the visible spectrum to which each type of cone responds. For example, a red cone will respond to some extent to green light, and vice versa. Indeed, colour vision is made possible only because the sensitivities of the three receptor classes do overlap. This means that, by comparing the relative outputs from cones of the different classes, the visual system is able to extract information about light of any wavelength.

Opponent processes
The long, medium and short wavelength information from the cone receptors is re-coded almost as soon as it has been generated. Different cone systems act as so called opponent pairs.

    At a simple level, the cone mediated signals going from the eye to the visual cortex may be thought of as belonging to three categories:

1.)   a category of information relating to the difference between the long and medium receptor activity levels. This is often referred to as the red-green opponent process;

2.)   a category of information relating to the difference between the combined activity of the long and medium receptors, and the activity of the short wavelength receptors. This is referred to as the blue-yellow opponent process;

3.)   a category of information relating to the combined activity of the long and medium sensitive receptors. This channel codes the intensity or luminance of an input. Note that the short wavelength (blue) receptors do not make any input to this luminance channel.

In general terms, the peripheral visual system processes the image of the real world formed on the retina, and extracts and preserves information about areas where change occurs. A lot less information is preserved from areas over which the visual input is the same.

6.4.2   The effect of luminance on colour perception

Varying the luminance of a coloured light whose wavelength is held constant will usually cause a perceived hue shift. This is known as the Bezold-Brucke effect after the original researchers of the effect (see Purdy, 1931, 1937, Walraven, 1961). An explanation for the effect is that the colour detecting mechanisms of the eye have a non-linear response to differing intensities of light. Increasing the intensity of coloured lights will cause colours with a strong wavelength component greater than about 510 nm (green light) to shift towards a percept of yellow and those with wave-lengths shorter than 510 nm will shift towards blue.

A more pronounced effect is that, with increasing intensity, all colours will shift towards a percept of white; that is, they will appear more desaturated. A related effect is that some colours are named differently as they change in luminance. Perhaps the best example is provided by decreasing the intensity of a bright yellow light: below a certain point, the yellow will appear as brown, even though it has exactly the same spectral composition and dominant wavelength.

The above findings may sound rather esoteric, but, like many other colour guidelines, they set a trap for the unwary display designer. This is because most colour monitors have some form of brightness and contrast controls. This implies that different users can and will use different settings: it's no good telling users to all use the same settings. Anything the user is able to adjust will get adjusted. For this reason, a designer has to exercise care when choosing colours for a display. For example, if a system involved a coloured screen which used a yellow which could appear brown at a low brightness setting, then an instruction to select a yellow item might be highly confusing to a user working with a low brightness setting on his/her monitor. The user might sit for hours waiting for some yellow items to appear, whilst patiently staring at a screen full of rather dim brown looking prompts!

6.4.3   The effects of the surround on colour perception

It is not possible to define what a colour will look like to an observer without taking into account the nature of the background against which it is presented. Three main effects operate in conjunction: a simple luminance contrast effect, and two more complex colour-specific effects.

6.4.3.1 Luminance contrast

The apparent brightness of a visual stimulus is determined to a large extent by the brightness of its surround. This type of effect becomes important if a screen has areas with dark and light backgrounds in different areas. Some grey text might look quite black against a light background, whilst appearing a soothing mid grey against a dark area of the screen. In order to tell the user what colour to be looking for on the screen, we therefore need to know what background it is appearing against.

6.4.3.2 Simultaneous colour contrast

The perception of a coloured object or patch on a colour screen can change enormously depending on the colour of its surrounds in the field of view. This effect is known as chromatic induction, because the surrounding colours induce a perceived change in the colour of the central patch. These perceived changes are in the direction of the complementary colour to the one that produces the effect. So, for example, a green surround will produce hue shifts in the direction of red.

In general two mechanisms, simultaneous contrast and chromatic adaptation, cause this chromatic induction effect. The first mechanism, simultaneous contrast, is an ever present effect and is possibly produced by the neural units in the optical system which underlie edge detection (Walraven, 1976, 1977). The second mechanism, chromatic adaptation, begins to appear after more prolonged viewing of a coloured area. This effect is generally attributed to a selective desensitisation of colour mechanisms in the optical system.

6.4.3.3 Colour assimilation, or 'bleeding'

Just to make things complicated, there is also an opposite effect to that of chromatic induction, where coloured areas take on something of the colour of their surrounds. This effect is known variously as colour bleeding, colour assimilation or the more exciting sounding 'Von Bezold spreading effect', after Von Bezold (1874) who first reported it. It is not entirely clear why chromatic induction occurs in some instances and the opposite effect of colour bleeding occurs in others. Chromatic induction tends to occur in visual images in which a block of colour is surrounded by another colour, whereas colours tend to bleed into one another where patterned detail of a particular colour covers a sizeable part of the background.

The effect can be created on a colour monitor by drawing up saturated red bars on one area of an otherwise blue screen. If the bars are narrow, red become purplish; however, if the bars are wide the bars remain saturated red. The effect also works if the colours of the bars and the background are reversed. The effect is a lot easier to see than to describe in words, so we have included two photographs (Plates 3 and 4) which should produce the effect if viewed in bright light at the suggested viewing distance.

You will notice that if you move away from the photographs so the retinal image of the bars becomes smaller and finer, the chromatic induction effect turns into to one of colour bleeding. The change from a perception of chromatic induction to one of colour bleeding appears to be related to the spatial dimensions of the pattern.

Burnham (1953) concludes that there is no convincing explanation for the colour bleeding effect. Walraven (1984, 1985) also reports that the mechanism is not well understood but suggests that the explanation may lie in some sort of cross-talk between colour signals generated in the edge detection process, which then become extrapolated beyond those edges. In this process however, the perception of the edges themselves remains clear and unaffected and therefore the illusory colour can certainly not be explained by the simple optical mixing of light as occurs when image elements become too fine to resolve. Walraven (1984, 1985) gives a colour plate example of the colour bleeding effect. White and black alphanumerics are seen side by side on a blue background, and these are seen to cause the background to appear to be divided into lighter and darker blue areas.

6.4.4 Colours of the same luminance differ in apparent brightness

In some cases, you might want to make two items on a display seem as bright as each other. For example, you might be developing a system in which green and yellow items are presented against a dark background, and have similar status. In this case, you could want each colour to be as noticeable as the other. It was mentioned above that luminance is supposed to represent the perceptual effects of physical light intensity, and so it would seem right to make the two sets of items have the same luminance, so they appear as bright as each other. Unfortunately, the luminance correction does not work too well for some coloured stimuli, so there is a further complication to be taken into account.

It has long been recognised that some colours appear brighter than others even when their physical energy output is equal. Early experiments tried to produce a measurable quantity 'luminance' which was supposed to relate to the perceived quality of brightness. In 1927 the Commission Internationale de l'Eclairage (CIE) introduced a spectral luminous efficiency function of the eye called $V\lambda$ (V lambda), which still provides the basis for the photometric quantity of luminance (see CIE publication no. 41 and Walraven, 1984, 1985). The problem with using the measure $V\lambda$ is that, in fact, when colours of equal $V\lambda$ are presented side by side they often appear different in brightness. This discrepancy has been termed the Helmholtz-Kohlrausch effect, and is due in part to the experimental technique used to determine the luminance function.

Guth & Lodge (1973) report that if blue and yellow lights of equal luminance are placed side by side, the luminance of the blue will have to be reduced by a factor of two or more in order to obtain a brightness match.

Murch, 1984 carried out flicker photometry matches and heterochromatic matches and gives a table of equal colour/brightness ratios. He suggests that if the screen white is set to a value of 10 cd/m^2 then yellow should be set to 7.6 cd/m^2, cyan to 7.4, green to 7.1, red to 4.9, magenta to roughly 3.7 and blue to 2.7. A designer of an information display would probably attempt to balance colours for brightness when using colour codes so that particular items of information did not stand out as brighter than the rest and misled the observer into thinking brightness carries some significance. The best way to balance colours for brightness is to ignore light meters and do the job by eye.

Guth & Lodge (*op. cit.*) have explained the discrepancy between measured luminance $V\lambda$ and perceived brightness as being due to the separate processing

of achromatic and chromatic information by the human brain. You may remember this from the discussion of the 'wiring' of the rod and cone systems
above. These achromatic and the chromatic mechanisms are differentially sensitive to movement and size, however, they both contribute to the perception of
brightness. Because of the particular method by which the CIE $V\lambda$ is determined, it disproportionately reflects the sensitivity of the achromatic channels
(Walraven, 1984, 1985). Since the brightness percept for coloured stimuli also
involves responses from the chromatic channels, the $V\lambda$ measure becomes inaccurate. These inaccuracies increase with highly saturated colours because of
their higher chromatic content.

To sum up:

> *If you want two brightly coloured items of different colours on a display
> to appear as bright as each other, the best way is to trust your eyes rather
> than any numerical measures.*

6.4.5 The problem of small blue objects

The development of high-resolution terminals has greatly increased our ability
to use computers to display fine detail, such as small text, intricate detail in
engineering drawings, and so on. This opens up another problem area for the
unwary display designer, since it becomes possible to draw information which
is too detailed and too small for the eye to make out.

A further related problem with the human colour vision system is that it is
not equally good at detecting fine detail at different wavelengths within the visual spectrum. A major cause of this effect is that there are fewer short wavelength colour receptors in the eye. In consequence, these are more widely spaced
than those responsible for detecting the red to green regions of visual spectrum,
so fine detail becomes blurred and difficult to localise in space. This effect is
especially pronounced at the fovea of the eye, where the density of other colour
receptors is highest.

Because there are fewer blue-region receptors in the eye, a patch of blue has
to be either larger or brighter to be as visible as a similar patch in a different
colour. To put it another way, the eye is not well equipped to detect small blue
objects. The effect comes into operation at sizes less than around 0.25 degrees
of visual angle (around the width of a match head viewed at a distance of
700mm). The name of the phenomenon, *small field tritanopia*, alludes to the
fact that the human visual system behaves as if it is blue-blind for small
objects: tritanopia is the term used to describe the condition where the short
wavelength (blue) receptor system in the visual system is absent or defective.

Another manifestation of the same effect is that there is a difference in perceived colour between a large blue patch and a small patch which is physically
identical. The smaller blue patch will typically appear to be more washed out,
or desaturated, than the larger one, again because of the relative paucity of blue
detectors. Since a small object does not activate enough blue receptors, the
relative output from the more densely packed red and green receptors (which are
also excited to some extent by blue stimulation) is therefore greater than for a
larger object of the same colour, leading to the 'washed out' effect.

This phenomenon, which can be related back to anatomical experiments
which assess the relative numbers of different detectors in the eye, has

important implications for the display designer. Blue, especially a fairly pure, saturated blue, should be avoided where possible for the display of fine spatial details, such as small text or intricate graphics. Also, care must be exercised if blue is used as part of a colour code which is used for items of different sizes which are to be interpreted in the same way: in certain cases, items of different size might be perceived as belonging to different colour name categories, and hence an important association might be missed when a user is working under pressure.

6.4.6   The problem of isoluminant colour boundaries
A naive display designer might take his or her new colour monitor, and decide to make a display as colourful and effective as possible by using different bright hues for text and background information. Unfortunately, a strong hue difference without a brightness difference can lead to severe perceptual problems.

A number of studies have indicated that the human visual system has difficulty resolving edges created by colour alone. Edges and boundaries require a reasonable luminance difference, or a perceived brightness difference, in order to appear sharp and clearly defined (Wolfe, 1983).

The effects of isoluminance are demonstrated in Plate 5. Here, text of three different brightnesses is shown against a blue background which increases in intensity. For each brightness of text, there is a point in the column at which it gets very difficult to read the text. This is the point at which the text and background are isoluminant. The isoluminant colours are indeed very different, but in the absence of a luminance difference at the edges of the characters, the text is hard for the visual system to process, since only the chromatic channels are being used.

6.4.7   Movement illusions with colour
Few present colour systems make much use of movement, but it is worth mentioning a movement-related effect which can occur. It could crop up, for example, if a particularly exotic on-screen cursor were developed for a colour graphics workstation.

If, for example, a red and blue 'object' on a computer screen is moved around from side to side, the red and blue components may appear to become dissociated, and to move relative to each other in a disturbing manner. This effect occurs because the blue component of the object does not make an input to the fast acting luminance channel of the visual system.

A related effect can be seen without recourse to a colour monitor. If you are driving a car at night-time, along a road with no street-lights, and you shake your head from side to side slowly (try not to swerve off the road when conducting this experiment!), the lit instruments on the dashboard appear to move out of step with the darker outline of the windscreen. In this case, the instruments activate the chromatic system, whilst darker areas such as the edge of the windscreen do not.

6.4.8   Depth illusions
When widely separated spectral colours such as red and blue are presented on a screen, they will often appear to be in slightly different depth planes. The same effect is sometimes seen when viewing stained glass windows. There are two

possible explanations for this effect; the first involves the optical artifact, *chromatic aberration*; the second is mediated by stereoscopic depth detecting units in the visual cortex and is called *colour stereoscopy* or *chromo stereopsis*.

6.4.8.1   Chromatic Aberration

The image in the human eye is formed on the retina by a simple lens. In common with other lenses, this works by bending the incoming light. Any simple lens has the property that it will produce an image at slightly different depths for different wavelengths of light. Long wavelengths such as red are brought into sharp focus at a greater distance from the lens than shorter wavelength blue or violet colours.

This effect is of concern to the designer of a display for two main reasons. Firstly, the fact that items of different wavelengths are focussed at different depths means that a display which combines such items may produce curious percepts, with one part of a display appearing to float in front of another part. On occasion, this could be a desirable effect, but in most cases such a phenomenon would be both disturbing and distracting for the user of a system.

The second, and related, way in which chromatic aberration can be of concern to a designer of a colour interface occurs when colours which are focussed on at different depths actually abut (*eg*. a bright red text highlight in a passage of small blue text). In this case, the eye may repeatedly attempt to pull each colour of image into sharp focus in rapid succession. In this case, there is no wholly correct depth to focus at, and there is evidence that the process of hunting around different focus depths is fatiguing.

One technique which can be used to alleviate the problems caused by chromatic aberration at least partially is to make use of desaturated colours, especially for those whose dominant hue is close to one or other end of the visual spectrum. In cases where this is not possible (for example, where the colour graphics hardware does not allow the user to mix a particular colour) the juxtaposition of colours from opposite ends of the visual spectrum should be avoided where possible.

6.4.8.2   Chromo Stereopsis

The second depth related effect is interesting, since the nature of the effect differs from person to person. A lens will pass light of all wavelengths through itself directly, provided the light is aimed along its optical axis. However, if the light source is not on the optical axis of the lens, different wavelengths of light are affected differently, with shorter wavelength light being formed into an image further away from the axis than longer wavelengths.

In order not to make things too easy for the display designer, nature has contrived to make people with eyes which have the optical axes either aimed inwards or aimed outwards. In the former case, blue images in each eye will be further apart than similar red images, and will therefore appear to be closer to the observer. A person with the opposite alignment would see a blue part of an image further behind any red parts.

Since this effect varies between different people, it is not possible to provide a simple correction. The best way to avoid the problem is to not use colours from opposite ends of the spectrum near to each other.

6.4.9   Colour deficiency

Approximately 8% of the male population and 0.2% of the female population have congenital impairment which affects red-green or blue-yellow vision or both systems. Many other individuals have acquired colour deficiency, gained through illness, smoking, medication or alcohol consumption. These individuals cope perfectly well in their daily lives and many assume their colour vision to be normal.

Colour deficient people often distinguish different colours by using brightness cues. For example, a red-green colour defective person may see a green traffic light as being much brighter than the red one. In this case, there is also a position cue in operation: the green light is always below the red light. If colour is used on a computer display, the display will be easier to use for most colour-deficient people if some other cue, such as brightness is added to complement the colour code.

Many natural objects contain a range of wavelengths which combine together to produce an impression of a particular colour. For example, a red tile viewed in daylight will reflect a wide range of wavelengths. The red phosphor in a colour CRT, on the other hand, has a sharply peaked spectrum, and has most of its energy at two particular wavelengths. There may therefore be particular problems for colour deficient users when a colour difference has to be detected on a colour CRT.

6.5 CONCLUSIONS

6.5.1   Introduction

In this final section, we shall examine some of the other ways of coding information besides colour, and then go on to think about some of the problems which can crop up when the crunch comes, and you actually have to implement a colour interface, using all the guidelines at the same time, in a real setting, rather than consider them one at a time as in a book chapter such as this.

6.5.2   Other coding dimensions

It is useful to consider other coding dimensions which can be used besides colour, in order to gain an overview of how and why such systems run into difficulty in certain situations.

6.5.2.1 Flash or blink coding

One possible way to separate different items of information on a computer screen is to make some items flash. This can be a useful technique in a simple situation where the intention is to attract the user's attention to a particularly important item of information. If the need is for segregation rather than highlighting, flash coding runs into a problem. Flashing items tend to be much more noticeable than static items, and can even appear to be overpowering in certain circumstances. The extra salience of flashing items makes it an unsuitable coding dimension for segregating equal status display items from each other.

Flash coding might also be considered for coding the level or value of an item, with, for example, a rapid flash rate coding a severe overload in an industrial control setting.

There are two main problems with this approach for this type of use. Firstly, the visual system is relatively poor at absolutely encoding different temporal patterns, or flash rates. The best that could be achieved might be a two step process, with a very slow and a fast flash rate. Users would not be able to discriminate more rates than this with an acceptable level of accuracy.

The second problem is more related to limitations in the equipment which is used: it is often not possible to have more than one flash rate in any case. On some graphics systems, flashing is not synchronous across the monitor screen, so that disturbing apparent movement effects can be perceived.

6.5.2.2 Brightness coding

One obvious way to code information on a graphics screen is by using different levels of brightness. This can be a useful technique for separating foreground and background information on a screen. For example, it could be useful to separate the row and column markers which define the cells in a spreadsheet from the data items which had been entered. In this case, the background, or 'frame', into which data is to be entered is of lower importance than the actual data items themselves, and so it could be appropriate to present the background items in a dimmer colour than the data items. Similarly, brightness can be used to accentuate a particular area of the screen, such as the next data entry field.

As is the case with flash coding, brightness is not particularly useful for absolute encoding of the value or level of an item: the human visual system can only accurately encode around four levels of brightness. It is therefore not possible to show, for example, a value which changes in seven steps using brightness alone.

Brightness is adequate as a two level segregation mechanism, but runs into further difficulties if it is necessary to define several different sub-areas on a screen. For example, it might be necessary to show a title, a dialogue area where text can be entered, and a system message box, where items such as error messages may appear as separate areas.

6.5.2.3 Image polarity

Most recommendations on whether to use bright alphanumerics on a dark background or the reverse contrast polarity are based on research that considered monochrome screens. Pawlak (1986) argues that not only do the advantages and disadvantages of the image polarities change as technology advances, but that the entire operator environment has to be taken into account when making a recommendation. The recognition of a coloured text, either on a coloured or on a 'black' background, depends mainly on the luminous contrast between the letters and the background. The colour used on the screen plays a comparatively minor role in influencing the legibility of the text (Bouma, 1980, Foster & Bruce, 1982, Van Nes, 1986). Since this is the case, it is probably worth applying general guidelines gained from studies of luminance effects on legibility from monochrome screens to colour screens.

Early visual display units were restricted for technical reasons to the image polarity of bright alphanumerics on a dark background. The fashion now seems to be more in favour of the reverse polarity, with bright positive screens with dark text similar to the printed page. Pawlak (1986) suggests that this is mainly due to an intuitive belief that an image polarity which is similar to typed scripts must be better.

In a study of monochrome screens, Kokoschka & Fleck (1982) suggest that where a negative polarity is used (*ie.* bright characters on a dark background) the character luminance should be selected to be between 5 and 10 times brighter than the background after reflections on the screen are taken account of. They go on to recommend that an average luminance ratio of 3:1 is sufficient for the perfect reading of text when the background luminance is more than 10 cd/m². With positive polarity screens (*ie.* dark characters on a light background), preferred luminance ratios are similar to those suggested for negative polarities. Kokoschka and Fleck (*op. cit.*) 1982, recommend luminance ratios of between 5:1 and 10:1.

The VDU operator often has to read from the printed page as well as the screen. It has been argued that if the screen were the reverse polarity from the printed page that the operators' eyes would continually have to be re-adapting to different contrast polarities and that this may reduce legibility (Radl, 1980). However, Kokoschka & Haubner (1985) have shown that average luminance differences of up to 20:1 between document and screen hardly affect legibility.

The use of dark text on a bright background has another advantage. A dark screen background can often reflect distracting images of the user and the surroundings. This glare effect is especially pronounced if light from a window falls directly on the screen. A light background will make any such refelctions much less annoying.

6.5.3   Don't rely on colour coding alone: redundant coding
Colour becomes essential when the range of other encoding mechanisms available to the designer becomes exhausted. However, with the majority of displays the designer can use a mixture of coding by position, size, spatial pattern, temporal pattern and colour. Hudson (1985) stresses the importance of these other cues and concludes:

> "...with complex tasks and complex displays, colour may offer far
> and away the best mechanism to help the user [but that] colour
> does not however add anything that could not have been done
> in some other way if we were ingenious enough."

Using redundant coding can greatly increase the accessibility of information on the screen. A trivial example would be to separate different categories of information into different columns and then to accentuate the difference by showing these categories in different colours.

The London Underground map is colour coded with a key, but the nature of the information shown means that there is inherent position coding. A useful exercise, for those interested in the relative merits of pattern and colour coding, is to compare the black and white pattern coded version of the London Underground map (often found in diaries and books) to the colour coded version (see Plates 1 and 2)

There are several good reasons for using redundant coding on colour displays. Some pattern, size and position coding is important to the structuring the information on the screen. These mechanisms become more essential as the information on the screen becomes increasingly complex. Thinking about how to use codes other than colour becomes a useful exercise in itself and reduces the risk of over using or misusing colour.

Perceived colour of an item can change depending on the surrounding colour array, size of that item on the retina, the brightness and contrast settings on the monitor and ambient illumination. Because of this, using a few colours chosen from widely spaced points in the colour spectrum will minimise possible colour confusions. Redundant coding will also reduce the risk of confusion.

In some cases the users of software may be using one of several categories of display; monochrome, restricted colour and full colour. The software designer must be aware of this possibility and use redundant coding accordingly. A commercial software package which depended on colour to the extent that it was unusable without colour might well be unacceptable, since potential sales would be restricted to those users who have colour systems.

Perhaps the most important reason for using redundant coding, but one very often ignored, is that some viewers are colour deficient and will have difficulty in discriminating some colour combinations. Although many of these individuals will have some colour vision and will be able to identify many colours, redundant coding using pattern, shape, size and contrast will be useful if not essential to them.

6.5.4   How to begin to use colours

Colours are often added to a screen as an afterthought to make a display more eyecatching, with no consideration of the difficulties that this may cause to users who try to ascribe meaning to the way that colour is used. In one recent commercial software package, information was presented in three dimensional block charts with the front, side and top of each block drawn different clashing colours. Needless to say the information content of the display was difficult to grasp. When colour is used in an arbitrary manner to code irrelevant information it can be a powerful distractor (Hudson, 1985).

So far in this chapter we have talked in general terms about the use of colour in computer screen design and the importance of other forms of coding. We have not talked about which particular colours to use on the screen. Of course, the types and numbers of colours used on the screen depend very much on the specific task that the designer has in mind. Some guidelines which should help are given in this section. It is important to use guidelines as general aids and not as rules, the final choice is up to the designer. Some research papers give specific examples of which colours to use and not use together, based on the relative legibility of texts using these colours (eg. Matthews, 1987). These papers, however, often refer to specific products which have restricted numbers of foreground and background colours. It is difficult to generalize from these papers because different products produce different colour outputs; for example different phosphors may have been used. It may even be unwise to generalize between different examples of the same product; phosphors degrade with age, contrast and brightness settings may be set differently, and ambient illumination may be different.

Another major difficulty in recommending specific colours to be used or not used in combination is that colours are very difficult to define precisely. The guideline might read something like:

> *"...with characters of a magenta colour avoid using red as a*
> *background, instead use blue or white as a background"*
>   (Bruce and Foster, 1982)

On some screens magenta on red may be illegible; however, the two sets of colours that can be labelled magenta and red are fairly large, and some particular combinations of magenta on red may be perfectly acceptable. In order to be able to define colours more precisely and to begin to predict why some magentas and reds work together and others don't, we have to explore the concept of colour a little further.

An object which is either reflecting or emitting light can be described as having a particular colour. Mostly, a colour description is sufficient, and in fact much detail about the quality of that colour can be given by using descriptive terms such as, sky-blue, lavender-blue, royal-blue. But still these terms are rather vague when the number of just noticeably different shades are considered. If you go into a paint shop with the description "a darkish royal blue" you are still likely to have several shades to choose from. The problems become compounded if you happen to be looking for your paint in a foreign country which, for example, has the wrong climate for growing lavender. There is another way to describe colour which is more satisfactory if precise details about a colour are required. This system uses the qualities of hue, lightness and saturation. (see 6.2.1 above)

The three qualities of hue, lightness and saturation can be defined numerically, and represented on an internationally agreed standard colour space. People working in the area of colour commonly use one particular colour space called the CIE (Commission International de l'Eclairage) chromaticity diagram (see 6.2.3 above). This system was basically developed to enable the manufacturers of dyes and paints to define and communicate about the exact colours of their products. It has also latterly been used to define the colours of CRT emissions.

The major drawback of using the CIE system to define and communicate about colours is that it requires very sophisticated colour measuring equipment. The cost of these systems is often greater than that which a university or a company could afford.

The problem of how to define colours is becoming something of a problem to designers of colour displays. Even basic colour workstations now offer 16 simultaneously usable colours out of a palette of 4096, and a choice of 256 simultaneously usable colours out of a palette of 16.7 million is becoming common.

6.5.4.1 Number of colours used on the screen

We cannot attend selectively to *sub sections of colours,* only to nameable hue groups (Hudson, 1985). Colours used for coding should be easily discriminable. A rule of thumb is to use combinations of colours that are going to be named differently over a wide range of the possible computer colour monitor brightness and contrast settings. For example, as the brightness setting is decreased, a bright yellow changes to a darker brown. Therefore the use of a yellow and an orange which are easily discriminable at high brightness may lead to problems for the user who sets his or her brightness control low and sees both colours as brownish.

6.5.4.2 Combinations of colours to use

Recommendations of which colours go well with each other, or perhaps more importantly which colours to avoid using together are useful but can be contradictory. If this type of guideline is applied rigorously the designer can quickly run out of colours to use on the screen. The problem with most guidelines on which colours work together on the screen is that the colours are not precisely defined. In fact it is very difficult to define a colour using a verbal description. The word blue could be used for different intensities of blue, different greyish qualities of blue and different colours that ranged from purplish to greenish blue.

6.5.4.3 Contrast

It is important to remember that, if the contrast difference between two colours is sufficiently great, then most colours can be used together. In order to pick out detail shown against a background, there should be a luminance as well as a hue difference.

6.5.4.4 Colour meanings

Many colours have a particular set of meanings or associations. For example, red is often associated with danger, or a stop state, or with heat, green is associated with safety or a go state, and blue is associated with coolness, and with water.

It is important to bear these factors in mind when designing a system: the use of colour in a man-machine interface should be as consistent as possible with everyday usage. Where a strong stereotype exists, and is exploited in one part of an interface design (for example, using a bright red colour to produce warning messages on a screen), care should be take not to weaken this effect by unnecessary or contradictory use of the same colour for another purpose (for example, it would not be appropriate to use the same bright red colour for a menu title which appears all the time).

6.5.5   Further problems with combinations of guidelines

It is important to consider the relationship of guidelines for colour display designers to the primary source material from which they are derived. The key conclusions from an article in a research journal, or from a series of such reports, will, of necessity, be distilled into a terse and accessible phrase. In doing this, positive findings, and findings common to a range of investigations, tend to be emphasised and preserved, whilst negative results, and odd results which are not in accord with the general pattern can tend to be ignored. Much of the richness of discussions about conclusions which can be drawn in the individual research papers is lost, as are any caveats and analyses of the scope and general applicability of the results of particular investigations.

Another effect is that findings collected in completely different settings can be amalgamated together to produce a single, simple guideline. For example, experiments on flicker perception have been carried out in different environments using different techniques, using office workers and military staff as subjects (Laubli et al., 1980, Knave, 1983). Care has to be taken not to combine evidence from incompatible sources when producing a guideline.

The same experimental methodology which is used to derive the guidelines which we have been examining often makes it difficult to apply them in a practical setting. Typically, it is only possible to examine one guideline area at a time: an experiment in which a whole range of factors are co-varied would take a prohibitive length of time to complete. In the laboratory, it is easy and acceptable to hold all but one variable constant, and then systematically manipulate a single factor and determine the effects on user performance. The real world is, however, very different from the controlled environment of the psychophysics laboratory.

An example will help at this stage. The literature on computer displays contains a substantial body of work on image polarity, and on screen flicker. The first area involves studies in which light text on dark background (negative polarity) images are compared with dark text on light background (positive polarity images). This evidence has been reviewed already in Section 6.5.2.3 above. Experiments using these different image polarities have shown a preference for positive polarity images. There are several possible reasons why, in isolation, this might be so: a positive image is more like the usual types of paper printing we are so used to and a positive image is of a similar brightness to paper documents which will often be used in conjunction with a computer display. Detailed experimental investigations of image polarity have therefore been distilled into a general guideline to the effect that positive image polarity is to be preferred.

Work on screen flicker has shown that many of the computer monitors which are currently available appear to flicker when they display a large area of light colour, such as a full screen white background for text. Flicker is produced because a CRT image has to be continuously refreshed: a still image on a CRT tube is really made up of a succession of frames which each flash on nearly instantaneously, and then quickly start to decay in intensity. If the rate of refresh of the image is too low, the visual system can detect the individual frames, which is distracting for the user of the screen, and is reported to cause eye-strain and a range of other problems.

Guidelines on flicker tend to recommend one of two courses of action. The first, preferred, option is to use a computer monitor which is refreshed at a high enough rate for flicker perception not to be a problem. A rate of 80 to 100 frames a second is often recommended. This contrasts with the 50 or 60 frames a second of most computer monitors in current use. Equipment which meets the higher specification tends to be specialised and expensive: the guideline is not really relevant to the majority of systems which are actually used, although it could be argued that it may put pressure on manufacturers to improve the performance of their products.

The second type of guideline on flicker acknowledges that we live in an imperfect real world, where equipment has to be bought now rather than later, and for as low a price as possible. Flicker is perceived most strongly if a large area is brightly illuminated, so the other way to avoid flicker perception is to avoid the use of bright backgrounds.

There is therefore a conflict between the guidelines on flicker avoidance, and those on image polarity, with one suggesting we should use exactly the paper-white background that the other would have us avoid. Although these individual guidelines are clear enough, their generality is limited by the controlled nature of the studies that produced them. Some skill is therefore needed to combine guidelines about different factors to produce a workable practical solution which satisfies all the relevant constraints at the same time. In some cases, guidelines about different aspects of a display simply cannot be reconciled, and one is then presented with the problem of assessing the merits and coherence of the evidence behind each of the guidelines involved.

An understanding of the limitations of colour graphics equipment, coupled with an understanding of the limitations of the human visual system gives a designer a sound framework within which to assess colour display guidelines. When proper attention is paid to these two sets of limitations, it is possible to design displays which are acceptable to users, and which allow the designer of a system to present different types of information clearly.

6.6 GLOSSARY OF TERMS

Ambient illumination: the light which is incident upon an object. In the case of a self-luminous computer display, this refers to the light falling on the monitor screen, usually from artificial light in the room, or daylight coming through the windows.

Brightness: the subjective correlate of intensity of light. Brightness can only be inferred by experiment, whereas intensity may be measured directly.

Colour contrast: the difference in colour between two areas of a visual stimulus. See also Luminance contrast.

Cones: cone shaped cells in the retina of the eye which convert light into changes in neural activity. There are normally three types of cones, which are tuned to be most sensitive to different wavelengths of light. Cones are responsible for colour vision, and are only effective at higher levels of illumination.

CRT emissions: the light given off by CRT phosphors.

Discrimination: A measure of how easy it is to detect the difference between two items. For example, a persons colour discrimination would be good if two coloured patches could be seen to be different even though they only differ physically by a small amount. Discrimination typically changes with the physical nature of the input: e.g. the same physical difference in wavelength might be easily detected in the blue-green region (good discrimination) but very hard to detect in the red region of the spectrum (poor discrimination).

Fovea: The central portion of the retina of the eye, where the density of receptors is generally highest, allowing good detail resolution.

Luminance: An approximate measure of the effects of the physical intensity of light as detected by a human observer (see Brightness). This transformation from intensity is needed because the eye is only sensitive to a band of wavelengths of light, and is differentially sensitive to different wavelengths. The correction is only a rough one: colours with the same measured luminance can seem to be different brightnesses.

Luminance contrast: the difference in luminance between two areas of a visual stimulus.

Nanometre: the unit used to measure the wavelength of visible electromagnetic radiation. A nanometre is one thousandth of a millionth of a metre.

Perceptual grouping: a term used to describe associations between different objects.

Phosphor: a substance used to coat the inside of a CRT tube, which gives off a particular colour when excited by an electron beam. Different phosphors give off light made up from different wavelengths. A colour monitor uses three phosphors which give off light which looks red, green and blue respectively. Other colours are produced by mixing outputs from these individual phosphors.

Pixel: the smallest addressable part of a graphics display. The size of a pixel is determined by the resolution of the equipment concerned.

Redundancy: a technique for coding a single attribute using more than one coding dimension. In this way, a distinction can be made even if one of the coding dimensions cannot be detected, and information from each dimension used reinforces that obtained from the others.

Resolution: a term used to describe how well a CRT can show fine detail. Most computer CRT displays are made up of points (pixels) which can be addressed individually. The more pixels there are on the screen, the higher the resolution, and the finer the detail that can be shown.

Retina: the array of receptor cells and interconnecting nerves at the back of the eye.

Rods: rod shaped cells in the retina which convert light into nerve activity. These cells are highly sensitive, and are responsible for night vision, but cannot detect colour.

Wavelength (of light): related to the hue of a pure (monochromatic) light. The wavelength of blue light is short, whilst that of red light is longer. Wavelengths are measured in nanometres.

7

Evaluating user interface designs

MARTIN LEA
Department of Psychology
University of Manchester

7.1 INTRODUCTION

The purpose of this chapter is to provide a general introduction to the field of user interface evaluation. There are two themes which are addressed throughout:

1.) The first theme is concerned with the place of evaluations in the design process and the recent (since 1984) trend towards a more thorough integration between evaluation and design. It is now (1988) more common for evaluation to occur throughout the design process, allowing more frequent, more rapid, and earlier evaluations of the design.

2.) The second theme concerns the increased importance of evaluation, from what was an informal discussion between designers to a planned, careful and methodical enquiry in which the rules of social science research are applied.

In evaluation research a distinction has traditionally been made between *formative* and *summative* evaluations. This view of evaluation can be traced back to Scriven (1967) who, in the unrelated field of educational research, used the terms to distinguish the role of evaluation in designing a new educational course from its role in assessing the impacts of the course once it had been run. This distinction appeared to be a useful one to apply to the emerging field of human-computer interaction, where formative and summative evaluations have

referred respectively to evaluations that feed back into the design process in order to further system development, and evaluations that seek to provide an
overall assessment of the final product.

Although these terms are still in widespread use (*eg*. Hewett, 1986), recent
changes in the nature of interface design argue against their continued use. It is
becoming increasingly clear, for instance, that a sharp contrast can no longer be
drawn between a design development stage and the final adoption of the design
by the user. More and more systems continue to be refined long after they have
become generally available to users, and many of these refinements are to the
user interface. Since about 1982, developments have also meant that evaluation
of the interface has become possible at earlier stages in the design than was the
case only a few years earlier. The blanket term "formative evaluations", if
applied today in 1988, would have to cover a range of different approaches to
evaluation, carried out at different stages in the design process.

One consequence of the shift in the focus of evaluations to earlier stages in
the design cycle has been a re-appraisal of its concerns which hitherto had been
almost exclusively with the 'lower levels' of the interface. By 'lower levels of
the interface' I refer to the input/output level, or device level of the interface (the
physical link between the user and the system), and the dialogue level (which is
concerned with the syntactic elements of the language which the user uses in
order to interact with the system). The 'higher (conceptual) levels' (*ie*. the conceptual representation by the interface of the application system and the tasks
that can be performed) have also become subjects for evaluation.

Formative and summative evaluations are terms used to distinguish not only
between stages, but also between *objectives*(*eg*. to refine the design or to describe a system) and these different meanings are discussed separately in this
chapter in order to clarify the objectives of evaluations and their role in the design process.

A second trend that can be traced is the development of evaluation from an
intuitive approach to one of scientific enquiry. This has followed a route that is
common to the emergence of many new scientific disciplines. To begin with,
evaluation usually consisted of informal discussions between the system designers who used their own experiences to provide intuitive notions of what
constituted good and bad user interface design. Subsequently, there was a recognition that general principles were required to guide evaluation and that
information about the requirements of users and their actual behaviour with a
computer was needed. Paetau (1984) has described how this phase was charac-
terised by discussions of the general notion of "user-friendliness", and by the
rapid growth in the application of social-scientific methodology.

This phase was rapidly followed by a greater awareness of the methodological issues inherent in empirical evaluations. This included an awareness of the
importance of providing adequate operational definitions for variables, and the
introduction of functional evaluation criteria. The most recent advances in evaluation research can be seen in attempts to provide theoretical underpinnings to
evaluation criteria (*eg*. Paetau, 1984), and in the development of conceptual
frameworks which provide a view of the wider context in which any evaluation
of the user interface takes place (*eg*. Howard & Murray, 1987).

These two themes are dealt with in the following pages under four headings.
The chapter begins with a brief overview of the general objectives of evaluation

of the user interface. This is followed by a section in which various approaches to evaluation are described within the context of traditional and more recent approaches to user interface design. A brief review of evaluation criteria is presented in another section. Thereafter, the remainder of the chapter is taken up by a consideration of methodological issues in evaluation research, and a description of the major evaluation techniques that can be used.

7.2 OBJECTIVES OF EVALUATION

There are three general objectives which can be identified in any evaluation of the user interface, irrespective of the type of interface, the hardware or software, the stage in the design, the use or not of human subjects in the evaluation, the method used, and the type of data gathered. These objectives are:

1.) the assessment of the capabilities of the design,
2.) the assessment of the impacts of design decisions,
3.) the diagnosis of problems with the design.

7.2.1 Assessment of design capabilities
The first objective is to assess the capabilities of a design by evaluating it against the requirements of the users, and this has been approached in two ways which differ in their orientation to the user or the system. The more user-centred approach assesses capability in terms of the tasks which the user can perform using the system, and the interface, and the extent to which the range of tasks meets the users' *task-requirements*. The more system-orientated approach assesses the features of the system and the interface and matches these to the *feature-requirements* of the user. These two approaches relate to top-down and bottom-up approaches to design that refer to different levels of the interface, the evaluation of which will be discussed later.

While both approaches have their place, a tasks approach to assessing design capabilities is more user-centred (see also Chapter 2) than a features approach, for several reasons. To begin with, a features approach assumes some knowledge of the range of design options and their relative feasibility either on the part of the user (*eg.* through his/her experience with similar systems), or by the evaluator (who may not be a computer scientist), whereas the tasks approach assumes familiarity by user and evaluator only with the range of tasks that the user might wish to perform. Also, a tasks approach improves the continuity between design and evaluation since it becomes possible at any stage to evaluate the emerging design against an earlier specification of the user-requirements irrespective of the extent of the design changes. On the other hand, the features approach potentially places more direct control for the *way* in which the user-requirements are implemented in the hands of the users (and the evaluator), by enabling them to constrain the design options.

The assessment of design capabilities, more than any other evaluation objective, requires that both the interface, and the software system which it fronts, are involved in the evaluation.

7.2.2   Assessment of impacts

The second objective of evaluation is to identify the effects of an interface design upon the user and the user's interaction with the system. The assessment of both intended and unintended effects is important. Intended effects are those that the designer desires or expects to occur because of the nature of the design. Unintended effects may arise as a cost which accompanies the benefits of a particular design feature, or as a result of applying different combinations of design features.

Most user-centred evaluations, whether they are approached from a sound theoretical basis and tested in carefully controlled experiments, or from a functional perspective and carried out in informal trials, have impact assessment as their objective. In the evaluation of interface design, the major impact that is usually given most attention is the degree of effort required on the part of the user in order to use the system capabilities.

7.2.3   Diagnosis of problems with the design

Diagnostic evaluations are systematic attempts to identify and clarify the scope of specific problems. They differ from impact assessment in their single focus upon the negative effects of specific design decisions. Frequently they view the interface through the interactive dialogue between user and computer, and pinpointing and investigating interaction failures in which the dialogue breaks down or takes an unexpected turn.

7.3 APPROACHES TO EVALUATION

7.3.1   The design–evaluation cycle

It is a generally accepted principle that evaluation should take place during the interface design to ensure that the developing interface does not depart significantly either from the design objectives or the user requirements and to make any needed changes to the design.

Precisely how this relationship between design and evaluation is achieved at different time-points in the development of the interface depends upon the approaches that are taken to design. For example, how explicit and firmly-fixed the design objectives are; whether any attempt is made to model the design, and from what perspective; the availability of prototype designs for evaluation, and so on.

In traditional system design, the process begins with the production of a specification for the design based upon the design objectives and user requirements. A design solution is then worked out and is implemented. This is evaluated and the results fed back into the original specification, leading to refinements to the design which are re-implemented and re-evaluated. The process is represented in Fig. 7.1 below.

In smaller projects, this simple approach in which the evaluation is performed upon the software implementation may be adequate. It has the obvious disadvantage that no evaluation takes place until *after* the effort has been expended in coding the design in a programming language, and any refinements to the design that the evaluation suggests will usually require modifications to be made to the program code.

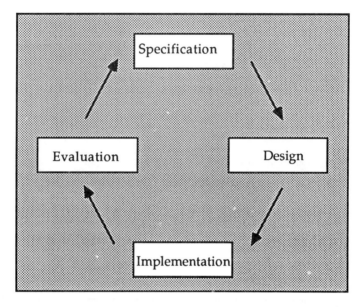

Fig. 7.1 –   The design–evaluation cycle.

In larger and more complex projects, it may be impractical to incorporate the results of evaluations that are left until this late stage, particularly if large modifications to the design are required. In large-scale design projects, late evaluations – *ie*. evaluations of the implemented design – tend to reduce the role of evaluations to small-scale tinkering with the design, and the full range of human factors considerations are ignored. In order to reduce this problem, designers and evaluators may consider *simulating* some aspects of the interface before they are embodied in a programming code. This is considered in the next section.

7.3.2   Evaluation through simulation
Simulation is an important approach which allows the interface to be evaluated in advance of its implementation, in order that changes to the design can be made quickly and less expensively than they could otherwise. Simulations take a variety of forms ranging, for example, from drawings of screen designs to dynamic and interactive displays. They can be constructed from design specifications and guidelines, but may involve considerable work that does not directly contribute to the implementation. Consequentially it may be sensible to limit the simulations to simple ones. Indeed, many useful evaluations can be performed with very simple simulations. For example, a simple simulation may consist of presenting users with some feature of the interface, such as the command structure, in the form of a written manual, or guide, or as a taught course, and asking the 'users' to 'perform' set tasks by describing the strategy they would adopt, or the commands they would use, and the results they would expect from the system. In its most basic form the simulation resembles a questionnaire. Simulated activity data can be analysed in much the same sort of

ways that actual activity at the user interface is analysed. That is, measures can be taken of the frequency of use of commands, the correct use of commands, error rates and error types, and so on.

However, the complexity of the simulation often determines the usefulness of the evaluation, since the more accurate the simulation is, the more it can be confidently assumed that the results of the evaluation would apply to the real interface. Most simple simulations, though useful, suffer from the major drawback of being *static* and unable to simulate realistically the dynamic process of interaction between a user and an interface. Static simulations do not provide any feedback from the system to the user, and in the absence of any feedback it is difficult to evaluate larger units of activity such as command sequences or entire user tasks, or to simulate error correction procedures that would normally involve the presentation of diagnostic messages to the user.

A more realistic alternative is *dynamic* simulation. In this, a mock-up of some aspects of the interface is presented, usually on a computer terminal, and the user interacts with the mock-up by entering commands and receiving feedback on them. The 'system' appears to carry out the tasks instructed by the user, but this is a deliberate deception, and the true course that the user-session takes is either pre-determined by the evaluator through appropriate programming, or else the 'system' is spontaneously driven by the user's activity.

A guiding principle in this approach is that the simulations should require much less effort to develop than the full software implementation, because they are discarded and do not themselves go to form the eventual system. Simulations of the interface allow different ideas to be tried out on users, and problems to be identified at an earlier stage than if the evaluation is left until implementation, but there exists nevertheless an important drawback to basing the evaluation upon simulations of the interface. It is that there is necessarily a trade-off between the saving in programming effort and accuracy of the simulation of the design. It may be easy to draw an intended screen design, but the usefulness of any evaluation of the simulated screen design for the actual design will depend upon how well the simulation captures the essential features of the intended design. A major problem in the use of simulations for the evaluation of complex user interfaces is how to capture accurately the complexity of the interaction between the user and the system.

7.3.3.   Evaluation through prototyping
More recently (since 1980), the development of fourth generation technology has allowed prototypes of systems to be produced very rapidly, with the consequence that the sharp distinction between the design and implementation stages of design has been eroded. Prototypes are rather like dynamic simulations, but use specially developed software tools to provide a more complex interface which has a greater correspondence with the actual design.

Prototypes are becoming a major focus of attention for the evaluator. However, the exact purpose of a prototype, and the number that may be produced during the design, depend upon a multiplicity of factors. Hekmatpour & Ince (1987) have identified three main types of prototyping.

1.)   *Evolutionary prototyping* is a process in which an initial early prototype is incremented and refined until it forms the final product. Evaluation

takes the form of assessing the prototype against various evaluation criteria, derived from the design objectives.

2.) *Incremental prototyping* can be distinguished from 1.) because here the
interface is built and evaluated from its initial design (possibly one section at a time), with minimal changes to the original design taking place.

3.) *Throw-it-away prototyping* is a process in which a version of the interface
is built that lacks some of its intended features and in which the capabilities are constrained. It is used to assess user requirements and for
evaluating alternative designs, but is then discarded and does not itself become incorporated in the final interface.

In rapid prototyping the relationship between design and evaluation is made
more complex because the design approach is also dependent upon the results of
evaluations. For example, evaluations can reveal changes in the user-requirements, leading to a reformulation of the design objectives and thereby turning a
design that was proceeding through incremental steps towards a defined solution
into an evolutionary design in which the design remains much more fluid.
Alternatively the evaluation can determine whether the design proceeds through
the refinement of existing solutions, as planned, or whether these need to be
discarded in favour of a search for alternative solutions.

Evolutionary prototyping provides an opportunity for the integration of
evaluation with design in a design–evaluation cycle, in which the results of the
evaluations of a first prototype feed forward into a second, refined prototype,
which is evaluated, and further refined into a subsequent prototype, this process
continuing until the final prototype emerges, (see Fig. 7.2 below).

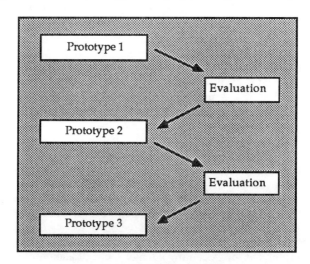

Fig. 7.2 –   Evaluation in evolutionary prototyping.

7.3.4   Evaluation through modelling

At an earlier phase of the design, attempts may be made to describe in a formal
way different aspects of the human-computer interaction, from one or more perspectives. A bewildering variety of models have been developed (see also chap-

ter 2 for some more discussion on this matter), and various attempts have been made to classify them (*eg.* see Murray, 1987; Sutcliffe & Old, 1987; and Whitefield, 1987). These taxonomies have tended to classify models along two major axes, *viz.*: (1) who or what is being modelled, and (2) who or what is doing the modelling. For example, Whitefield (1987) identifies five entities that can be modelled: the system, the program, the user, the researcher, and the designer (axis 1); and four agents who might hold the model: the program, the user, the researcher, and the designer (axis 2). Thus for instance, the designer holds a model of the user, the user holds a model of the system. Some other classifications include a third axis (who the model is intended for) and second-order classifications have also been suggested.

Incidentally, while the status of the researcher in Whitefield's classification is not very clear (since researchers may occupy a variety of different roles), a possibly useful addition to the classification would be the *evaluator,* whose function is clearly defined and who certainly can be thought of as holding a unique set of models. For example, the evaluator's models of the system and of the user can often be very different from those held by the software designer – indeed it is precisely for these reasons that evaluators are employed from different backgrounds and training. Evaluators, as well as designers, clearly also hold (different) models of users, and evaluation criteria can be thought of as products of such models.

The process of developing a formal model of the interface (which may then be evaluated) is characterized by a number of procedures. First, a task is selected which is representative of tasks that the system will be used for. This may be done informally, or through a task analysis which involves the preparation of a full description of the task and identification of its generic components (*cf.* Chapter 2). The task analysis phase is followed by a procedure in which the actions which the user is required to perform in order to accomplish the task (the 'methods') are represented. These methods are generally organized into a hierarchy of levels of representation beginning at the top with the task level, and proceeding down through a number of levels to an interaction level and finally an input/output level. The hierarchical structure of one model (Moran, 1981) is illustrated in Table 1.

Component	Level
Conceptual component	Task level Semantic level
Communication component	Syntactic level Interaction level
Physical component	Spatial layout level Device level

Table 7.1 –   Moran's hierarchical level model.

A common way of representing the interaction is to code the actions using a representational grammar, known as a task-action grammar (TAG – Payne, 1984) or a task modelling language such as TAKD (see Chapter 2).

Evaluation of the modelled interface can be based upon this formal description (known as formal methods of evaluation), or else carried out using empirical methods. The lower levels of models have been more adequately specified than higher levels, and consequentially evaluations have also focussed on these levels. Various performance measures have been derived from the device level and the interaction or dialogue level, for example. Some recent models, however, enable the higher (conceptual) levels to be evaluated too. For example, Kieras & Polson (1985) have developed from their model a formal analysis of the cognitive complexity of the interface in terms of knowledge required, and transfer of user knowledge (see Bennett *et al.*, 1987). Kellogg (1987) has defined the consistency of the interface at every level (as modelled by Moran) from the task level down to the spatial layout level, and described some empirical methods which can be used to evaluate conceptual consistency.

One of the advantages of evaluating conceptual models of the interface is that evaluation can occur very early on in the design process, before the more detailed (lower level) description of the interface has been specified. In a top-down, bottom-up approach to design and evaluation, both levels of description can be evaluated independently, and in relation to one another, before they become amalgamated in the design.

7.3.5 Evaluation throughout the design process

Evaluation throughout the design process is possible using the different approaches described above. In order to do so effectively, however, a fully integrated approach to design and evaluation is required in which the evaluations are tailored to the different stages in the design process, and consideration is given in advance by the designers and the evaluators to the ways in which the results of evaluations feed into the design. This can be done by identifying at the outset the stages through which the design will pass during its development, and specifying a number of evaluation points. Integration is achieved by specifying one or more design-evaluation cycles at each stage. Evaluation at each stage in the design is more useful and efficient in complex designs than the simple approach, outlined at the beginning of this section, which postpones evaluations until an implemented design has been produced.

Three types of evaluation cycle can be identified in general terms. In the first cycle, shown in Fig. 7.3 below, evaluation takes place within a single stage. That is, the output from a given design stage (N) is evaluated, and the results are fed back into the same stage; the output is refined accordingly, and the modified output can be re-evaluated.

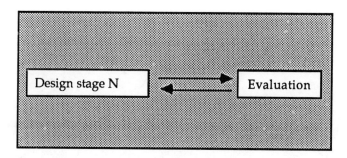

Fig. 7.3 –   Evaluation within a design stage.

In the feedback cycle (Fig. 7.4), the output from a given design stage (N) is evaluated and the results fed back into an earlier stage in the design (N–1), which is refined accordingly, leading eventually to a re-design of the later stage.

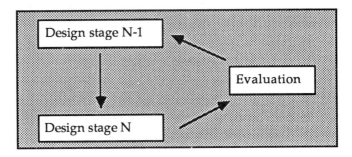

Fig. 7.4 –   Feedback cycle.

In the feed-forward cycle (Fig. 7.5 below), the design proceeds independently from the evaluation into the next design stage. Here, the output of design stage (N) is evaluated, but the original design is maintained and development proceeds concurrently with evaluation. The results of the evaluation are fed forward into the next design stage (N+1). This cycle is useful when development time is short, and it is not possible to pause the design for evaluation to take place. Instead the design progresses, but with the expressed intention that the evaluation results will catch up with the design at a later stage.

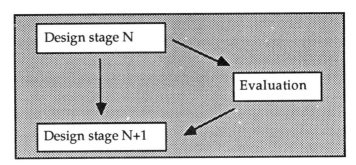

Fig. 7.5 –   Feed-forward cycle.

These basic design-evaluation cycles can be combined with a rapid prototyping approach to design to feed the results of the evaluation at a particular design stage in one prototype into the equivalent (or an earlier) stage of a subsequent prototype. This process is illustrated for just one design stage in Fig. 7.6. Here, evaluation of Prototype 1 occurs at design stage (N) and the results are fed forward into Prototype 2 at the equivalent design stage (N), and at an earlier stage (N–1). Similar design-evaluation paths can be traced for each stage in the design of a series of prototypes.

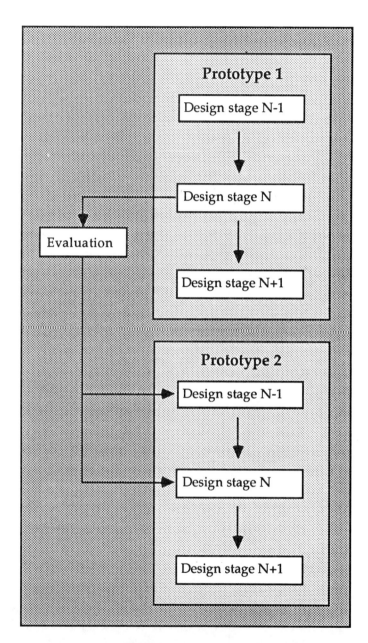

Fig. 7.6 —   Evaluation feeds forward into a subsequent prototype.

At some point in the process of designing an interface, the prototyping activity finishes and the design becomes frozen as the 'final' interface for a production system. The work of evaluation does not finish here however, since it is likely that only at this point will the interface be available for use by a wide variety of people over a significant time-period. At this stage in evaluation, it is possible to step back and evaluate wider aspects of the design and to implement some longitudinal studies that look at the long-term impacts of the design. The results of these evaluations feed forward into the modifications of the software for an updated version, and they may benefit the future design of interfaces by informing the HCI community at large.

7.3.6   Criteria for evaluation

Evaluation research requires explicit criteria against which to measure the quality of the user interface design. These criteria relate to the objectives of evaluation, discussed previously. For an integrated approach to design and evaluation, initial evaluation criteria need to be set early on in the design, beginning with the specification (product definition) stage. They can be refined subsequently, as the development work proceeds, to correspond with changes in design decisions.

Currently, the most frequently adopted criteria are *functionality* and *usability*. Functionality relates primarily to the general objective of assessing the capabilities of the design, and refers to the tasks that the system enables the user to perform. Usability relates to the assessment of the impacts of specific design decisions and refers to the ease of use of the interface.

Depending on the aims of a particular evaluation, criteria can be defined as performance measures, or subjective measures, or both. They generally relate to the communication and physical levels of the interface, but more recently, criteria have begun to be specified for the conceptual level as well, in line with recent developments in design.

Shackel (1986) has proposed an operational definition of usability along four factors: effectiveness, learnability, flexibility, and attitude. *Effectiveness* is defined as performance which is better than some required level (measured, *eg.* in terms of speed and errors), and achieved by a required proportion of the user population in a range of usage environments. *Learnability* is criterion performance achieved within some specified time based upon a specified amount of training and user support. *Flexibility* is defined as adaptation to some specified range of variation in user tasks. The fourth factor, *attitude*, which refers to acceptable levels of human cost (fatigue, discomfort, frustration, personal effort, *etc.*), and perceived benefits (which promote continued and enhanced usage of the system), is defined in subjective as well as performance terms. Subjective measures, collected primarily through questionnaires and rating scales, are important in evaluation since they provide information about the quality of the interface that are difficult to obtain in any other way.

Criteria may also be defined in absolute terms, using pre-specified levels that have been judged to be acceptable for the design, or they may be expressed in relative terms, involving comparisons between alternative design options, or alternative available software.

The guidelines relating to system response time, described in Chapter 3, are examples of absolute criteria. The comparative approach is clearly illustrated in a study by Cohill *et al.*. (1986) who have developed a normative approach towards the comparative evaluation of systems using subjective ratings of functionality, usability, and system performance as the main criteria.

Paetau (1984) working from a knowledge-based approach to interface design has presented a set of criteria for human-computer dialogue which includes *task-adequate usability* (*ie.* the system supports user tasks without demanding extra work due to specific system characteristics); *self-description* (*ie.* the dialogue is directly understandable, or else the system provides sufficient information for the user to develop an adequate representation of the system features suitable for accomplishing their tasks and *user-control* (*ie.* the user can influence the speed of the dialogue and the order of the steps). *Correspondence with user expectations,* and *tolerance of user input errors* are further criteria.

Consistency of the interface has been defined by Kellogg (1987) at various levels (as described earlier), and she has suggested a number of criterion measurements for its evaluation. These include user performance variables, users' perceptions of the clarity of the conceptual structure of the interface, and subjective measures of users' feelings of competence and satisfaction with the interface. Elsewhere, Tullis (1986) has defined criterion measures for consistency at the spatial-layout level of a green-screen interface, such as the overall density of characters on the screen, and the number of visual groupings of characters on the screen.

There is increasing recognition of the importance of designing interfaces that enable the user not merely to operate the interface, but to build an adequate conceptual model of it so as to to learn how to master it. As a consequence, there is a pressing need for designers and evaluators to agree upon a set of standard criteria for evaluating the user interface which can be defined at every level of the interface, from the conceptual level downwards.

7.4 FORMAL METHODS IN EVALUATION

Having briefly considered the aims of evaluation and its relation to design, we must now consider the methods that are available for evaluation. No review of evaluation methods would be complete without a brief description of the application of formal methods to evaluation. These methods, it will be recalled from 7.3, emerge from attempts to model user interaction with the interface. Empirical methods of evaluating the interface will be considered in the next section (7.5), beginning first with some general discussion about methodology, followed by descriptions and examples of the methods themselves.

The choice of a single method to present as an illustration in the section that follows was decided by the centrality of the concepts and approach to formal methods generally, and by the explicitness with which the application of the method to evaluation has been formulated. Both historically and conceptually, Command Language Grammar (CLG, Moran, 1981) shares a close relationship with the GOMS model which developed around the same time (Card & Moran, 1980; Card, Moran, & Newell, 1983). As a result there are considerable overlaps between the two representational frameworks. The CLG framework, like that of GOMS, consists of a set of operators and methods, and a set of goals, called tasks, which are organized functionally. The notion of level is also present in CLG. The symbolic notation of CLG is similar to that used in GOMS, but in the interests of brevity will not be described here; the interested reader is referred to Moran (1981). CLG and GOMS were both forunners for several more recent models (*eg.* Kieras & Polson, 1985; Payne, 1984).

CLG has three fundamental components: the conceptual component, the communication component, and the physical component. The conceptual component contains the abstract concepts around which the system is organized; the communication component contains the command language and the conversational dialogue; and the physical component contains the physical devices that the user sees and comes into contact with.

The components are stratified into distinct levels. Each level provides a complete description of the system at its own level of abstraction. The descriptions consist of procedures for accomplishing tasks addressed by the system in terms of the actions available at that level (*eg.* methods).

Beginning with the top-most level, the *task level* analyses the set of tasks that the user wishes to accomplish and that the user has set for himself or herself without the aid of the system. It is used to structure the task domain in a way that is both amenable to an interactive system and caters for the user's needs. The *semantic level* lays out the conceptual entities and conceptual operations that are useful for accomplishing the user's tasks. These represent the system's functional capability so, viewed another way, these are the methods for *accomplishing* tasks. The *syntactic level* lays out the command language (commands, arguments, *etc.*). Whereas the meaning of a command is represented at the semantic level, it is re-coded at the syntactic level into a form that the user uses to communicate with the system. The *interaction level* specifies the dialogue conventions – the physical actions associated with each of the *syntactic level* elements and the rules governing the dialogue. It specifies the sequences of key presses and other device manipulations by the user, and display actions by the system. The *spatial layout* level describes the arrangement of input/output devices and the display graphics. Lastly, the *device level* describes all the remaining physical features (see Chapter 5).

Formal descriptions assume that the Designer's Model (DM) of the system (see Chapter 2) can be a reasonable approximation to the user's conceptual model. This view is justified to the extent that the user can easily assimilate the designer's model (from explicit training and/or documentation), and/or induce the model from the behaviour of the system. Moran (1981) has described some of the evaluation measures that can be derived from formal descriptions. Briefly stated in general terms, these include:

learning – the length of a formal description of a system may provide an estimate of the overall time it takes a user to learn the system.

efficiency of the system – derived from a summative equation of the times taken by a user to perform the physical actions associated with a given task. A similar index can be computed at the syntactic level by counting commands and arguments.

optimality – the optimal use of state variables and default values in the system design can be found by computing different values of a 'redundancy index' for different methods.

memory load – it is possible to compute indices of the user's memory load from formal descriptions to the extent that they make explicit what information the user needs. CLG specifies command arguments and display layouts, and these, together with empirical measures such as the timing of the user's looks at the display (time–memory trade-off), can provide such an index.

Other evaluation measures derived from formal descriptions are possible, but methods of evaluating higher levels of a formal description such as CLG have not been fully worked out. Kieras & Polson (1985) apply cognitive complexity theory to GOMS, and use a task modelling language from which the interface can be evaluated for ease of learning and transfer of user methods (in terms of knowledge required and generality of the knowledge), as well as ease of use. One weakness of evaluation through formal descriptions, at present, is that they do not handle user-error conditions well, although, of course, normal human-computer interaction is far from error-free.

7.5 EMPIRICAL METHODS – GENERAL CONSIDERATIONS

The availability of formal methods for evaluation does not obviate the need for empirical methods of evaluation (indeed, the development and refinement of formal approaches in itself requires empirical data in order to validate the methodology). For example, models can only provide an incomplete representation of the user's interaction with the interface, and simulations and prototypes of the design provide an opportunity for evaluating the design using actual users.

In this section I shall address the question of how evaluation data about the user interface can be collected, and, once collected, how it can be analysed. There are a number of methodological issues to be considered in choosing between evaluation methods. These are described here in addition to the major evaluation methods: experimentation, observation, and survey. Brief outlines of the major categories of methods are provided. For each, I have tried to provide a description of the general techniques for collecting data from users, and the major applications to which they can be put. The type and range of data which they provide, together with the general approaches for analysing and interpreting the data are also described, and finally the chief limitations of each method are considered.

7.5.1   Choosing methods

It should be clear by now that the question of the appropriate method to employ in evaluation cannot be answered until some of the more fundamental issues about the evaluation have been settled. Once the objectives of the evaluation have been set, a suitable approach has been agreed with the designers, and appropriate criteria have been decided upon, the choice between appropriate applicable methods can more easily be made.

In addition to those factors which are determined by the specific evaluation study, there are a number of methodological issues which also have to be considered in choosing a suitable method. These factors affect the validity of an evaluation, and hence the confidence that can be placed in the resulting design recommendations. General appreciation of these issues is important to establish evaluation as a scientific discipline. Different evaluation methods possess different advantages and disadvantages. They differ considerably, for example, in their obtrusiveness to users (who may consider themselves, rather than the interface, to be the subject of the evaluation), and in the type of data they provide. Many of these issues can be simply expressed as opposing dichotomies (overt and covert methods, for example). In practice, most methods *tend* towards one or other extreme, rather than belonging irrevocably in one category or another – there is often a procedure available by which the attributes normally associated with a particular method can be changed (for example, qualitative interview data can be coded into a quantifiable form). In relating these issues to the choice of methods, it is more appropriate to consider them as dimensions along which different methods can be located, rather than as discrete categories. Some of the more important dimensions are considered here.

7.5.2   Overt and covert methods

This dimension refers to the obtrusiveness of the evaluation method, that is, the degree of awareness by the users of the evaluation method, and the measures being taken. Methods vary between being completely overt (full awareness) and completely covert (complete unawareness); most lie somewhere between these two extremes. Examples of relatively overt methods are interviews and rating scales. Experiments are relatively less overt in that users' awareness of crucial aspects of the method can be controlled until the end of the experiment when they are debriefed (see Section 7.5.7). Overt methods have the disadvantage that the user's awareness of the evaluation may influence their behaviour in import-ant ways that reduce the reliability of the results (*ie.* they are susceptible to subject bias). They may for example encourage the user to behave in ways that they consider to be either desired by the evaluator, generally desirable for social reasons, or else they may intrude upon the users' performances at a task, *eg.* by acting as a distraction from the task. An example of a completely unobtrusive (covert) method is system monitoring (see 7.6.3.4).

7.5.3   Retrospective and concurrent measurements

'Concurrent measures' refer to measures that are taken at the same time as the user's interaction at the interface; 'retrospective measures' refer to instances where an attempt is made subsequently to reconstruct the state the users would have been in during the interaction. Self-report methods such as questionnaires, that ask users to give a retrospective account of their behaviour, belong to this category of measures. The problem with self-report measures is that the data is based on a fallible reconstruction which relies on possibly faulty recall. How-ever, it is possible to build into the research design features that enable the evaluator to gauge some of the effects of memory on their data, and to allow for these in the subsequent analysis. Retrospection is a very popular approach, and is likely to remain so because it is very economical, particularly in comparison to longitudinal studies. Concurrent measures, on the other hand, frequently suffer from the disadvantages associated with obtrusiveness, noted above.

7.5.4   Qualitative and quantitative data

Most evaluation methods aim to record observations as quantitative data (from controlled experiments, questionnaires, and so on) that lend themselves to numerical analysis and summary. Qualitative data (such as protocols of unstructured interviews and notes from observations) on the other hand, can be less easily summarized in this form, but have compensating advantages: a better understanding of causal processes may be gained through intimate acquaintance with people and observation of their behaviour; numerical summaries tend to dehumanise people.

The distinction between these two types of data is a fuzzy one, and procedures exist for converting qualitative data into some quantitative form (and vice-versa). A compromise approach commonly taken by researchers is to attempt a numerical summary of qualitative data, through content coding. This retains some of the richness of the data while facilitating its consistent interpretation. However, the major drawbacks of qualitative data, (that it is expensive to gather uniformly and subject to bias and misinterpretation), limit its use in evaluation primarily to exploratory studies and to in-depth diagnosis of specific design problems.

7.5.5 Objective and subjective data

Subjective data differs from objective data in that a degree of human interpretation is required, either by the user or the evaluator, or both. Subjective evaluation data is acquired using questionnaires, rating scales, interviews, and by human observation. The greater reliance that is placed upon humans for the acquisition of subjective data increases the probablity of introducing biases of various sorts. By comparison, objective measurements of user performance, such as time taken to complete a task, or frequency of use of different commands, have a high degree of accuracy attached to them. Subjective data is often obtained through retrospection, which introduces further reliability problems, but some data is difficult to obtain by any other method. The distinction between objective and subjective data is not always clear in evaluation studies, particularly where the collection of data is automated, as in system monitoring, in which a log of the user's interactions with the interface is recorded. Apparently objective records of behavioural measures may make use of subjective category systems that are incorporated into the monitoring or data analysis software.

7.5.6 Practical considerations

Various practical considerations enter into decisions about the evaluation method to be employed. Frequently, evaluations have to be conducted quickly if they are to keep pace with the design development and produce recommendations that can be incorporated into the design. Restrictions on the available time may limit the thoroughness of the data analysis that can be performed. Observation methods are very costly in this respect, but the problem can be circumvented to some extent by making prior decisions about the type of events that are of interest and the range of analyses that are to be performed.

A second consideration is the financial cost of the evaluation, which may limit the available equipment or the size of the study. System monitoring and video recording methods require relatively expensive equipment. Questionnaires and interviews, on the other hand, are relatively cheap methods to implement. The general approach that is advocated *here* is to choose whichever method is best for the type of evaluation that is required, taking into account the practicality and feasibility of the method.

7.5.7   Ethical issues

There are ethical issues in evaluation research, as in all research involving the use of humans to provide the raw data for study. The choice of evaluation methods should attempt to reduce to a minimum the degree of stress which the subject might experience, and the degree of deception that might be required. In order to control certain variables, experimental design sometimes requires the true purpose of an experiment, or the nature of the experimental measures, to be concealed from the subjects; observation methods may require concealed video cameras, and so on. Thorough debriefing should always follow participation in such circumstances.

Similarly, confidentiality of the information that subjects provide is a neccessary consideration in the choice of survey methods, and there is a also a legal requirement to preserve the anonymity of subjects in computer held data records.

7.5.8   Choosing subjects

Finally, brief mention must be made of the important topic of the choice of subjects for the evaluation. It is important for the accuracy of any evaluation study that the subjects resemble in important ways the eventual users of the interface. A number of general demographic variables, such as age and level of education, are relevant. In addition, for most studies, some estimates of a subject's relevant experience or knowledge are required. The traditional approach to this problem has been to try to develop an informal category system to describe users in these terms. Thus, for example, users have been classified as novices, or experts, or casual users, and subjects for evaluation studies have been chosen using these criteria (see Chapter 2).

Since the late 1970's, the general computer user population has shifted dramatically, of course, with the result that most users belong to the category of 'casual users' (where casual, refers both to frequency of use and experience with the computer system). In addition, 'knowledge workers' are a category of users that are commonly found now. These are people who use the system sporadically (as a tool) to help them accomplish their tasks, which also involve a number of other activities, such as planning and decision-making, which are accomplished away from the system (Paetau, 1984). Current approaches to modelling users pay attention to identifying the wider areas of knowledge that users may bring to the interface. In addition to knowledge about specific tasks, gathered from similar situations, these include 'worldly knowledge' about problems in general, or about the general context of the task. Thus, subjects for evaluation studies need not be computer users at all. It is sometimes more important to use subjects who are representative of other populations, such as task experts, or employees of a particular establishment.

The size of the sample is another important consideration. It is not unusual to see reported in the literature, evaluation studies which have employed only a very small number of subjects. For certain studies, those which have problem diagnosis as their central objective, for example, a small number of subjects can be entirely appropriate. For most evaluation studies, however, the chosen subjects are intended to be representative of some larger population, and because subjects are usually randomly sampled from this population, the sample size must be large enough to provide a reasonable chance for this condition to be met. Statistical tests are mainly very robust against bias effects produced by small sample sizes. However, sample sizes smaller than, say, two dozen subjects begin to run into serious problems in the analysis, and this problem is exacerbated by certain sorts of experimental designs, which require the sample to be assigned to a number of smaller groups.

7.6 SPECIFIC EMPIRICAL METHODS

7.6.1 Meta–evaluation

The first evaluation method to be considered does not involve the evaluator in gathering data from users. Meta–evaluation consists of trawling the existing evaluation literature for evidence relating to the design feature, or whatever it is, that is under evaluation, and using the results obtained from previous studies as evaluation data. Meta–evaluation can be performed either as an alternative to carrying out new evaluation studies, or as a useful supplement to new empirical work.

Most evaluations involve carrying out some empirical work with the design. However, in some cases, where a specific feature of the design is under study, or a particular problem is being investigated, there is much to be gained from reviewing the existing evaluation literature to see what, if any, previous work has been carried out. After all, it is inefficient in evaluation research to conduct experiments that merely repeat what has already been done; a literature review offers the potential for a more wide-ranging evaluation than a single study could achieve, since the differences, as well as the similarities, between studies can be the subject of the review. In order to evaluate the existing literature effectively, the evaluator requires an appreciation of some of the methodological issues involved in carrying out evaluation research, which were described earlier.

Meta–evaluation does not rely only on a critical review by the evaluator to draw conclusions from the results of reported studies. Techniques exist which treat the results as raw data for input into a meta–analysis that produces statistical summaries of the results. For the meta–analysis, the relevant studies are coded along the dimensions on which they differ (for instance, sample size, methods used, independent variables, controls used, and so on), and then submitted to a multivariate analysis in which the independent variables are the coded dimensions and the dependent variables are the effects measured by the studies. The results provide an estimate of the effects observed, while controlling for the ways in which the studies differed from each other.

The advantage of employing a meta–analysis is that it can summarize the results of the findings of a batch of individual studies whose results might appear contradictory unless they were examined systematically together. Fitz-Gibbon (1984) provides a general introduction to this methodology. Although little used at present (1988), this method of evaluating user interface design is set to mushroom, as the results of more and more empirical evaluation studies are published and become widely available.

7.6.2 Experimental methods

A wide variety of experimental methods can be used for evaluation purposes, and from this vast topic it is appropriate only to outline the important features of experimentation in general terms in this section, and to give a few examples of its application to user interface design. For readers who require more information than a brief outline can provide, there are many texts available on this topic – the references cited should be followed up.

Experiments may be used in any of the approaches to evaluation described in the last section. They are most appropriate for making comparisons between alternative implementations or simulations of interfaces. Techniques also exist for experimentally testing user conceptual models (UCMs).

Experimentation always follows a series of prescribed steps:

1.)　statement of hypotheses;
2.)　design of experiment;
3.)　running of experiment;
4.)　analysis of data.

7.6.2.1 Statement of hypotheses

Experimentation begins with a statement about the general aims of the experiment and the development of some hypotheses to be tested. These are expressed as alternative predictions for the outcome of the experiment. For example, the aim of an experiment might be to compare different input devices for text selection in a word-processing package (*eg.* arrow-jump keys or a mouse) the hypothesis might be that there is a difference between the devices in the speed and accuracy of cursor movements that they produce; the *null hypothesis* would predict no differences between the two devices. Sometimes, as a result of prior knowledge, it is possible to state directional hypotheses, for example predicting that the arrow-jump keys will produce more accurate cursor movements, but the mouse will be quicker to use.

7.6.2.2 Experimental design

Having decided upon the hypotheses, the next step is to design the experiment. This is usually the most difficult part of the experimental process, and involves many considerations. However, if the design has been adequately thought out, the experiment will run smoothly, and the data easily analysed to produce meaningful results. The two main aims of experimental design are control and randomization of irrelevant variables that may confound the results and prevent meaningful interpretation. Experimental design involves linking the selection of samples of individuals for the experiment with the experimental procedure so as to maximize these factors. Descriptions of a number of experimental designs can be found in texts on evaluation research (*eg.* Rossi & Freeman, 1985). The strongest designs for evaluation are *randomized* and *repeated measures* designs.

In a basic randomized design, individual subjects are allocated randomly to two groups, one of which receives experimental manipulation, and the other acts as a control group for comparison purposes against which the magnitude of the experimental effect is measured. More complex designs use more than one experimental group. In a repeated measures design, the same subjects participate in every condition. In a further variation, the *matched subjects* design, control is achieved by allocating subjects who have been statistically matched on relevant variables (age, sex, experience with computers, for example) to the different groups. Ewing *et al.* (1986) chose to employ a repeated measures design in their experiment, *ie.* all subjects performed the experimental tasks using the arrow-jump keys and the mouse, and the order in which the two devices were used was counterbalanced so that half the subjects used the keys first and then the mouse, and half used the mouse followed by the keys.

Among the weakest evaluation designs are *before-and-after* studies. These are sometimes employed to evaluate the effects of instruction or training upon human-computer interaction. In essence, the design involves a comparison between subjects at two points in time, the interval between having been filled with the training course under evaluation. Despite the considerable intuitive appeal of before-and-after studies, there are numerous problems in the interpretation of results from this design because of the absence of control over any variables which may have an effect at the same time as the training course during the intervening period. A better option for this type of evaluation is to construct a control group which matches the experimental group on crucial variables, but which does not receive any training. Both groups are pre-tested (to measure the degree of match, and to identify any remaining differences) and post-tested, and a comparison is made between the groups at post-test (while statistically controlling for any differences that were observed at pre-test) in order to determine the effectiveness of the training.

Experimental design also involves operationally defining the measures, that is, deciding upon a set of appropriate dependent measures that relate to the hypotheses, and ways of obtaining the measures during the experiment. In our example study, the dependent measures were time taken to complete a standard task (relating to the speed hypothesis) and a count of the errors made in completing the task (relating to the accuracy hypothesis).

7.6.2.3 Running the experiment
Piloting of the experimental procedure is recommended to iron out any problems and to ensure that all measures are working correctly. Given a successful pilot test, the actual experiment should run smoothly. In running the experiment it is important to avoid introducing experimenter bias, that is, effects that result from the differential treatment of subjects in different conditions. The use of a standard administration procedure, and training of experimenters, help to reduce experimenter bias. Another useful procedure to adopt is the *double-blind technique* in which the experimenter (as well as the subject) is unaware of the experimental condition to which the subject has been allocated.

7.6.2.4 Data analysis
Consideration of the size of the experimental sample has been left until now for discussion since it crucially determines the type of data analyses that can be performed, and thereby the generalisability of the results. It is, however, something that must be decided upon at the design stage of the experiment. It is quite common in evaluation studies to find that a very small sample (frequently in single figures) has been used. In such cases the sample can hardly be said to be representative of the population of users (or potential users) from which they were drawn. Due to this, the results of the experiment cannot be generalized to the population of users, and the usefulness of the evaluation study is consequentially severely limited. The means by which the generalizability of

the experimental effects can be measured is by statistical analysis of the results, which can provide a numerical statement of the probability of the effects having occurred by chance, and the confidence with which their results could be expected to occur again, in a replication of the experimental conditions.

7.6.3   Observational methods

Observation of user performance is a general method that is in widespread use. The basic technique consists of giving a user a specific task to perform on a system and observing him or her carry out the task. Observation of user performance at a user interface can be achieved by four methods:

1.)   direct observation;
2.)   video recording and analysis;
3.)   protocol analysis;
4.)   system monitoring.

These methods, which are described in some detail below, are capable of providing the evaluator with plenty of data from which a range of useful measures of the user's interaction with the interface can be calculated. Some examples of the type of measures that might be made are shown in Table 2 below.

Focus of evaluation	Example measures
Task completion	Number of tasks correctly completed. Number of tasks completed in a given time. Time taken per task.
Command usage	Frequency of use of different commands. Use of command sequences. Use of special commands (*eg.* 'Help').
Command abbreviations	Use of abbreviations for particular commands. Occurrence of mistyped command names.
Use of visual display	Time spent looking at display. Comparative data for different display formats.
Use of keyboard	Time taken to execute command. Comparisons with other input devices (*eg.* mouse).
User errors	Classification of error-types Frequency of error types across tasks. Time spent in error situations. Time taken to correct errors.

Table 7.2 –   Useful measures for different foci of evaluation.

The choice of any particular observation technique depends upon a number of considerations. Each method possesses a slightly different set of general attributes of the type described above. That is, they differ from one another in terms of the objectivity of the data they provide, and the intrusiveness of the data capturing process, and in other attributes. It should also be noted that some methods are to be preferred over others depending on what type of data or level of information about user performance is required. The nature of these differences can be gathered from the description of the methods given below.

It is often useful to employ one observation technique in combination with another. This is because two methods can provide complementary data on a particular aspect of the interaction or else because they can be used to triangulate on a particular measure (see multi–method approach, at the end of this section). This is particularly desirable in the case where the measure that is taken is implied by, rather than directly related to, the data. Measures of cognitive activity, for example, are only implied by observation data since they are based on an assumption that the occurrence of cognitive activity relevant to the task is reflected in a particular observable activity (or apparent non-activity). One way of measuring cognitive activity, using system monitoring techniques, is to measure the length of pauses between entering commands. Another way, this time using video recording and analysis, is to measure the time spent looking at a terminal display. A third approach, exploited in protocol analysis, is for the user to tell the evaluator that he or she is engaging in a particular cognitive activity. The use of more than one technique to provide data on the same construct improves the validity of the measure.

Evaluation studies that employ observation methods tend to adopt a case study approach rather than opting for statistical sampling. Most observation studies reported in the evaluation literature have used only a handful of subjects at most. This is partly due to the considerable time that is required for coding and analysing observations of user performance, which limits the sample size simply for practical reasons. However, it is also to do with the objectives of the observation study. In cases where the primary purpose of the study is to pinpoint problems in the user-computer interaction, in-depth study using a few carefully selected users provides more revealing data than a less detailed study with a larger number of individuals.

7.6.3.1 Direct observation

Direct observation is a method of observation in which the evaluator watches the user as he/she performs activities at the terminal. The evaluator may be seated next to or slightly behind the user so that both the user and the display screen can be observed. Normally, the evaluator takes notes on the user's performance, and may use a stop-watch or timer as well. Apart from the quality of the view afforded by this method of observation, the other advantage is that the evaluator can interject questions to clarify aspects of the user's behaviour that may not be comprehensible from passive observation alone, or else can prompt the user who is irretrievably stuck at a task.

The major disadvantage of direct observation is that it is a very intrusive way of observing behaviour and hence likely to cause interference with that behaviour. A less intrusive means of direct observation, but with costs in terms of the quality of view, is to observe covertly via a one-way mirror. There is an additional advantage to this method in that two or more evaluators can be used to observe the performance, in order to reduce any systematic biases that are likely to be introduced into a record of user behaviour that is generated by just one evaluator, but direct observation, even by only one observer is costly in terms of time.

Direct observation is sometimes used in conjunction with other observation methods. For example, the system may be used to monitor some aspects of the user's activity (*eg.* time to do something) thus freeing the evaluator to concentrate fully on the content of the activity, or else direct observation may be combined with the collection of a verbal protocol. The advantage of this combination is that the user can be readily prompted when he or she falters, and so it ensures that a complete protocol is generated.

7.6.3.2 Video recording and analysis

An alternative to direct observation is the allied technique of video recording and analysis. A good example of its application is provided by Davis (1983) who video-recorded users attempting to run SPSS jobs via a high speed batch-processing facility, and to correct the errors using an interactive editor. The camera was set up to provide a display of the user's head and hands, and the camera output mixed with the output from the computer terminal. The output from a video timer was added to the recording, and a synchronized sound track was also recorded.

There are a number of advantages to recording the user session. It provides a fairly full and permanent record of the session that can be edited, watched by the user or by independent observers, analysed, and correlated with data collected by other methods. By recording the session the evaluator can perform a comprehensive analysis that might include, for example, timings (*eg.* of command execution, inter-command intervals, keystrokes, *etc.*) and frequency counts of different activities (*eg.* screen glances, references to manuals, error rates, *etc.*). Thus, more opportunities for analysis are afforded by video recording than by direct observation.

In the Davis (*op cit.*) study, the recorded sessions averaged 2 to 3 hours in length and the principal analysis was of error rates and types. Five event-time recordings were taken for each session which were used to assess factors like the speed of feedback generated by the system, the utility of error messages, speed of error recognition, and the speed and latency of correction. Five types of error were identified and the frequency of each error type was related to the sub-system or mode in which the error was committed.

The chief problems attached to the video method are:

1.) that the recording can be highly intrusive upon the user's activity unless carried out covertly,
2.) that analysing the recording (which may be several hours long) can be very time-consuming. As a rough estimate, for detailed analysis it may take a minimum of 10 hours for every one hour of tape.

In addition there are the problems that are associated with the chosen methods of analysis (*eg.* choice of coding categories, allocation of events to categories, *etc.*).

7.6.3.3 Protocol analysis

With this method of observation the users are required to generate a verbal account of their current thoughts and actions as they carry out set tasks at the user interface. To effect this, users are usually instructed to think aloud and to report their reactions and responses to the output from the system, the strategies they are using, plans for subsequent activity, and so on.

Protocols are often collected as part of a video and sound recording of the user session. In the study by Davis (*op. cit.*) described above, verbal protocols of user activity were recorded in addition to the video recording of their activity. These were then used to facilitate the identification, classification, and timing of user errors.

Protocols may also be obtained by direct observation, which has the advantage mentioned earlier that the user can be prompted and guided, but there is a danger that prompting may alter the user's decisions and actions, and the likelihood of further experimenter effects creeping into the protocol is quite high in such a situation. An alternative approach is to video and audio record the session, but have an experimenter present to provide minimal prompting when the user is absolutely lost (*eg*. Lund, 1985).

Another method of collecting a protocol is by adding it to the video recording on a subsequent occasion. The protocol may be generated by the user acting as observer and viewing the tape recording of his or her own actions and the screen display. This has the advantage that the process of generating the protocol does not interfere with the user's completion of the task, but at the cost of lowered reliability from the now retrospective, verbal data. Post-session, user-generated protocols are likely to contain biases due to faulty, selective recall and after-the-event rationalizations of their behaviour.

An alternative is to use observers to generate the protocol from a simultaneous viewing of the user's actions from a remote monitor and terminal, or from subsequent viewing of a video tape. This procedure introduces a degree of extra objectivity into the protocol-generating process, but at the expense of lowered reliability because the observer is no longer the actor and may be unable to understand the significance of all the user's actions. However, an advantage of this approach is that a structured or semi-structured protocol can be generated from *a priori* schemes for coding behaviour, and these schemes may be used to determine the level of analysis of user behaviour.

The advantages of adding a verbal protocol to the video recording of user activity are clear: they provide an insight into some types of cognitive activities (see Bainbridge, 1979, for a description), and inform the evaluator about the user's conceptual model of the system, and the goals and plans associated with the user's observable actions. But the problems with verbal protocols are also clear: the verbal report may not correlate well with the user's cognitive activity, and may well interfere with it, and the various techniques that may be used to help with these problems are themselves problematic. Nevertheless, video recording and protocol analysis are very popular evaluation techniques since they are very effective in pinpointing problems in the user interface design.

7.6.3.4 System monitoring

The term system monitoring is used here to refer to the method in which the system itself is employed to record some aspects of the user session (*eg*. Neal & Simons, 1983). A wide variety of data can be captured by this method. For example, the occurrence of certain events such as errors or the use of particular commands can be monitored and their frequencies of occurrence calculated.

System monitoring possesses a number of methodological strengths. First, a degree of accuracy is attached to the data which is greater than that obtained from the use of subjective techniques· such as questionnaires. Secondly, the data is collected automatically, and reliably (*ie.* in a standardized way), once the system has been set up. With little expenditure of effort, large quantities of cumulative and time-related data can be gathered that describe the interactions. These can form the basis for objective comparisons between interfaces on standard performance variables. The data collection period can be quite substantial, which makes this method particularly useful for gathering longitudinal data. Lastly, the data is obtained unobtrusively without disrupting the users' performance.

On the other hand, some types of information about the interaction would be impossible to obtain from this method alone, and it is not surprising therefore to find that it is often used in combination with other methods, such as video recording and survey methods. Interface studies that have employed this method have often concentrated on exploiting the ability of on-line systems to time events to a high degree of accuracy. A prime example is in the use of keystroke data to evaluate formal descriptions of the user interface. Accurate timing is particularly important in this kind of study because, whereas the unit of activity that is timed may be very small (inter-keypress intervals, for instance), and hence the level of measurement is very low, the basic units are usually combined to represent some larger unit of activity (such as execution of a specific command) and the level of analysis is correspondingly higher. In compounding measured units of time, one necessarily compounds any errors associated with the inaccuracies in the timing method, and it is therefore important that a high degree of accuracy is obtained, in order to pinpoint problems with the user interface or to compare performance times with prediction times derived from formal descriptions, and system monitoring has the advantage over other methods of being able to measure inter-keypress intervals with an accuracy of a millisecond or less (*eg.* Allen & Scerbo, 1983).

7.6.4   Survey methods

Surveys of users, or potential users, are an important source of data that are very useful in all kinds of evaluation studies. Surveys are useful at any stage in the design. Early on, they can provide useful information on user requirements to be compared with the design objectives. At a later stage, they can be used to test the accuracy and utility of conceptual models of the user and of the design. User opinions of the interface can be gathered from either a simulation or an implementation, so that the impacts of a design, and the extent to which user requirements are being met, can be measured. Lastly, surveys provide an opportunity for the evaluator to gather user reports of their actual experience of the system and its interface.

The employment of a survey method usually involves the evaluator in first constructing a survey instrument. Three of the principal types of survey instrument that will be described here are:

1.)   Questionnaires
2.)   Rating scales and judgemental tasks
3.)   Interviews

Survey instruments are indispensable for evaluation, since they offer a rapid means of determining users' attitudes and opinions towards computer software. They do possess a number of limitations, however, and it is important that these are recognized by the evaluator both in the construction and administration of the instrument and the analysis of the data they produce. These limitations relate to the general methodological issues that were discussed earlier in this chapter.

In contrast to experimental methods (described earlier), which are used to gather objective data about the user interface, survey instruments are used to gather subjective data. Their coverage of evaluation topics is similar to the range covered by experimentation, but the approach is fundamentally different. Rather than measuring behaviour and performance, as experiments are designed to do, survey instruments might ask users to describe their experience of using the interface, and their attitudes and opinions towards it. Survey instruments may therefore contain questions such as, "Did you feel frustrated or annoyed at any point during the session?"; "Was it easy to remember the commands?". Alternatively, they may ask for a report of the user's behaviour, such as, "How often did you use this command?"; "How long did it take to learn how to perform that task?"

Some evaluators have suggested that subjective data is the most important type of information that the evaluator can have. They argue that knowing what the user *thinks* about the system response time, to take one example, is more revealing than objectively measuring the response time, or how much a user achieves at a given task. Any aspect of the user interface can be evaluated using survey methods, which therefore allow different aspects of the total evaluation to be synthesized by a common methodology.

This approach pays less heed to the limitations of survey data for the sake of a common methodology, and therefore starkly opposes the multi-method approach outlined earlier, in which the strengths and weaknesses of different methods and data types are exploited in the total evaluation. Survey methods do possess a number of weaknesses. To begin with, their usefulness is restricted to asking questions to which users can readily formulate answers. However, their principal weaknesses result from the type of data they collect. For no matter what purpose they are put to, survey instruments yield subjective rather than objective data. If a self-report of the user's behaviour is requested, then they yield retrospective data, and if the user's opinions about the interface are requested, they yield judgemental data. These types of data are lower in *reliability* and *validity* than many types of objective data produced by controlled experimentation and observation methods described earlier.

Reliability and validity are two problems that are well known in survey research, and they apply equally to evaluation research. The usefulness of any evaluation involving a survey instrument is increased if the instrument is known to be both reliable and valid. Reliability is a concept that refers to consistency and stability. Stability over time is the power of the survey instrument to measure the same thing in the same way on different occasions. Stability can be increased by giving careful consideration to the wording of questions in the instrument, and by providing users with a standard set of instructions for completing the instrument. Internal consistency means that all the items that are intended to be measure a particular topic *do* measure that topic and do not relate to some other topic which may or may not be of interest. Consistency can be increased by employing several related questions to approach a given topic, rather than a single question, and by weeding out questions that appear to produce answers that are affected by extraneous factors, that is, factors that are not intended to be measured.

There are a number of ways in which an instrument can be said to be valid. Firstly, it possesses construct validity if there is an adequate conceptualization of the topic area to be surveyed. Unless the underlying concepts are clearly defined, it is unclear what a survey instrument may be measuring, even though it may be measuring something very reliably! An instrument is said to possess criterion-related validity if responses on the questionnaire relate to or predict users' actual behaviour with the interface. In a questionnaire on user satisfaction, for example, satisfied users identified by the questionnaire would be expected to be more likely to continue to use the interface than dissatisfied users who might be expected spontaneously to express dissatisfaction while using the interface, and to discontinue use as soon as a viable alternative presented itself. The general process by which the reliability and validity of a newly constructed survey instrument is improved is known as *item analysis*. Item analysis is usually carried out through initial pilot studies of the survey instrument with subjects from which various summary statistics are calculated to measure reliability and validity.

Survey methods are flexible regarding the range of subjective data they yield. They can provide qualitative data, for example, from answers to open-ended questions; or they may be used in what is, strictly speaking, not a survey application at all, namely to provide ideographic data from a single user. These types of data are useful for exploratory studies, where the impacts of a particular aspect of the design are unknown, and for pin-pointing specific problems with the design. They can also provide quantitative data which is more amenable to a nomothetic approach to the data and multivariate analysis to reveal the statistically significant effects in the data.

One reason why it is important to understand the limitations of survey methods is that few standard survey instruments exist at present, and the evaluator is necessarily forced into constructing new ones to meet the needs of the moment. Short descriptions of the most important survey instruments are provided below, but the reader who is seriously interested in constructing a new instrument should consult one of the standard texts on survey methods. Some suggestions for further reading in this area are provided at the end of the chapter.

7.6.4.1 Questionnaires

Questionnaires can be used to elicit user's cognitions about the interface, or self-reports about their own behaviour when interacting with a user interface. Questionnaires usually consist of a short series of questions on a given topic. The questions may be open-ended, requiring the user to write some notes, or even a short essay in response; or else they may be closed. Closed questions usually require users to respond by selecting an answer from a range of provided options (multiple-choice format), or they require the user to indicate agreement or disagreement with a statement. Examples of these question types are illustrated in Fig. 7.7.

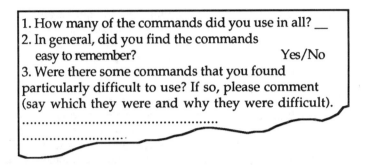

1. How many of the commands did you use in all? __
2. In general, did you find the commands
   easy to remember?   Yes/No
3. Were there some commands that you found
   particularly difficult to use? If so, please comment
   (say which they were and why they were difficult).

Fig. 7.7 –   Examples of closed questions.

Survey instruments such as questionnaires (and rating scales) are usually administered to a sample drawn from a population of users – or one that is representative of an intended user population. The same sort of considerations apply to the selection of samples for survey instruments as were considered earlier under experimental methods. Questionnaires may be administered to users either individually, or in groups. Responses are statistically analysed to provide a summary of the responses from the group. Simple analyses may involve the calculation of percentages of the sample that choose different responses; a more complex analysis would also look at the relationship between user's responses to the different questions; while the most sophisticated analyses involve the computation of multivariate statistics to provide more accurate estimates of the relationship between variables in a statistical model.

It is sometimes convenient to administer a questionnaire on-line, for example at the end of an interactive session with a user interface. Although little used in evaluation studies so far, on-line questionnaires offer a number of advantages over conventional paper forms. The questionnaire may be presented as a text file into which responses are written using a conventional text editor. This offers the evaluator easier and standardized administration, and in situations where a conventional postal survey would have been used, it is appropriate to distribute the questionnaire using electronic mail, with consequent savings in response times, and (at least according to some recent research) better response rates.

A good example of this approach, in which users made their responses concurrently with their performance of the evaluation task, was an evaluation by Bannon & O'Malley (1984) of an on-line help program. Users were required to indicate their success or failure to obtain the information they wanted each time they used the program by means of a simple menu of commands. Care was taken to make the questionnaire as unintrusive as possible. In order to quit the program, users typed upper case Q(uit) if they found the facility useful, and lower case q(uit) if it was not. In addition they could provide more detailed feedback by typing c(omments) which put them in an editor where they could type their comments and then return to the on-line help entry.

More sophisticated questionnaires may be generated under software control, which provides greater advantages, such as individually tailored administration (in which automated branching to different questions occurs dependent upon the user's responses to previous questions) and on-line analysis of the responses.

7.6.4.2 Attitude and rating scales
Rating scales refer to a particular type of questionnaire item, one that requires the user to indicate a judgement about the item by using an 'interval' scale. The advantages of having the user respond on an interval scale are that the response can easily be converted to a numerical value, facilitating a quantitative analysis of the data, and at the same time the scale provides a more sensitive response measure. The rating-scale provides the user with more freedom of response than a simple 'yes/no' answer (making it a more sensitive item), while maintaining reliability by 'anchoring' the user's response to the scale-points that are described.

A considerable literature has grown up around the subject of rating scales, and advice on the construction of this type of item is available in texts on questionnaire design. The commonest types of rating scale are described here:

The step scale
The user selects one of a graded series of intervals. The intervals are usually numbers or adjectives.

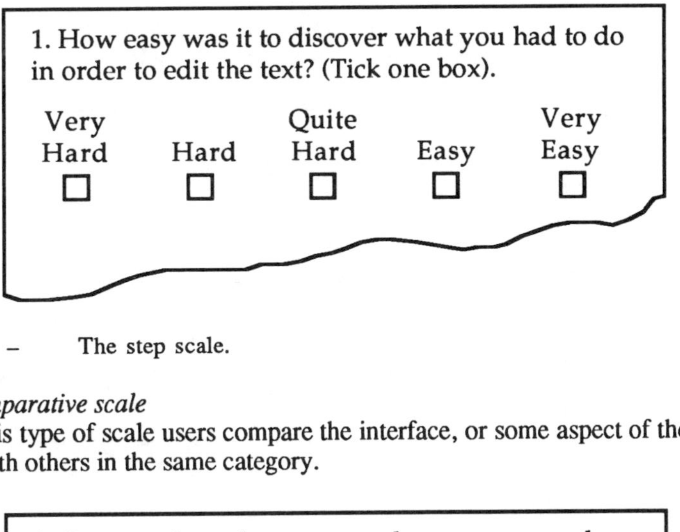

1. How easy was it to discover what you had to do in order to edit the text? (Tick one box).

| Very Hard | Hard | Quite Hard | Easy | Very Easy |
| □ | □ | □ | □ | □ |

Fig. 7.8 –   The step scale.

The comparative scale
With this type of scale users compare the interface, or some aspect of the interface, with others in the same category.

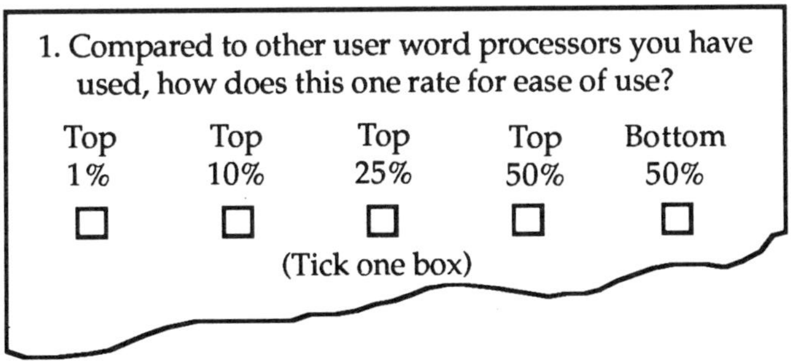

1. Compared to other user word processors you have used, how does this one rate for ease of use?

| Top 1% | Top 10% | Top 25% | Top 50% | Bottom 50% |
| □ | □ | □ | □ | □ |

(Tick one box)

Fig. 7.9 –   The comparative scale.

The Likert–type scale
Named after its original developer, this type of scale requires users to indicate the extent of their agreement or disagreement with a statement.

> 1. Generally speaking, the commands were
>   easy to remember.
>   Strongly agree ☐
>   Agree ☐
>   Undecided ☐ (Tick one box)
>   Disagree ☐
>   Strongly disagree ☐

Fig. 7.10 –   The Likert–type scale.

The semantic differential scale
Users are required to provide ratings along a set of dimensions, which are defined at the extreme points by single opposing adjectives.

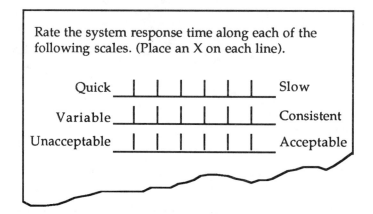

Rate the system response time along each of the
following scales. (Place an X on each line).

Quick _|_|_|_|_|_|_ Slow

Variable _|_|_|_|_|_|_ Consistent

Unacceptable _|_|_|_|_|_|_ Acceptable

Fig. 7.11 –   The semantic differential scale.

The rank–order scale
Rating scales are normally linear scales. However, another type of scale that is sometimes used is a rank–order scale. Responses on rank–order scales are not as easy to interpret as those on rating scales, however, they are usefully for recording users' preferences.

> 1. How useful to you were the sources of information
>   listed below. (Put a 1 in the box opposite the
>   most useful, a 2 opposite the next most useful,
>   and so on. Put a 0 opposite any you did not use.
>   On-line manual   ☐
>   Help   ☐
>   Reference manual ☐

Fig. 7.12 –   The rank–order scale.

Rating scales are very often employed in evaluation studies, and are frequently combined with other items in a composite questionnaire.

7.6.4.3 Interviews

Interviewing is another useful method of finding out about a user's attitudes and opinions. It is more flexible than the questionnaire approach, and can be used to probe more deeply into issues than is possible with a questionnaire. There are of course many different ways of conducting interviews and one decision that must be taken is whether to impose a degree of structure on the interview session.

Structured interviews are ones in which a pre-determined set of topics is discussed in a set order. Replies may be coded against a set of possible answers: in their most structured form they resemble questionnaires. The advantage of structure is it ensures that the topics of interest are covered and that useful, and possibly quantifiable, responses are obtained. However, these advantages are achieved at the cost of possibly restricting the scope of the interview. It imposes the evaluator's conceptual framework on the interview to a high degree, and may thereby prevent some important, but unexpected information from coming to light. Unstructured interviews are the most useful in this latter respect, and semi-structured interviews represent a compromise between the two approaches.

Case studies may be regarded as a special form of the interview method. It involves detailed interviewing of just one subject. Since only one subject is surveyed in the case study, the ability to generalize from the data is severely limited, but this is compensated for by the quantity and depth of the data that can be obtained. Case studies are useful for exploratory work and diagnosing problems with designs.

Group discussions are another useful type of interview, this time involving a number of people in an informal and relatively unstructured session. They offer a considerable saving in administration time, and the interaction between participants can throw up more comments and ideas, compared to one-one interviews.

Details of interviews are rarely supplied in reports of evaluation studies. This makes it difficult to assess the significance of the information they turn up. Interview data is notoriously unreliable – as an interactive process between interviewer and interviewee, the interviewee's responses are naturally subject to biases introduced by the interviewer. Tape-recording the interview for later transcription, rather than taking notes during the interview, helps to reduce one source of bias.

Interviews, questionnaires and rating scales are complementary techniques to use in evaluation surveys. An example of this is illustrated in Fig. 7.13.

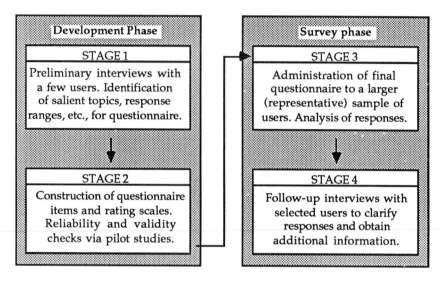

Fig. 7.13 –   How questionnaires, rating scales and interviews can be complementary.

Interviews are especially useful early on in the design for clarifying user requirements. Later on, questionnaires tend to be preferred over interviews as a means of collecting subjective evaluation data, because of the saving in administration time that they offer and the quantitative data they produce; however, the better questionnaires will use interview data as a basis for their construction.

Interviews are a useful procedure to administer subsequently to selected users on the basis of their questionnaire responses. Used in this way they can often clarify the reasons for certain responses, including the subjective basis for making ratings, and it provides users with an opportunity to convey additional comments that the questionnaire may have prompted.

Interviews can be usefully combined with other evaluation methods too. For instance, an interview can be conducted after video recording a user's performance with an interface. Replaying the video either prompts the user to describe the experience of the interaction, or else the user can be asked to explain his or her actions at particular points in the interaction, where problems were experienced, for example.

7.6.5   The multimethod approach
Each of the methods described in this chapter has a number of different strengths and weaknesses, and for many evaluations the use of several techniques will be better than just one. The multimethod approach uses more than one method in a convergent approach to answering evaluation questions. Rather than attempting

to find the optimum evaluation method for a given situation, the multimethod approach utilizes the evaluator's knowledge and appreciation of methodology to select methods which provide complementary data types. This approach to data in evaluation research is sometimes referred to as triangulation Thus, for example questionnaires which may be used to survey a large number of users can be complemented by in-depth interviews with a few; objective data from system monitoring techniques can be supplemented by subjective rating-scales. Some instances of a multimethod approach can be identified in the studies described above; many more are to be found in the general literature in this field.

7.7 SUMMARY

Let us end the chapter by clarifying what the preceding discussion has revealed about the meaning of the phrase used in the title – "Evaluating user interface designs". First, (borrowing from Moran, 1981) "user interface" refers to any aspect of the system that the user comes in contact with – physically, perceptually, or conceptually. Secondly, by "design" it is meant that (given the appropriate tools) evaluation can be carried out potentially at any point in the process of developing the interface, and that whatever form the interface takes during this process is the legitimate subject for evaluations. Thirdly, evaluations are user-centred; that is, they provide information about users or potential users of the interface, from study of those users, and the ultimate benefactors of the evaluations are the users. The aim of user-centred evaluations of the user interface design is to steer the design in ways which minimize the intrusion of the system upon the task that the user is attempting to perform.

8

So you want to be a professional?

8.1 INTRODUCTION

The working title for this chapter was 'Confessions of a Human Factors Specialist' but I decided against it in the end for fear it might attract undue (and undesired) attention. This chapter is aimed at: (i) students of all disciplines who would like to either become professionally employed as ergonomists or human factors specialists, and (ii) people, who though not directly employed in such a role, see themselves as representing the user to some degree in the design of computer systems. So, if you're reading this book for useful insights into the design of user interfaces, there should be something in the previous seven chapters that might be of use to you, but you'll find little specific design advice in *this* chapter. Indeed, some of the advice offered in this chapter can be found in many other text-books dealing with presentation skills and communicating with others. I am certainly no expert in these areas, but I feel my advice, based on the mistakes that I have made and the 'rules' that I have discovered are valid and useful to new entrants into industry – whatever subject they specialise in.

I hope to provide some insights into the role you might be asked to play, mainly by recalling events that have occurred to me, or to colleagues, over the seven years between 1981 and 1988. This sort of information is seldom recorded in such a permanent form, which means either it is difficult to present, or it is not worth presenting at all – I'll let the reader decide. When I was a studying for my MSc in Ergonomics, the one thing I wanted to know more about, that I could not obtain from the literature, was what it was like to work in Ergonomics. Case studies are one way of obtaining some information, but you really need to have such case studies presented in a lecture, so that you can pester the speaker afterwards with all sorts of difficult and embarrassing questions!

If *I* was curious about such things, my guess is that at least some of you are too. All my working experience has been gained in industry, working for one company. I am not the best qualified in terms of industrial experience or variety of jobs, but in the absence of anything better my recollections and experiences will have to do. Perhaps it will spur others, with a richer and more varied set of experiences, to put pen to paper.

We should also set matters straight right at the start regarding the word 'professional'. There are many people working in academia that are qualified in at least one discipline that would make us regard them as having pertinent things to say on the subject matter of this book. I have spent a considerable amount of time in the last two years (1986 to 1988) working closely with researchers in both psychology and computer science departments in three UK universities, in the cause of a collaborative project. These people were just as professional as any industrial researcher or consultant I have come across. Their styles of working are refreshingly different but nonetheless valid. I say all this, before I embark upon tales that are almost entirely industrially based. This is in part due to my aforementioned work experience, but also because there are pressures in industry that many people in university departments either are not subjected to at all, or are subjected to in relatively mild ways. That is not to say the pressures upon academics are in any way illusory. University departments suffer very real and painful pressures, particularly financial ones. No, the point is that the pressures in industry are different and, since most students have more experience of academia than industry, it is better that this chapter is weighted in favour of the latter than the former.

Having seen the arrival of many 'raw recruits' at the Human Factors Division at British Telecom Research Laboratories (BTRL) I would estimate that, on average, it takes six months for newcomers to start to think and act as industrial professionals. (It took me longer, maybe I was slow on the uptake, or merely hankering after the academic life!). I am not attempting to justify the required change in attitude, nor am I condemning it, it just *happens*, because of environmental pressures, like evolution. I am also not attempting to pass judgement on the relative merits of either environment, they both have their good and their bad points. What I am saying to those of you who are likely to join the ranks of the industrially employed, in whatever discipline, is: 'Be prepared!'

8.2 THE DEPARTMENT

When you join a company, you will, unless the company is very small, almost certainly be placed into a sub-division of the company that is the equivalent of an academic 'department'. It may be called a 'unit' or a 'division' or a 'section' but let us, for the sake of argument, call it a department. A department can be defined as the largest sub-division of the company in which you are likely to find other people with similar qualifications to yourself. It might be the Industrial Psychology Department, the Human Factors Department, the Computer Design Department or any of a hundred variations on this theme. Of course, in large multi-national (or even large national) companies, there may be several departments employing human factors specialists across the country or the world. However, let us concern ourselves with the actual department you find yourself in soon after you start work.

You would do well to find out how many of 'you' there are and what positions they hold in the company. If the human factors department is new and therefore probably quite small, you might be faced with a contradiction to academic life straight away.

At university there is a hierarchy, not only of rank and age, but also of knowledge. The 'Professor' is usually an acknowledged expert in his or her field, the 'Readers' and 'Research Associates' have PhD's sticking out of their back pockets, and the lecturers have a wealth of experience of students *and* subject matter. In an industrial department however, *you*, yes *you*, with the ink on your degree certificate not yet dry, might well be one of the most knowledgeable people on the subject of human factors in the department. There may well be many experienced 'company people' who have converted or drifted from another discipline such as electrical engineering or computer science, into the department. They might all be more highly ranked than you, but you will be one of the main founts of theoretical knowledge. There may be no long line of wisdom, of years of experience and expertise, reaching up into the misty heights of the higher ranks of the department, waiting to guide you, help you, train you. People will ask you questions, *and expect answers* . The trouble is, you cannot telephone your academic mentor or supervisor every time this happens (though I tried, believe me I tried!). In the end you just have to cross your fingers, give them an answer and wait. Depending upon the question and the quality of your answer, you may very well send them away happy - until the next time they need your advice.

In all seriousness, having such a responsibility can be a bit daunting, but the 'throw them in at the deep end' mentality is common in industry, and it is not all bad. This common state of affairs comes about because the discipline is relatively young (and relatively slow-growing compared to say, computing) and many of its industrial disciples are still young and low down the company hierarchy. If you do find yourself employed by a company which is new to human factors, you should certainly take a positive attitude and see it as an opportunity to make a lasting impression on the design practice of the company, and to make others notice you and your talents. In many ways the opportunities available in newer departments are greater than in the older, well established, departments employing a number of ergonomists and cognitive psychologists.

In the larger human factors departments there will be a wealth of experience and expertise for the new recruit to draw upon (but again most often bunched in the middle to lower echelons of the management hierarchy). If the department is large enough there will probably be a slow trickle of new entrants, as some people leave or move upwards in the company, or as the department itself expands. Seek out the last person to join before yourself; their memories of their first weeks will still be clear and untarnished by either cynicism or rose-tinted spectacles. Try to get a feel for the internal workings of the department, and especially the intra-departmental politics. You will of course assimilate this knowledge, almost by osmosis, during the first few months, but being on the look-out for hints about how the department ticks can never be a bad thing.

8.3 WORKING WITH OTHERS

8.3.1 Working in teams

Academic life for students tends to provide a high degree of socialising outside work hours, but because of the competitive nature of most western hemisphere educational systems, the work itself is very individualised. You attend lectures with many others, you will work in groups in the lab, but when it comes to study, for an essay, thesis, report or examination, you are on your own. Working in groups does provide a useful insight into how well you might work with others, but at university it is rarely more than an artificially imposed grouping with very short-term goals.

At work, in some respects, the opposite is true. You will be expected to work closely with others, often as part of a team. Reports that you write will often be produced co-operatively with your immediate supervisor or manager. You will often attend meetings (internal and external to the company) where you and one or two colleagues might be representing 'the company' or 'the department'. You will be required at times to suppress your individualism and act as a 'team player'. I found this a particularly difficult thing to do and one small anecdote here might help make the point.

Within six months of my arrival at work, I had to attend a meeting with my 'Head of Group' (two levels above me) at which we met two other company people from another department. We were attempting to obtain money from this other department in order to perform some research we considered interesting and valuable. Halfway through the meeting I quite innocently mentioned how much money we were getting from another department within the company. Immediately I felt a throbbing pain in my left shin – my boss had literally kicked me under the table for opening my mouth! You can criticize my former boss for not briefing me sufficiently before the meeting, and for the sharp physical rebuke inflicted, but you cannot cover all eventualities, and I was a rather headstrong young man.

Some people take to working in a team better than others, and often the make-up of a team (the personalities involved) needs careful planning. At its best, team working produces more than the sum of the individual's efforts - a synergy between team members results in the generation of ideas that no single member would have produced working by themselves. At its worst, team working produces conflict, rivalries and can be unproductive and de-motivating for all the team members.

8.3.2 Making yourself heard

The reader should not gain the impression that working in a team is a constraint that will affect you and your ability to produce good work - and obtain due recognition for it. Working in a team is a constraint only if you allow others to dominate the work of the team. You should be prepared to fight for the right to be heard and make your point of view known to the team, it is one thing to make a suggestion and have it rejected after consideration, it is quite another to fail to make the suggestion in the first place.

It is probably best to consider working in a team as a game, with its own rules and regulations. If you learn to play within the rules, you will find that team working may not be a hindrance or a constraint at all. It might even be an advantage since you are guaranteed a captive audience.

In order to make yourself heard both literally and metaphorically, here are one or two hints that might help.

8.3.2.1 Have something to say

There is little point in making yourself heard unless you have something to say. Interjecting at a meeting first and then thinking up what you want to say second is likely to end in disaster. You should always let your need to say something rule your desire to be heard. Such a state of affairs is sometimes referred to as 'putting your mouth into gear before engaging the brain'.

8.3.2.2 Know when to say it

It is probably true to say that having something useful to contribute at a meeting almost always stems from listening carefully to what the others are saying. Attending a meeting determined to make a specific point is fine, provided the opportunity arises for you to make that point, *in context*. Changing the focus of the group's attention by stating your point irrespective of the preceding discussion (besides breaking the normal 'rules' of conversational discourse) is bad manners and more likely to be seen as disruptive than constructive. Timing is therefore important, make sure you have the rest of the people's attention and that the context is right.

At international standards meetings protocol is particularly important, not for any pompous reason, but for sound practical purposes. Meetings with simultaneous translations or with people who do not speak English as a first language take longer, and transitions between speakers need to be clearly signalled. At CCITT[†] meetings that I have attended, it is normal to request 'the floor' by raising one's hand and, after being granted the floor to start all contributions with: "Thankyou, Mr Chairman."

8.3.2.3 How to say it

This is not intended to be a section on 'Public Speaking': there are many publications and courses that are geared specifically to improving those skills. However, here are one or two pointers that you might do well to observe. You should follow any custom that has been established for the meeting, *ie.* stand up, thank the Chair, come to the front *et cetera*. Speak clearly and at a volume that all can hear comfortably. Do not rush (especially at international meetings) and if the point you are making is complicated, make it slowly, going through the arguments one by one. Do not go on interminably; if you have little to say do not repeat yourself more than once. If you have much to say, inform the audience and the Chair that you have several points to raise and then raise the most important point. If the Chair is at all alert he will prompt you for the other points, or not, depending on the amount of response there is to your first point - at least you will have neither usurped the Chair's authority nor hogged the floor excessively.

---

[*] The initials CCITT stand for the French equivalent of :
' The International Telegraph and Telephone Consultative Committee'

8.3.2.4 Visual aids

There will often be occasions when you will attend meetings whose agenda is known well before the actual meeting itself (though all too frequently I have attended and, alas, occasionally chaired, meetings where the first item on the agenda is 'to draw up an agenda'). Such meetings may not necessarily be formal affairs, but informal 'team discussions' where a number of work items are considered, perhaps to measure how work is progressing. If you know in advance that you will be asked to make a contribution or that you decide you have something to say, preparing some visual aid is an excellent means of enhancing your contribution.

In some cases just a series of headers written down and photocopied (one per attendee) will suffice. In other cases a flip chart with some ideas and diagrams already written down is best. At larger, and usually more formal, meetings, overhead transparencies might be considered, though always check that projection facilities will be available. The preparation and use of 35mm slides should be avoided except for conference presentations and lectures. If lights need to be turned off at a meeting people cannot see their papers easily and it is an open invitation, especially after lunch, for some people to 'rest their eyes'.

Whatever the occasion, I always try to prepare some form of visual aid or 'hand out', and it is not only for altruistic purposes either. Preparation for meetings is itself important. Therefore it suits my purpose to set down my ideas or thoughts beforehand. This allows me to get my own thoughts in order and, when I hand out my diagram or list of headings, they act as a prompt for what I want to say. It is easier to conjure up a series of thoughts when prompted by some notes made at the time the ideas were generated, than to go to a meeting thinking 'I'll know what to say, when it comes to my turn', because often you don't.

8.3.2.5 Formal presentations

Much of what I have said earlier in this section applies equally well to formal presentations only more so. Being prepared is not just a good idea, it is essential. Appropriate, and well designed, visual aids are indispensable. However, *the* most important thing is *knowing, understanding* and *believing in*, what you are saying. One of the most awful experiences of my working life occurred when I forgot this simple tenet.

The group members were each required to make a presentation to a group of people who were attempting to assess the validity of an approach we were planning to use to evaluate how people worked at a particular task using a new computer system. We were planning to video the subjects, monitor their keyed inputs to the system and feed all this and their verbalization of their interaction with the computer onto a synchronised video tape. We hoped to interview typical job-holders before and after the introduction of this technology and assess them across a range of well known scales used in occupational psychology in order to measure any effects such an introduction might bring about. We also, due in part, to my physiological background, planned to measure their mental workload by monitoring their heart-rate and calculating their heart-rate variability when performing the computer-based tasks.

Each group member was assigned a part of the presentation, the video and verbal protocols, the occupational psychology, the mental workload calculations. Of course it was my job to present a justification for the heart-rate monitoring. Such monitoring is quite well reported in the literature, especially for aircraft pilots and others who routinely perform tasks that are particularly stressful. The literature on heart-rate variability however, was too vast and comprehensive for me to gain a useful understanding in a short space of time. Besides that, I really was unconvinced that asking these guys to wear a heart-rate monitor for 24 hour periods and to log their activities was going to provide a meaningful metric of how their mental workload was affected by computer use. Consequently, come the great day, video cameras were set-up, microphones were installed and the guests were ushered in to their seats. I rose and begun my well practised presentation with these immortal words:

> "There are three advantages to measuring heart rate variability as means of assessing mental workload..."

I remembered the first two advantages, but when it came to the third one, I paused, prepared to speak, but... nothing, not a thing, my mind was a complete blank! I must have stood there for 20 seconds (an eternity when you are 'on camera') before my boss prompted me from the front row. Needless to say rebuke was swift! In the end, for reasons other than those based upon my doubts, the work was shelved. I learned a valuable 3-part lesson that day:

1.)   always prepare more thoroughly than you feel you need to;
2.)   always 'know your stuff';
3.)   always have confidence in what you are saying.

8.3.3   Writing reports

It would be pointless for me to take up a lot space on this topic by attempting to make specific recommendations about how to write reports once you are em-ployed. Every organization, every department and every smaller sub-department will have different 'house-styles' of report writing. There will be a set of in-ternal rules for structuring and presenting such reports, and you will have to conform to such rules, or change them. Despite such rules there is still room within all house styles for writers to show individualism and to develop their own method of presentation - again it is a matter of using the rules of the game to their fullest potential. I shall offer just a few thoughts of my own on the subject which are general and therefore applicable in most cases.

In the first place you should realise that writing internal reports is unlikely to be like any writing you have done before, or at least most recently. The aca-demic prose required for PhD and MSc theses and for 3rd year undergraduate projects is rarely acceptable in industry, some of the reasons for rejecting a style you have been encouraged to develop during your years in adult education are given here, the others you'll have to work out for yourself.

Suppose you are asked evaluate some screen designs for a new piece of software and are required to produce a report both for the designers and for your boss which make suggestions for improvements. You might wish to validate the measures you made or criteria you applied by referring to the literature on the subject. Your boss will point out to you that provided you can, if required, show precedent for the judgements you make, there is no need to include them in a report to the designers, for several reasons:

1.) the more concise (clear and economical *not* deficient) a report the more likely it is to be read;
2.) the quicker you produce the report the more likely it is that it will have an effect upon the design;
3.) short turn around times for reports mean that you will be available for more work more quickly, no company can afford to have its specialists engaged in report writing at the expense of outstanding work.

All this sounds harsh, but it is usually the case. Another tip is that you should always strive to be positive about any recommendations you suggest. If you really feel your suggestions should be implemented then make that quite clear. Prefixing suggestions with phrases such as; 'perhaps it would be slightly better if...' casts doubt on your judgement, raises doubts in the designer's mind about how worthwhile such a suggestion is, and generally demonstrates a lack of confidence. If you are really unsure that a suggestion will improve matters then do not include it in that part of the report. Instead, have a separate section that deals with marginal issues and clearly provides the designer with a choice of equally valid options

8.4   DEFENDING HUMAN FACTORS

It is my hope that one day a section such as this will be redundant. The sad truth is that in many UK industries, and in my experience, other industries in Europe and the USA, the role of human factors in the design of computer systems is still questioned in some quarters. Sometimes it is cost effectiveness that is questioned, sometimes, though happily increasingly rarely, it is an ignorance of the domain and what it offers. Whatever the reason, I promise you that in your time working as a specialist in interface design, or cognitive ergonomics or any other label given to those that represent the user's position during the design process, you will be called upon to defend any combination or all of the following: your position, your role, your department, your profession and at times the whole of psychology.

Why should this be so? Why should this particular specialism be so frequently held to account? The answer is simple; *because cognitive ergonomics is difficult.* It is difficult to understand for informed non-specialists. It is difficult because it deals with elusive qualities rather than concrete quantities – (what answer do we give to the question "... but *how much* better is this screen design than that one?" ?). It is difficult because it deals with people, and people, confound them, are complicated entities. You can debug a program (by looking at each component or line of code) so that it works properly, rewrite it in another language, compile it so that it runs faster, modularise it so that you can add to it later, document it so that you know what happens at each stage of the process... *etc.* Humans just aren't that accessible. We need to use abstract and indirect processes to understand what people do in certain circumstances – and non-psychologists find that hard to deal with.

Another problem, we as profession, have to face, is that it can be difficult to demonstrate *positively* the value of our input. I have used and heard used the following justification many times:

> "...the cost of a mistake by the user, a wrong decision, an invalid assumption, would be many times greater than the cost of our in volvement in the design of an X"

It is a valuable and strong weapon in the human factors specialist's arsenal and should be used when appropriate. However, it is, and always will be, a rather negative justification for our involvement. It is difficult to sell insurance and it is difficult to sell your expertise for exactly the same reason; unless the stakes are high, risks will be taken. People under-insure their property if they think the chances of burglary are low, but you'll be hard pressed to find an under-insured bank or jewellers shop.

'Accentuate the positive', is an easier doctrine to preach than to adhere to but here are some of the things I do or consider worthwhile in presenting a positive face to designers:

1.) the first thing to do is to be confident about your contribution to the design, if you are full of self-doubts, then you have little chance of convincing others of your worth,

2.) never forget how much lousy software there is around, so get to know some extreme and ludicrous examples and use them whenever possible but especially in the presence of software designers, it will sow a seed of doubt in their mind about their ability to 'do it all themselves', or that interface design is 'just common-sense',

3.) if the designers tell you all they need is a copy of a book such as this one then, ask them, as a friend and the co-author of Chapter 5, Dr Nick Milner, did in a letter to the weekly industry paper 'Computing', whether they would be happy to have their gall bladder removed by a hospital architect using a copy of 'Gray's Anatomy' – remember you are a *specialist*,

4.) make and remember a list of the things you can offer a design team (knowledge of human limitations and abilities for example),

5.) establish the ways in which you will be able to work with the designers both during the design and during any evaluative stages.

You will no doubt find other ways of justifying your existence as you gain experience of dealing with the issue. Discuss the matter with colleagues – how do they cope?

8.5   CONTRIBUTING TO THE KNOWLEDGE BASE

An unfortunate and unnecessary reluctance to communicate findings, ideas and concerns seems to beset many newcomers to industrial ergonomics departments.

It is not clear whether the cause is due to a general malaise based upon the notion that once employed in industry, contributing to the human factors 'knowledge base' can and should be left to the universities and related academically respectable bodies. Alternatively, perhaps there is some feeling of 'unworthiness' or 'impurity of approach' because of the nature of the work performed in industry.

These excuses for any failure to contribute are related, but equally unacceptable, because the domain is essentially applications oriented rather than theoretically and philosophically interesting. The target for research is 'The User', more often than not 'The User' is using equipment supplied by 'The Employer' for the purpose of performing tasks that 'The Employer' requires to be performed in order for 'The Business' to run and to succeed. Most research findings in this domain are worth little if they cannot be applied to 'real-life' situations, machines and environments. University laboratories run experiments which, by attempting to hold many variables constant, result in the oft heard (and often self-invoked) criticisms such as: 'unrealistic' or 'too abstracted from the normal work environment'. Thus the improvement in techniques, the applicability of research, and the general approach of ergonomics depends, crucially, upon a synthesis between academia and industry. Neither environment is more valid than the other, their interdependency is undeniable.

It should be clear from the last paragraph that human factors specialists working in industry do have an important role to play in increasing the width and depth of knowledge that others in the field can draw upon. You should see it as part of your job, and make it clear to your superiors, that attending and contributing to the occasional conference, will, first and foremost, benefit the company, as well as you, and your profession.

Finally, you should be aware of your debt to the discipline and to other fellow practitioners. Make any techniques you discover or develop available to others, publish, give talks, attend workshops. It is only by the steady growth of our knowledge base that we can hope to progress. When deciding to publish, select outlets that will give your ideas wide circulation, which is not always an academic journal. Newspapers and industry-based magazines are increasingly publishing material that is written by specialists in all sorts of fields including human factors – use them. You might even get paid for doing so!

8.6   CONCLUSION

Everybody's experiences are different, there will no doubt be human factors people whose industrial experiences are vastly different from mine. However, there are some commonplace expectations placed upon all new employees in whatever discipline they are qualified. This chapter attempted to give some pointers, to what those expectations might be, and how you might fulfill them. If you are really 'into' human factors or ergonomics, then being employed to work in that area is in itself a very satisfying experience. That in itself will allow you to cope better with any new regimes imposed upon you.

I hope this book conveyed some of my pleasure at being employed in a discipline I firmly believe in. It is my fervent wish that by reading this book you, the reader, have also become, in some sense, a 'human factors person'. If that is so, then I shall feel I have achieved something worthwhile.

References

Allen, R. B., & Scerbo, M. W. (1983). Details of command language keystrokes. *ACM Transactions: Office Automation Systems* 1, 159-178

Antin, J. F. An evaluation of menu systems for space station interfaces. (1986) *Proceedings of Human Factors Society, 30th Annual Meeting* pp. 679-683

Apperley, M. D. & Field, G. E. (1984) A comparative evaluation of menu-based interactive human-computer dialogue techniques. In B. Shackel (Ed.). *Proceedings of the IFIP Conference on Human-Computer Interaction - INTERACT '84*. London, 4-7 September. London: North-Holland

Apperley, M. D. & Spence, R. (1983) Hierarchical dialogue structures in interactive computer systems. *Software-Practice and Experience* 13 777-790

Aretz, A. J. & Reising, J. M. (1983) Colour coding in fighter cockpits: It isn't black and white? In: *Proceedings of the Second Symposium on Aviation Psychology* pp 1-7, Columbus, Ohio, 1983

Bainbridge, L. (1979). Verbal reports of process operator's knowledge. *International Journal of Man-Machine Studies* 11, 411-435

Ball, R.G., Newton, R.S. & Whitfield, D. (1980) Development of an off-display, high resolution, direct touch input device: the RSRE Touchpad. *Displays*, 203-207

Bannon, L., & O'Malley, C. (1984). Problems in evaluation of human-computer interfaces: a case study. In B. Shackel (Ed.). *Proceedings of the IFIP Conference on Human-Computer Interaction - INTERACT '84*. London, 4-7 September. London: North-Holland

Beaumont, J. G. (1985) Speed of response using keyboard and screen-based microcomputer response media. *International Journal of Man-Machine Studies* 23, pp 61–70

Bennett, J. L., Lorch, D. J., Kieras, D. E., & Polson, P. G. (1987). Developing a user interface technology for use in industry. In H. J. Bullinger & B. Shackel (Eds). *Proceedings of the Second IFIP Conference on Human-Computer Interaction - INTERACT '87*. Stuttgart, Federal Republic of Germany, 1-4 September. London: North-Holland

Bergman, H. (1985) *Definition of Help Systems*. A Contribution to CCITT SGII, Working Party 2 meeting in Munich, September 1985

Beringer, D. B., & Petersen, J. G. (1985) Underlying behavioural parameters of the operation of touch-input devices: biases, models and feedback. *Human Factors* 27, 4, pp 445–458

Bezold, W. von. (1874) *Die Farbenlehre*. Westerman, Braunschweig

Black, J., & Moran, T. (1982) Learning and remembering command names. In: *Proceedings Human Factors in Computer Systems*, 15–17 March 1982, Gaithersburg, Maryland, pp 8–11

Bobko, P., Bobko, D. J. & Davis, M. A., (1984). A multidimensional scaling of video games, *Human Factors* 26 pp 477-482

Bouma, H. (1980) Visual reading processes and the quality of text displays. In: Grandjean, E. & Vigliani, E. (eds) *Ergonomic Aspects of Visual Display Terminals*. Taylor and Francis, London, England

Brown, C. M., (1986). *Human Computer Interface Design Guidelines*, Ablex Publishing Co., Norwood, NJ.

Buckley, P., & Johnson, P. (1987) Analysis of communication tasks for the design of a structured messaging system. In: Diaper, D., & Winder, R. (eds), *People and Computers III. Proceedings of the third conference of the British Computer Society Human-Computer Interaction Specialist Group, University of Exeter, 7-11 September 1987*, Cambridge University Press, pp 29–40

Cakir, A., Hart, D. J., & Stewart, T. F. M. (1980) *Visual Display Terminals*. John Wiley, England

Card, S. K., & Moran, T. P. (1980). The keystroke level model for user performance time with interactive systems. *Communications of the ACM* 23 396-410

Card, S. K., Moran, T. P. & Newell, A. (1983) *The Psychology of Human-Computer Interaction*. Hillside, New Jersey, Lawrence Erlbaum Associates

Card, S.K., English, W.K. & Burr, B.J. (1978) Evaluation of Mouse, Rate-Controlled Isometric Joystick, Step Keys and Text Keys for Text Selection on a CRT. *Ergonomics* 21, 8, 601-613

Carroll, J. M. (1982) Learing, using and designing filenames and command paradigms.*Behaviour and Information Technology* 1, 4, pp 327–346

Carter, R. C. (1982) Visual search with colour. *Journal of Experimental Psychology* 8 pp 127-136

Chambers 20th Century Dictionary (1983)

Christ, R. E., (1975) Review and analysis of color coding research for visual displays, *Human Factors* **17**, pp 542-570

Cohill, A. M., & Williges, R. C. (1982) Computer-augmented retrieval of HELP information for novice users. *Proceedings of Human Factors Society 26h Annual Meeting*. pp 79–82

Cohill, A. M., Gilfoil, D. M., & Pilitsis, J. V. (1986). A methodology for evaluating application software. *Proceedings of the Human Factors Society 30th Annual Meeting*, pp 14-18

Comerford, R. (1984) Pointing-device innovations enhance user/machine interfaces. *EDN* July 26, 54-66

Davis, R. (1983). User error or computer error? Observations on a statistics package. *International Journal of Man-Machine Studies* **19**, 359-376

Dumais, S. T. & Landauer, T.K. (1983) Using examples to describe categories. *CHI '83 Conference Proceedings* pp 112-115. Boston. MA.

Durrett, J. & Trezona, J., (1982) How to use color displays effectively. *BYTE*, April issue, pp 50-53

Dvorak, A. (1943) There is a better typewriter keyboard. *National Business Education Quarterly* **12**, 2, pp 51-88

Eason, K. D., & Damordaran, L. (1981) The needs of the commercial user. In: Coombs, M. J., & Alty, J. L. (eds), *Computing Skills and the User Interface*. Academic Press, London, pp 115–142

Emmons, W.H. (1984) A comparison of cursor-key arrangements (box versus cross) for VDUs. In: Grandjean, E. (Ed), *Ergonomics and Health in Modern Offices*. Taylor and Francis, London and Philidelphia

Engel, S. E., & Granda, R. E. (1975) Guidelines for man/display interfaces. *Technical report 00.2720*, IBM, Pughkeepsie, N.Y.

Engelbart, D.C. (1973) Design considerations for knowledge workshop terminals. *Proc. NCC, AFIPS,* **42**, 9-21, June 1973

English,W.K., Engelbart, D.C. & Berman,M.L. (1967) Display selection techniques for text manipulation. *IEEE Transactions on Human Factors in Electronics* HFE-8, 1, pp 21-31

Erlandsen, J. & Holm, J. (1987) Intelligent help systems. *Information and Software Technology*, **29** 3 April 1987

Ewing, J., Mehrabanzad, S., Sheck, S., Ostroff, D. & Shneiderman, B. (1986) An experimental comparison of a mouse and arrow-jump keys for an interactive encylopedia. *International Journal of Man-Machine Studies* **24** 29-45

Fitz-Gibbon, C. T. Meta-analysis: an explication. *British Educational Research Journal,* **10**(2), 135-144

Foley, J.D. & van Dam, A. (1982) *Fundamentals of interactive computer graphics.* Addison-Wesley, Reading, MA.

Foley, J.D. (1983) Cit. in Shneiderman (1987) – see below

Foster, J. J. & Bruce, M. (1982) Looking for entries in Videotex tables: a comparison of four colour formats. *Journal of Applied Psychology* **67**, pp 611-615

Galitz, W. O. (1980) *Human Factors in Office Automation.* Life Office Management Assn., Atlanta

Galitz, W. O. (1978). *Screen Format Designers Handbook,* CNA, Chicago

Gallaway, G. R. (1981) Response times to user activities in interactive man/machine computer systems.In: *Proceedings of Human Factors Society 25th Annual Meeting.* Rochester, New York, October 1981, pp 754–758

Giroux, L. & Belleau, R. (1986) What's on the menu? The influence of menu content on the selection process. *Behaviour & Information Technology* **5** No. 2, 169-172

Gomez, A.D., Wolfe, S.W., Davenport, E.W. & Calder, B.D. (1982) LMDS: lightweight modular display system. *NOSC Technical Report* **7**67, Naval Ocean Systems Center, San Diego, CA.

Gould, J.D. & Grischowsky, N. (1986) Does visual angle of a line of characters affect reading speed? *Human Factors* **28**, 2, 165-173

Greenstein, J.S. & Arnault, L.Y. (1987) Human Factors aspects of manual computer input devices. Chapter 11.4, 1450-1489. In: Salvendy, G. (Ed) – see below

Guth, S. L. & Lodge, H. R. (1973) Heterochromatic additivity, foveal spectral sensitivity, and a new colour model. *Journal of the Optical Society of America* **63** p 450

Haller,R., Mutschler,H. & Voss,M. (1984) Comparison of input devices for correction of typing errors in office systems. In B. Shackel (Ed.). *Proceedings of the IFIP Conference on Human-Computer Interaction - INTERACT '84.* London, 4-7 September. London: North-Holland

Hart, D.J. (1976) The Human Aspects of working with visual display terminals. *INCA-FIEJ Research Report* No 76/02, 1-61, Darmstadt, W.Germany

Hauptmann, A. G. & Green, B. F. (1983) A comparison of command, menu-selection and natural language computer programs. *Behaviour & Information Technology* **2** No. 2, pp 163-178

Hekmatpour, S. & Ince, D. C. (1987). Evolutionary prototyping and the human-computer interface. In H. J. Bullinger & B. Shackel (Eds). *Proceedings of the Second IFIP Conference on Human-Computer Interaction - INTERACT '87*. Stuttgart, Federal Republic of Germany, 1-4 September. London: North-Holland

Hewett, T. T. (1986). The role of iterative evaluation in designing systems for usability. In M. D. Harrison & A. F. Monk (Eds.), People and computers: designing for usability. *Proceedings of the Second Conference of the British Computer Society Human Computer Interaction Specialist Group*. University of York, 23-26 September. Cambridge: Cambridge University Press

Hill & Knowlton (1987) International Public Relations Counsel, London WC1X 8SH

Hilz, R. L., Huppman, G. & Cavonius, C. R. 1974. Influence of Luminance on Hue Discrimination. *Journal of the Optical Society of America* **64**, pp 763-766

Hirsh, R. S. (1976) *Human Factors in Man-Computer Interfaces*. IBM Human Factors Center, San Jose, California

Hirsh-Pasek, K., Nudelman, S., & Schneider, M. L. (1982) An experimental evaluation of command names. *Behaviour and Information Technology* **1**, 4, pp 359–370

Hodge, M., & Pennington, F. M. (1973) Some studies of word abbreviation behaviour. *Journal of Experimental Psychology* **98**, p 350

Howard, S., & Murray, D. (1987). A taxonomy of evaluation techniques for HCI. In H. J. Bullinger & B. Shackel (Eds). *Proceedings of the Second IFIP Conference on Human-Computer Interaction - INTERACT '87*. Stuttgart, Federal Republic of Germany, 1-4 September. London: North-Holland

Huckle. B.A. (1981) The Man-Machine Interface: Guidelines for the design of the end-user/system conversation. Savant Institute Studies, Lancashire, England

Hudson, P. T. (1985) What does colour add to a display that can't be done in black and white? In: *International Conference on Colour in Information Technology and Visiual Displays (Publ. 61)*, 27-28th March, 1985, Guildford, England

Jackson, A. (1982) Some problems in the specification of rolling ball operating charateristics. RSRE, UK

James, E. B. (1981) The User Interface: How we may compute. In: Coombs, M. J., & Alty, J. L. (eds), *Computing Skills and the User Interface*. Academic Press, London, pp 337–372

Jenkins, W.L. & Karr,A.C. (1954) The use of a joystick in masking settings on a simulated scope face. *Journal of Applied Psychology* **38**, 457-461

Johnson, P. & Johnson, H. (1987) Practical and theoretical aspects of human computer interaction. To appear in: Aleksander, I. (ed.) *The World Yearbook of Fifth Generation Computing Research and Development*. Kogan Page, London

Johnson, P. (1985) Towards a task model of messaging: an example of the application of TAKD to user interface design. In: Johnson, P., & Cook, S., (eds), People and Computers: Designing the interface. *Proceedings of the conference of the British Computer Society Human-Computer Interaction Specialist Group, University of East Anglia, 17-20 September 1985,* Cambridge University Press, pp 46–62

Johnson, P., Diaper, D., & Long, J. B. (1984) Tasks, Skill and Knowledge; Task Analysis for Knowledge Descriptions. In: Shackel, B., (ed.) *Proceedings of the IFIP Conference on Human-Computer Interaction - INTERACT '84.* London, 4-7 September. London: North-Holland

Karat, J., McDonald, J. E. & Anderson, M. (1984) A comparison of menu selection techniques: touch panel, mouse and keyboard. In B. Shackel (Ed.). *Proceedings of the IFIP Conference on Human-Computer Interaction - INTERACT '84.* London, 4-7 September. London: North-Holland

Karat, J., McDonald, J. E. & Anderson, M. (1986) A comparison of menu selection techniques: touch panel, mouse and keyboard. *International Journal of Man-Machine Studies* **25** pp 73-88

Kellogg, W. A. (1987). Conceptual consistency in the user interface: effects on user performance. In H. J. Bullinger & B. Shackel (Eds). *Proceedings of the Second IFIP Conference on Human-Computer Interaction - INTERACT '87.* Stuttgart, Federal Republic of Germany, 1-4 September. London: North-Holland

Kieras, D. E., & Polson, P. G. (1985). An approach to the formal analysis of user complexity. *International Journal of Man-Machine Studies* **22**, pp 365-394

Kiger, J. I., (1984) The depth/breadth tradeoff in the design of menu-driven user interfaces. *International Journal of Man-Machine Studies* **20** pp 201-213

Kinney, J. A. S. (1982) Brightness of coloured self-luminous displays. *Colour Research Applications* 8/12 p 82

Knave, B.G., (ed.), (1983), The visual display unit. In: *Ergonomic principles in office automation.* Ericsson Information Systems AB, Stockholm, Sweden.

Kokoschka, S. & Fleck, H. J., (1982). Experimenteller Vergleich von Negativ- und Positivdarstellung der Bildschirmzeichen. *Vortrag aus Lichttechnischer* Gemeinschaftstagung, Lugano, pp 507-531

Kron, H. & Rosenfeld, E., (1983). *Computer Images: State of the Art.* Stewart, Tabori & Chang Publishers, NY.

Lambert, L. J. (1984) A comparative study of system response time on program developer productivity. *IBM Systems Journal* **23**, pp 36–43

Landauer, T. K. & Nachbar, D. W. (1985) Selection from alphabetic menu trees using a touch screen: breadth, depth, and width. In L. Bormanand & B. Curtis (Eds.), Human factors in Computing Systems. *Proceedings of the CHI'85 Conference,* San Francisco, April 14-18. New York: ACM

Laubli, Th., Hunting, W., & Grandjean, E. (1980), Visual impairments in VDU operators related to environmental conditions. In: E. Grandjean & E. Vigliani (eds), *Ergonomic Aspects of Visual Display Terminals,* Taylor& Francis, London, 1980.

Lee, E. S. & MacGregor, J. N. (1985) Minimizing user search time in menu retrieval systems. *Human Factors* **27**(2) pp 157–162

Lee, A. & Lochovsky, F. (1985) User Interface Design. In: Tsichritzis, D. (ed.) *Office Automation.* Springer-Verlag, Berlin, pp 3–21

Levine, M. W. & Shefner, J. M. (1981) *Fundamentals of Sensation and Perception.* Addison-Wesley, London, England

Lewis, C., & Norman, D. A. (1986) Designing for error. In: Norman, D. A., & Draper, S. W. (eds) *User Centered System Design.* Lawrence Erlbaum Associates, New Jersey, pp 411–432

Lucas, A. (1987).*Desktop Publishing.* Ellis Horwood, Chichester

Lund, M. A. (1985). Evaluating the user interface: the candid- camera approach. In L. Bormanand & B. Curtis (Eds.), Human factors in Computing Systems. *Proceedings of the CHI'85 Conference,* San Francisco, April 14-18. New York: ACM

MacGregor, J. N. & Lee, E. S. (1987) Performance & preference in videotex menu retrieval: a review of the empirical literature. *Behaviour and Information Technology* **6** No. 1, 43-68

Magers, C. S. (1983) An experimental evaluation of on-line HELP for non-programmers. In: *Proceedings of the CHI'83 Human Factors in Computing Systems* Boston, 12-15 December. ACM, New York, pp 277–281

Marcus, A. (1983) Graphic design for computer graphics, *IEEE Computer Graphics Applications* July issue, pp 63-70

Marcus, A. (1984) Corporate Identity for iconic interface design: The graphic design perspective, IEEE Computer Graphics and Applications, December issue, pp 24-32

Martin, G. L., & Corl, K. G. (1986) System response time effects on user productivity. *Behaviour and Information Technology* **5**, 1, pp 3–13

Martin, J., Long, J. B., & Broome, D.(1984) The division of attention between a primary tracking task and secondary tasks of pointing with a stylus or speaking in a simulated ship's-gunfire-control task. *Ergonomics* **27** 4 pp 397–408

Matthews, M. L. (1987) The influence of colour on CRT reading performance and subjective comfort under operational conditions. *Applied Ergonomics* **18**, 4, 1987

McCormick, E. J. & Sander,M. S. (1983) *Human Factors in Engineering and Design.* (Fifth Edition) McGraw-Hill Inc, Tokyo, Japan

Mehr, M. H. & Mehr,E. (1972) Manual digital positioning in two axes: a comparison of joystick and trackball controls. *Proc. of the 16th Human Factors Society Conference,* 110-116, Santa Monica, CA.

Miller, G. A. (1956) The magical number seven plus or minus two: some limits on our capacity for processing information. *Psychological Review* **63**, 2, 81-97

Moran, T. P. (1981) The command language grammar: a representation for the user interface of interactive computer systems. *International Journal of Man-Machine Studies* **15**, 3-50

Murch, G. (1984) Human visual accomodation and convergence to multichromatic information displays. In: Gibson, C. P. (ed.) *Proceedings of NATO workshop "colour coded vs monochrome electronic displays",* Farnborough, England

Murray, D. M. (1987). Embedded user models. In H. J. Bullinger & B. Shackel (Eds). *Proceedings of the Second IFIP Conference on Human-Computer Interaction - INTERACT '87.* Stuttgart, Federal Republic of Germany, 1-4 September. London: North-Holland

Muter, P. & Mayson, C. (1986) The role of graphics in item selection from menus. *Behaviour & Information Technology* **5**, 1, pp 89-95

Neal, A. S., & Simons, R. M. (1983). Playback: a method for evaluating the usability of software and its documentation. In A. Janda (Ed.), Human Factors in Computing Systems. *Proceedings of the CHI'83 conference,* Boston,12-15 December. Amsterdam: North-Holland

Newman, J. R. & Brown, H. T. (1958) The effects of marker size and display control ratio on speed and accuracy on radar target acquisition with operators using a rolling ball. *Proc. American Psych. Assoc.* Washington, USA

Norman, D. A. (1986) Cognitive Engineering. In: Norman, D. A., & Draper, S. W. (eds) *User Centered System Design.* Lawrence Erlbaum Associates, New Jersey, pp 31–61

Noyes, J. (1983) The QWERTY keyboard: a review. *Int. J. of Man-Machine Studies* **18**, pp 265-281

Paetau, M. (1984). The cognitive regulation of human action as a guide-line for evaluating the man-computer interface. In B. Shackel (Ed.). *Proceedings of the IFIP Conference on Human-Computer Interaction - INTERACT '84.* London, 4-7 September. London: North-Holland

Parton, D., Huffman, K., Pridgen, P., Norman, K. & Schneiderman, B. (1985) Learning a menu selection tree: training methods compared. *Behaviour & Information Technology,* **4**, 2, 81-91

Pawlak, U. (1986) Ergonomic aspects of image polarity. *Behaviour and Information Technology* **5**, 4, pp 335–348

Payne, S. J. (1984) Task-Action Grammars. In: Shackel, B., (ed.) *Proceedings of the IFIP Conference on Human-Computer Interaction - INTERACT '84.* London, 4-7 September. North-Holland, Amsterdam

Payne, S. J. (1984). Task-Action Grammar. In B. Shackel (Ed.). *Proceedings of the IFIP Conference on Human-Computer Interaction - INTERACT '84.* London, 4-7 September. London: North-Holland

Perlman , G. (1984) Making the right choices with menus. In B. Shackel (Ed.). *Proceedings of the IFIP Conference on Human-Computer Interaction - INTERACT '84.* London, 4-7 September. London: North-Holland

Perry, L., & Lindgaard, G. (1985) What's in a name? Preferences and performance with three different sets of vocabulary for a message handling system. In: *Proceedings of the 11th International Symposium on Human Factors in Telecommunications.* 9–13 September 1985, Cesson Sevigne, France

Pfauth, M., & Priest, J. (1981) Person–computer interface using touch screen devices. In: *Proceedings of Human Factors Society 25th Annual Meeting.* Rochester, New York, October 1981

Pluke, M. A. (1983) Keywords on Prestel. *Proceedings of the 10th Annual Conference on Human Factors in Telecommunications.* Helsinki

Poulton, E. C. (1974) *Tracking Skill & Manual Control.* Academic Press, New York

Price, L.A. & Cordova, C. A. (1983) Use of Mouse Buttons. In A. Janda (Ed.), Human Factors in Computing Systems. *Proceedings of the CHI'83 conference,* Boston,12-15 December. Amsterdam: North-Holland

Purdy, D. M. (1931) Spectral hue as a function of intensity. *Am. Journal of Psychology* **43**, p 541

Purdy, D. M. (1937) The Bezold-Brucke phenomenon and contours for constant hue. *Am. Journal of Psychology* **49**, p 313

Radl, G. W. (1980) Experimental investigations for optimal presentation-mode and colours of symbols on the CRT-screen. In: Grandjean, E. & Vigliani, E. (eds) *Ergonomic Aspects of Visual Display Terminals.* Taylor and Francis, London, England

Reising, J. M. & Emmerson, T. J. (1985) Colour in quantitative and qualitative display formats: does colour help? In: *International Conference on Colour in Information Technology and Visiual Displays (Publ. 61),* 27-28th March, 1985, Guildford, England

Richards, G. T. (1964) *The History & Development of the Typewriter.* The Science Museum, London, HMSO

Ritchie,G. J. & Turner,J. A. (1975) Input devices for interactive graphics. *International Journal of Man-Machine Studies* **7**, 639-660

Robertson, P. J., (1980) A guide to using color on alphanumeric displays, *IBM Technical report G320-6296*, IBM White Plains, NY.

Rochester, N., Bequaert, F. N. & Sharp, E. M. (1978) The Chord Keyboard. *Computer* December 1978, pp 57-63

Rogers, J. G. (1963) *Human Factors* **5**, pp 379-383. Cit. in Jackson – see above

Rogers, Y. & Oborne, D. J. (1985) Some psychological attributes of potential computer command names. *Behaviour & Information Technology* **4**, 4, pp 349-365

Rogers, Y. (1986) Evaluating the meaningfulness of icon sets to represent command operations. In: Harrison, M. K., & Monk, A. F. (eds), *Proceedings of the second conference of the British Computer Society Human-Computer Interaction Specialist Group, University of York, 23–26 September 1986,* Cambridge University Press, pp 586–603

Rosenberg, J. K. (1982) Evaluating the suggestuiveness of command names. *Behaviour and Information Technology* 1, 4, pp 371–400

Rossi, P. H., & Freeman, H. E. (1985). *Evaluation: a Systematic Approach.* Beverly Hills, CA: Sage Publications

Rubinstein, R. & Hersh, H. M. (1984) *The Human Factor: designing computer systems for people.* Digital Press, Burlington, MA

Salvendy, G. (Ed) (1987) *Handbook of Human Factors.* Wiley Interscience, New York

Scapin, D. L. (1982) Generation effect, structuring and computer commands. *Behaviour and Information Technology* 1, 4, pp 401–410

Schell , D. A. (1986) Usability testing of screen design: beyond standards, principles, and guidelines. *Proceedings of Human Factors Society, 30th Annual Meeting,* pp. 1212-1215

Schulze, L. J. H., & Snyder, H. L. (1983) A comparative evaluation of five touch entry devices. *Technical Report No. HFL-83-6.* Virginia Polytechnic Institute and State University, VA.

Scott, J.E. (1982) *Introduction to computer graphics.* Wiley, New York

Scriven, M. (1967). The methodology of evaluation. In R. W. Tyler, R. M. Gagne, & M. Scriven (Eds), *Perspectives on curriculum evaluation.* Chicago: Rand McNally

Shackel, B. (1986). Ergonomics in design for usability. In M. D. Harrison & A. F. Monk (Eds.), People and computers: designing for usability. *Proceedings of the Second Conference of the British Computer Society Human Computer Interaction Specialist Group.* University of York, 23-26 September. Cambridge: Cambridge University Press

Shneiderman, B. (1983) Direct manipulation: A step beyond programming languages. *Computer,* August 1983, IEEE publication

Shneiderman, B. (1987) *Designing the User Interface.* Addison-Wesley Publishing Co., Reading, Mass.

Shneiderman, B.(1980) *Software Psychology.* Winthrop Computer System Series

Sisson, N., Parkinson, S. R. & Snowberry, K. (1986) Considerations of menu structure and communication rate for the design of computer menu displays. *International Journal of man-Machine Studies* **25** 479-489

Smith, D. (1983) A business case for subsecond response time: Faster is better. *Datamation* **18**, April 1983

Smith, D. C., Irby, C., Kimball, R. Verplank, W. & Harslem, E. (1982) Designing the Star Interface. *Byte* 7, 242-282

Smith, S. L., & Mosier, J. N. (1986) Design guidelines for user-system interface software. *Technical Report ESD-TR-86-278* The Mitre Corp., Bedford, MA.

Snowberry, K., Parkinson, S.R. & Sisson, N. (1983) Computer display menus. *Ergonomics*, **26**, pp 699-712.

Spragg,S.D.S., Finck, A. & Smith, S. (1959) Performance on a two-dimensional following tracking task with miniature stick control, as a function of control-display movement relationship. *Journal of Psychology*, **48**, 247-254.

Sutcliffe, A. G. & Old, A. C. (1987). Do users know they have models? Some experiences in the practice of user modelling. In H. J. Bullinger & B. Shackel (Eds). *Proceedings of the Second IFIP Conference on Human-Computer Interaction - INTERACT '87*. Stuttgart, Federal Republic of Germany, 1-4 September. London: North-Holland

Teitelbaum, R. C. & Granda, R. E. (1983) The effects of positional constancy on searching menus for information. *Proceedings of the CHI'83 Human Factors in Computing Systems* Boston, 12-15 December. ACM, New York, pp 150–153

Thomas, J., & Schneider, M. L. (1982) A rose by any other alphanumeric designator would smell as sweet. *Behaviour and Information Technology* **1**, 4, pp 323–326

Tijerina, L. (1986) Design guidelines and the human factors of interface design. *Proceedings of Human Factors Society, 30th Annual Meeting*, pp. 1358-1361

Tullis, T. S. (1986) Optimising the usability of computer-generated displays. In: Harrison, M. K., & Monk, A. F. (eds), *Proceedings of the second conference of the British Computer Society Human-Computer Interaction Specialist Group, University of York, 23–26 September 1986*, Cambridge University Press, pp 604–614

Underwood, B.J. & Schultz, R.W. (1960) *Meaningfulness and Verbal Learning*. Lippincott, Philidelphia.

Usher, D.M. (1982) A touch-sensitive VDU compared with a computer aided keypad for controlling power generated Man-Machine Systems. IEE Conf. Pub. No. 212

Van Nes, F. L. (1986) Space, colour and typography on visual display terminals. *Behaviour and Information Technology* **5** 2 pp 99-118

Walraven, J. (1976) Discounting the background, the missing link in the explanation of chromatic induction.*Vision Research* **16** p 289

Walraven, J. (1977) Colour signals from incremental and decremental light stimuli.*Vision Research* **17** p 71

Walraven, J. (1984) Perceptual artifacts that may interfere with colour coding on visual displays. In: Gibson, C. P. (ed.) *Proceedings of NATO workshop "colour coded vs monochrome electronic displays"*, Farnborough, England

Walraven, J. (1985) The colours are not on the display: a survey of non-veridical perceptions that may turn up on a colour display. *Displays* **6** January 1985

Walraven, P. L. (1961) On the Bezold-Brucke phenomenon. *Journal of the Optical Society of America* **51** p 113

Waterworth, J. A., & Talbot, M. (1987) *Speech and Language-based Interaction with Machines: towards the conversational computer*. Ellis Horwood, Chichester

Weerdmeester, B. A., Von Velthoven, R. H. & Vrins, T. G. M. (1985) Keywords for information retrieval on interactive videotex. *Behaviour & Information Technology* **4** No. 2, 103-112

Weitzman, D. O., (1985) Color coding re-viewed, *Proc. Human Factors Society* - 29th Annual Meeting, Santa Monica, CA, pp 1079-1083

Whitefield, A. (1987). Models in human-computer interaction: a classification with special reference to their uses in design. In H. J. Bullinger & B. Shackel (Eds). *Proceedings of the Second IFIP Conference on Human-Computer Interaction - INTERACT '87*. Stuttgart, Federal Republic of Germany, 1-4 September. London: North-Holland

Williges, R. C., Elkerton, J., Pittman, J. A., & Cohill, A. M. (1984) Providing on line assistance to inexperienced computer users. In: Shackel, B., (ed.) *Proceedings of the IFIP Conference on Human-Computer Interaction - INTERACT '84*. London, 4-7 September. North-Holland, Amsterdam

Wright, P. (1983) Manual Dexterity: A user-oriented approach to cretaing computer documentation. In: *Proceedings of the CHI'83 Human Factors in Computing Systems* Boston, 12-15 December. ACM, New York, pp 11–18

Young, R. M.(1981) The machine inside the machine: user's models of pocket calculators. *International Journal of Man–Machine Studies* 15 pp 51–85

Index

substitute technology, 28
sub-tasks, 69
summative evaluations, 134, 135
survey instruments, 160
survey methods, 161
surveys, 24, 159
syntactic level, 147
System Image (SI), 20, 21
system monitoring, 149, 155
system performance, 145
system response times, 36, 37
systems analysis, 23

TAG, 34, 141
TAKD, 31, 141
target item, 56, 57
target population, 24
target visibility, 78
task-adequate usability, 145
task analysis, 28, 141
task performance 29
task-requirements, 136
task - tool relationship, 34
textual descriptors, 71
throw-it-away prototyping, 140
time taken, 29
title bar, 100
touch screen, 81
trackball, 74, 87-88
truncation, 49
typewriter, 77

UCM, 153
undo, 47, 48, 63
unobtrusive (covert) method, 149
usability, 145
user-computer dialogue, 37, 53
user support and training, 35
user conceptual model, 20
user parameters, 28
user population, 23, 24
user productivity, 39
user requirements, 137, 140
User's Model (UM), 20, 21
user's view, 36

validity, 160
verbal protocol, 157, 158
video recording, 155, 157, 158

visual search tasks, 112

wavelength differences , 110
windows, 96- 97
WIMP, 52, 62, 65, 74, 94
word processing, 23, 29
writing, 29
WYSIWYG, 106

ELLIS HORWOOD BOOKS IN COMPUTING SCIENCE

General Editors: Professor JOHN CAMPBELL, University College London, and BRIAN L. MEEK, King's College London (KQC), University of London

Series in Computers and Their Applications

Series Editor: BRIAN L. MEEK, Computer Centre, King's College London (KQC), University of London

Computer Communications and Networking